Books by John Tarrant

CAREER STAGES
(with Auren Uris)

MAKING IT BIG ON YOUR OWN

LEAVETAKING
(with Mortimer and Gloria Feinberg)

THE VICTORY PRINCIPLE
(with Auren Uris)

DRUCKER: THE MAN WHO INVENTED THE CORPORATE SOCIETY

HOW TO NEGOTIATE A RAISE

THE NEW PSYCHOLOGY FOR MANAGING PEOPLE
(with Mortimer Feinberg)

SURVIVAL 2001
(with Henry Voegeli)

THE END OF EXURBIA

HOW TO KEEP FROM GETTING FIRED
(with Auren Uris)

GETTING FIRED

THE CORPORATE EUNUCH
(with O. William Battalia)

HOW TO WIN YOUR BOSS'S LOVE, APPROVAL—AND JOB
(with Auren Uris)

DATA COMMUNICATION AND BUSINESS STRATEGY

TOMORROW'S TECHNIQUES FOR TODAY'S SALESMEN

GREAT BATTLES OF WORLD WAR II

PERKS AND PARACHUTES

NEGOTIATING YOUR

EXECUTIVE EMPLOYMENT CONTRACT

John Tarrant

A STONESONG PRESS BOOK

LINDEN PRESS/SIMON & SCHUSTER   NEW YORK   1985

1   3   5   7   9   10   8   6   4   2

Library of Congress Cataloging in Publication Data
Tarrant, John J.
Perks and parachutes.

"A Stonesong Press book."
Includes index.
1. Executives—Salaries, pensions, etc.—Law and
legislation—United States. 2. Labor contract—United
States. I. Title.
KF1424.T37   1985   344.73'01891   84–19431
                          347.3041891
ISBN: 0-671-49851-7

CONTENTS

TO DOT,

WITH THANKS AND LOVE

PERKS AND PARACHUTES

1

INTRODUCTION: NOW YOU SHOULD GET IT IN WRITING

Growing numbers of middle- and upper-level American executives are confronting a profound new career consideration: *the negotiation of an employment contract.* The use of written agreements between employers and managerial, professional, and technical people is spreading. Managers in many levels of administration who until recently thought of contracts as the exclusive privilege of entertainers, athletes, labor unions, and the chairman of the board can now realistically expect to be offered their own contracts and, in cases where their employer is not forthcoming, to insist upon having one.

Ten years ago those pursuing careers in management signed contracts only in special cases. The accepted view of the manager's career was that it held the potential for power, status, and money. The down side of these prizes was the manager's vulnerability to abrupt firing without recourse, often for reasons having little or nothing to do with performance. The executive could be terminated because the economy had turned down, because the company was reorganizing, or because there was bad "chemistry" in the executive suite. The American manager, in this traditional view, lived always with the possibility that the ax might fall just so that an organizational glitch might be straightened out. And of course there was always the new-broom effect: when new management came in or the company changed hands, executives could be swept out simply

11

because they were identified with the old regime. (It is this last phenomenon that has recently given rise to the Golden Parachute, under whose benign shadow senior managers bestow lucrative severance agreements upon one another as insurance against post-takeover termination.)

But that's all changing. The unlimited right to fire is being curtailed, by policy, by law, and by employment agreements.

Not long ago, managers could be fired because they were too old. By 1967, however, Congress had passed the Age Discrimination in Employment Act, which decreed, in part, that "it shall be unlawful for an employer... to fail or refuse to hire or to discharge any individual or otherwise discriminate against any individual with respect to his compensation, terms, conditions, or privileges of employment, because of such individual's age..." The prohibition against firing people because they are too old, combined with comparable legislative restraints on discrimination against women and members of minority groups, proved to be the handwriting on the wall. Now there is an all-out assault on the unlimited right to fire anyone, regardless of age, sex, or race.

On September 13, 1983, the *Wall Street Journal* carried a front-page article about the surging wave of challenges to the company's right to discharge managers at will. The *WSJ*'s conclusion: "Firing isn't that easy anymore.... State courts from New Hampshire to California are setting new limits on firing involving about 60 million nonunion workers. The rulings, which often provide hefty cash awards to those fired, chip away at the already-eroding 'employment at will' legal doctrine allowing businesses to discharge people without cause."

Now that the right to fire has been eroded, the basic reason for resisting employment contracts loses strength. If courts are going to treat the manager–employer relationship as if it were a contract—whether there is a written agreement or not—then management might as well give actual contracts when they achieve some useful purpose, like assuring the retention of promising talent.

There are many other reasons for the increased use of employment contracts, however, not the least of them the heightened mobility of managers.

A few decades ago it was not uncommon for an executive to spend his entire working life with one company. Today such a career is highly unusual. At one time, a person who had worked for three companies in six or seven years was considered a job-hopper. Today movement from job to job, at least during the early years, is the prevailing career strategy.

Our present degree of executive mobility is underpinned by the concept of the interchangeable manager. In the old days you had to work for a firm for years and become thoroughly steeped in all the minutiae of its products and its markets before you qualified for senior management. This idea was replaced by the principle that the trained manager could carry his tools in his briefcase from company to company and be effective in just about any industry. The executive vice-president of a popcorn company could move into the top spot with a turbine manufacturer.

With the increased emphasis on the interchangeability of managers came the phenomenal growth in the executive-search industry. It became commonplace for firms to retain headhunters to find—and help to recruit—executives.

The executives who found themselves the objects of all this activity had to be motivated, and this could not be done via straight salary, so bonuses, stock options, etc., became popular as forms of incentive pay. Since the arrangement of sometimes complex compensation plans frequently involved letters of agreement and the like, managers and employers were, in effect, entering into contracts, even though these contracts covered just one area: compensation.

As corporations spread their nets and brought in managers whom they really did not know, there were a lot of mismatches. Executives simply did not work out. They had to be let go. So the recruited manager began to think about self-protection before taking a job. The individual who had to tear up roots in Chicago and move to a job in Los Angeles demanded insurance against being let go after a year. So written agreements on severance arrangements over and above those in the policy manual (e.g., one month's pay for every two years on the job) became a normal part of recruitment.

Executives no longer thought of themselves as freebooters who

made big money but who had to be content with the constant threat
of being fired to straighten out anomalies in the organization chart,
or because the chemistry wasn't right, or because they were identified
with the losing side in a palace revolution. The manager looked
with increasing envy at the unionized blue-collar worker, who was
not only protected by a contract but was sometimes not making all
that much less than the manager. In 1972 the American Management Association reported on a survey of its members. The survey
had asked for feelings about unionization. The report included the
finding that managers, whose frustrations and discontents were increasing, no longer felt that union membership was taboo. Nearly
half the line executives would welcome a change in the labor laws
to compel employers to bargain with management unions. Three
out of four managers endorsed the idea of informal associations of
managers for the purpose of collective bargaining.

Perhaps if organized labor had moved more aggressively into the
white-collar field there would now be picket lines of executives in
front of corporate headquarters. In the absence of any concerted
impetus toward white-collar unionization, managers have sought
protection through individual contracts.

Still another development that has given impetus to the spreading
use of contracts in the United States is the growth of international
business.

Employment contracts for executives are much more prevalent
abroad, particularly in Europe, than in the U.S. This is in keeping
with the general philosophy in foreign countries, where the manager
is regarded as a true professional and accorded much more respect
than here. In Germany and France, not to mention Japan, it is
practically unheard of to fire executives because the chemistry is
wrong or because a new broom is sweeping clean or to straighten
out glitches on the organization chart. In the rest of the world the
manager does not live from one day's combat to the next like a
gladiator. Unfortunately, in some firms in the U.S. the comparison
is apt.

Curiously enough, managers in foreign countries, who have less
need of the protection afforded by written contracts, are much more
likely to have them. Sometimes this is because government regu-

lations make it necessary. At other times the contract is simply a way of doing business, a normal stage in the hiring process, part of the business culture.

When American management was the hope and envy of the world it was possible (and popular) to dismiss business practices in other lands. But of course it's all different now. We no longer think that every aspect of U.S. business custom is superlative. We look to European countries, and particularly to Japan—the land of "lifetime employment tenure"—for answers.

Carl Menk, former president of Boyden Associates, the leading executive-search firm, points out that these days management is becoming an international vocation. Executives from other countries come to work in the U.S., either for branches of companies in their own countries or for American firms. American managers are, of course, working abroad. When they work for foreign companies they often sign contracts for the first time. When they go to work in overseas subsidiaries of American companies they may do so under contract, because local law and custom dictate the practice. And even if the American manager abroad does not have a written contract, he comes into frequent contact with managers who do. He becomes familiar with the concept and begins to see its advantages.

Mr. Menk remarks that when an American manager who has been exposed to the idea abroad is transferred back, or is recruited by another company, he is likely to think of the written contract as protection. He is, perhaps, taking a greater risk than he would be in making a move within the States. He wants to provide himself with a generous severance arrangement in case things don't work out. So he tries to negotiate a written contract, something which once would have seemed strange but now seems to him to be the natural order of things.

As movement of managers between countries accelerates, the use of contracts will grow. As noted elsewhere, the American who goes to work for a foreign company is sometimes shocked by vast differences in viewpoint and business practices. This is no less true for the foreign executive who comes to work for a U.S. company. He will look for the kind of agreement that will protect him against misunderstandings. With the barrier being pierced in this way, the practice of asking for written contracts will spread among managers who are making purely domestic shifts in employment.

Companies which resist the idea of written contracts will come to accept their use because they help to give uniformity to relationships between people and organizations of different countries and cultures.

Another factor in the spread of employment contracts down through the ranks of middle-management levels will be top management's desire to protect the Golden Parachute. The enormous amounts of money involved in these payouts, combined with the absence of stockholder approval, have generated a great deal of unfavorable publicity for GPs, and have put a huge amount of pressure on the senior-level personnel privileged enough to have them. Since senior managers are not likely to lessen their desire for protection in the case of takeovers, they will increasingly be forced to share the wealth and broaden the use of contracts to include people at lower levels in the organization. This will at least remove one of the most egregious features of the Golden Parachute, namely its availability only to an exclusive club at the very top.

Growth in the number of company secrets that must be kept has increased the number of written agreements whose primary purpose is to limit the revelation of confidential material. Such contracts have been commonplace in high-tech industries, and are now used more frequently in other industries where inside information is vital, for example the fashion business. Recently businesses of all descriptions have begun to write confidentiality clauses into contracts.

Another self-protective measure is the "noncompete" agreement, in which an executive agrees not to go to work for a competitor (or to start a competitive enterprise) for a specified period. As we shall discuss, such contracts, although not necessarily enforceable, can have a deterrent effect on potential employers.

And then, let's face it, today companies are making all kinds of written employment agreements with executives. The desire to motivate and the need to provide tax shelters have stimulated a proliferation of exotic compensation methods like incentive stock options, junior options, phantom options, etc. Moreover, bonus agreements are often based on fairly complicated formulas. These plans are frequently embodied in written agreements. Thus the executive is likely to be involved in a contractual relationship with the employer to cover at least part of his employment situation.

Above all, American business must find ways to attract and keep executive talent. This is why in so many firms the once somnolent Personnel function has been elevated to become Human Resources, a full-blown and important corporate staff function. Companies have tried for some time to lock in managers with "Golden Hand-cuffs"—deferred compensation, stock options and the like. Now the company must go further and offer a full-scale employment contract. Furthermore, since the middle managers of today are the policy-level leaders of tomorrow, the contracts must be given to those below the top echelon.

For all of these reasons, written contracts are being offered in ever-increasing numbers to American white-collar employees. And while the most highly publicized contracts are given to board chairmen and chief executives, countless thousands of people in the middle-management area are under contract today, or will be negotiating contracts soon. If you make $30,000 a year or more, before too long you are likely to be confronting questions like these:

Is a contract to my advantage?
What should it cover?
How long should it run?
What are the dangers?
Can I earn the performance bonus called for in my contract?
What happens if I want to break my contract?
How can I negotiate the best possible agreement?

Let's first examine the pros and cons of contracts from the employer's point of view.

Employers, by and large, dislike the idea of employment agreements with executives. They limit top-management authority. While the concept that executives should be dismissible at will has taken some hard blows, it is by no means dead. You can still fire a manager with, say, four years to go on a five-year contract, but the severance pay is going to be pretty steep.

Another reason that employers resist the broader use of contracts for managers is that it establishes precedents. When a certain number of executives have won contracts which provide them with extremely attractive stock option arrangements, it's almost inevitable that the pot will have to be sweetened for everyone else.

Many employers are highly reluctant to lose "the ultimate motivator," the right to fire. They fear that managers who are protected by contracts will no longer show the desired amount of drive. While industrial psychologists have insisted for years that motivation must lie in positive things, not in the threat of firing, somehow that idea has never really caught on with some bosses.

However, there are advantages as well for the employer who has a written contract with an executive.

The most apparent is the locking-in of the employee for the life of the agreement. It is becoming more important to a good many corporations to find ways to keep good managers on the payroll. This is true of certain companies that have never before worried about retaining talent. For example, a worldwide soft-drink firm, notorious for high executive turnover resulting from a sink-or-swim approach to management talent, decided in 1983 to take a bold new tack. Henceforth managers were to be trained, cherished and developed into the leadership cadres that would determine the company's future. The strategy of hiring promising executives and tossing them into a shark pool was not working anymore. For one thing, the company reasoned, there were fewer gifted young managers to choose from, since the crest of the post–World War II baby boom had moved past the entry level. (True, this calculation does not take into account the increased number of women seeking management careers, but the company's senior officers found it compelling nevertheless.) The new emphasis was to be placed on identifying good managers and trying to keep them as long as possible.

A second advantage to the employer of a contractual relationship is that it eliminates or at least reduces the friction and divisiveness caused by annual bargaining between employer and employee over salary and bonuses. When the issue of compensation has been minimized for, say, a five year term, there is reason to believe that the executive is freer to concentrate on meeting corporate objectives.

Contracts make it easier to do human-resource planning. One of the jobs of the director of human resources is to try to project what the organization chart will look like five years hence, plot the courses of managers who are earmarked to fill certain jobs, and identify the strengths and weaknesses of the executive corps of the company. While the existence of an employment contract is no guarantee that a particular person will be on board five years in the future, the likelihood of the person remaining is enhanced. The planners can make their calculations with more assurance.

Many contracts contain provisions which protect the employer by forbidding the employee to engage in competition for a stated period after the agreement ends. Other contracts bar the employee's use of "secret" information. In certain industries where confidentiality is important—the fashion business, Silicon Valley, etc.— such contracts have been commonplace for some time. The perceived requirement for confidentiality of product and marketing data in other highly competitive industries has impelled employers to ask key people to sign such pacts. As we shall see, the definition of breach of confidentiality in some agreements can extend to a few casual words exchanged with a friend who works for a competing company. Executives who are asked to sign such limiting contracts are of course likely to require quids pro quo in the form of money, perks, and severance protection. Thus in order to get the protection of the confidentiality clause the employer has to enter a written agreement covering compensation, conditions of employment, and so on.

There *are* meaningful advantages to the employer in setting up contractual relationships with executives. However, let's be clear about the fact that employers are not, by and large, jubilant about the increasing resort to executive contracts, nor are they eager to offer contracts to their managers. This is realistic. A *full-rounded, well-negotiated employment contract is more in the employee's favor than the employer's.*

The biggest advantage to the employee is the fact that the employer is *committed in writing* to the provisions of the contract. It
would of course be naïve to believe that all provisions of every
contract are voluntarily carried out to the letter. But one is a lot
more certain of the goodies when they're spelled out in writing.

When you have a contract you have assurance of a job and a
minimum income for the life of the agreement. If the employer
breaks the contract by firing you, you're entitled to collect the
severance money called for in the contract. When the employer
has established a complex compensation plan, you're able to review
its provisions to make sure you're getting all you're entitled to. In
case the company suffers reverses, people without written agreements may be at the mercy of events. Sincerely, with the best
possible wishes, the company may say, "We're sorry, but we're going
to have to cut you down or let you go." When you have a contract,
the company is under an obligation to honor it unless it goes bankrupt.

Your contract can protect you from unwanted transfers. It can
enhance the value of your estate. It can assure you of a piece of
the action if the company makes money, while limiting your downside risk when times are hard.

But what about the negatives? A contract ties you down. You're
locked into a situation which you may want to get out of before the
agreement has run its course. Younger executives in particular may
be leery about putting it in writing because they anticipate making
several career moves.

The fact is that a well-negotiated contract ties the employer down
far more than the employee. As we will see, there are ways in which
a company may try to avoid paying the full severance in case of a
firing, for example by threatening to allege that the employee was
fired "for cause," insisting on a long-drawn-out lawsuit that the
employee can ill afford, and then offering a "reasonable compromise" on severance.

However, the manager who has signed a five-year contract and
who wants to leave for a better job after three years creates a problem.
Maybe the company can insist on the terms of the contract. But is
it really useful to force the executive to stay unwillingly? Will not

the individual's talent be outweighed by anger and resentment? As for financial penalties, obviously the employer tries to build into the agreement as strong a set of "Golden Handcuffs" as can be forged, in the form of deferred bonuses, stock plans, and pension benefits. The idea is to make it so costly for the employee to leave that the decision to remain looks attractive, no matter how good an offer another company has made. But if the other company wants the manager badly enough they will offer compensation for the loss, at least partially, in the form of up-front bonuses, enhanced benefits, speeded-up vesting in the pension plan, etc.

As for noncompete clauses, which forbid the manager to work for a competitor for a specified period after termination of the manager's employment, we will see that this provision is hard to enforce. The situation varies from state to state, but on the whole, courts tend to look askance at this sort of limitation. This is not to say that anyone should ever sign anything with the intention of breaking one or more of the provisions, or that one should cavalierly flout a noncompete clause on the theory that it is unenforceable.

The point is that contracts overall favor employees more than employers. That is, the *concept* of a written contract favors the employee. If the employer is able to get the employee to sign an agreement which is skewed in the employer's favor in one or more important ways, then the employee has lost the advantage. For example, a contract may contain a fabulously lucrative severance provision, but if the language defining termination "for cause" is loosely drawn, then the employer may be able to get out of the agreement at will without paying a penny of the severance.

The strategic thrust of the employer in negotiating a contract will be for ironclad provisions in the areas favorable to the employer, e.g., protection of secrets and noncompete, while keeping the language as vague as possible and wide open to interpretation in areas like termination. The employee will want to optimize those sections that offer the greatest payoff and protection while whittling down the scope of the employer's discretion and control.

This book covers the issues you will be negotiating when you bargain for your first or next employment contract. It will help you to shape your negotiating strategy and sharpen the tactics you need to win a favorable agreement. It supports its points with a variety of excerpts from actual contracts existing today between companies and managers. Here also you will find the complete text of many contracts. While legal documents do not make for spicy or lively reading, it is nevertheless a good idea to look this material over, even if you know or care nothing about the individual or the company involved in the agreement. The more familiar you become with the varied provisions of a given contract and the many ways in which they can be worded to favor one side or the other, the better able you are to spot pitfalls and to secure the wording that works to your advantage.

2

WHAT THE TYPICAL CONTRACT COVERS

The basic elements of the employment agreement are:

- Term—how long the contract runs.
- Duties—description of the job and status.
- Compensation—salary, bonuses, stock options, etc.
- Benefits—life and health insurance, retirement, etc.
- Termination—who can discontinue the contract and for what reasons.
- Severance—what is to be paid the fired employee.

Golden Parachutes contain the "trigger clause" declaring that the arrangement comes into effect in case of a change of ownership.

Beyond these basic ingredients, contracts may cover a variety of items—perks like limousines and club membership, consulting provisions, noncompete and nondisclosure provisions, arbitration, etc.

The following pages carry a number of employment contracts that exemplify the points made in the text. All are actual agreements, public documents filed with the Securities and Exchange Commission. The Appendix carries many more examples of contracts of various types.

The following agreement is a useful example of a standard contract. It's short and covers most of the major points and some of the secondary points usually covered in the typical executive employment agreement.

The contract was signed by Charles L. Jarvie and Dr Pepper Company in February 1980, after Jarvie left Procter & Gamble to take over as president and chief operating officer of the beverage company.

Some comments on the provisions:

1. The contract runs for three years. Most employment agreements run three to five years.
2. This description of the executive's duties is fairly general. Some "duties" clauses are more elaborate and, as we shall discuss, can establish the basis for an employer's claim that the terms of the contract have not been met by the employee and can therefore be broken.
3. Compensation is the centerpiece of most contracts. Here the agreement does not establish specific amounts or a range, but rather sets a minimum—in this case, $200,000 per year. The establishment of minimums without limitations on the upside should be standard procedure in negotiating a contract.
4 and 5. Agreements signed when an executive joins a firm often cover one-shot relocation expenses. This contract does not call, as some do, for an up-front bonus.
6. Expense accounts are the standard perk. We'll see examples of more exotic perks.
7. This is a mild form of the noncompete clause designed to restrict the activities of the employee. Such restrictions remain in effect for a specified period of time after the employee leaves the firm.
8. Here the employee is assured of participation in the company's benefit plans. This is a relatively perfunctory clause. Some agreements go on at great length to spell out intricate profit-sharing and stock option plans.
9. The contract is declared to be binding upon any other company that merges with or acquires Dr Pepper. This, of course, is not a Golden Parachute, which would specify a severance

arrangement to come into force only on the occasion of a change in control of the corporation.

10. The fruits of the agreement are assured for the employee's heirs if he dies and for those entitled to receive them if he is incapacitated.

One element absent from the agreement, though present in most, is a section on possible causes or justifications for unilateral termination.

THE STATE OF TEXAS

COUNTY OF DALLAS

THIS AGREEMENT made this *20th* day of *February*, 1980, between DR PEPPER COMPANY, a Colorado corporation with its principal offices and place of business in Dallas, Texas (the Company), and CHARLES L. JARVIE (Jarvie):

WITNESSETH:

WHEREAS, the Company desires to employ Jarvie as an executive officer of the Company and he is willing to accept such employment and thereafter to perform the services hereafter described, upon the terms and conditions hereinafter set forth.

NOW, THEREFORE, it is agreed between the Company and Jarvie that:

1. *Employment.* The Company hereby employs Jarvie for the period beginning on the date that he reports for work at the Company's offices in Dallas and ending three (3) years after such date; provided that this agreement shall terminate and be of no force or effect unless Jarvie reports for work to begin his employment prior to *March 1*, 1980.

2. *Duties.* During the period that Jarvie shall be an employee of the Company, he shall have and exercise such duties, responsibilities, privileges, powers and authority as may be assigned to him by the Board of Directors of the Company.

He shall report and be responsible only to the Board of Directors and the Chairman of the Board. Jarvie agrees to perform the duties enumerated in this paragraph and to serve as an employee for three years from the date of the commencement of his employment.

3. *Compensation.* In consideration of Jarvie entering into and executing this agreement and his serving as an employee for said 3-year period, the Company shall pay to him during the period of his employment a salary at the rate of Two Hundred Thousand Dollars ($200,000) per year, plus such additional or increased salary, compensation or benefits as the Board of Directors may direct, payable in substantially equal semimonthly amounts on the fifteenth and the last day of each month. Should Jarvie die or become disabled after the commencement of his employment and prior to three years thereafter, the amount of the then unpaid compensation, including all bonus payments to which he is entitled, shall be paid in equal monthly installments to him or his estate.

4. *Moving Expenses.* Jarvie's expenses reasonably incurred in moving him and his family from Cincinnati, Ohio, to Dallas will be reimbursed to him by the Company in full in accordance with the Company's policy in connection with executive transfers, and Jarvie shall also be paid an additional amount in cash equivalent to his income tax liability attributable to receipt of his moving expenses.

5. a. *Purchase of Cincinnati Residence.* Concurrently with Jarvie's entering upon his employment with the Company, the Company will cause his residence in Cincinnati, Ohio, to be appraised by a competent appraisal firm and will purchase the residence from Jarvie at the appraised price less the amount of any indebtedness, liens or encumbrances burdening the property, which mortgages and encumbrances will, however, be assumed by the Company.

b. *Loan.* To assist Jarvie in acquiring a residence in Dallas or its suburbs, the Company will lend to him the amount of Two Hundred Thousand Dollars ($200,000) for a term of three (3) years, such indebtedness to bear interest at the rate of six percent (6%) per annum and to be secured by a first lien on said Dallas residence purchased by him.

6. *Reimbursement for Expenses*. Jarvie is authorized to incur reasonable expenses for promoting the business of the Company. At the end of each month, the Company shall reimburse him for all expenses, including entertainment, travel and miscellaneous other expenses reasonably incurred in promoting the business of the Company and in performing his duties as an employee hereunder.

7. *Restrictive Covenant*. During the term of this agreement, Jarvie shall devote his best efforts and his full time to advance the interests of the Company and to perform his duties hereunder, and during such period Jarvie shall not directly or indirectly, alone or as a member of a partnership, or as an officer, director or shareholder of a corporation, be engaged in or concerned with any other commercial duties or pursuits which are in any manner competitive with the Company. During the entire time of this agreement, Jarvie shall be furnished with a private office, a private secretary and such other facilities and services suitable to his position and adequate to the performance of his duties.

8. *Employee Benefits*. Nothing in this agreement shall be construed to impair or limit Jarvie's right to participate in all employee benefit plans of the Company of every nature and he shall, in fact, be entitled to participate in and be a member of all such benefit plans in proportion to his compensation hereunder. "Benefit plans" shall include, but not be limited to, group life, hospitalization and major medical insurance coverages, stock options, stock purchase or bonus plans, retirement programs, profit-sharing arrangements and other incentive compensation plans. Jarvie's eligible dependents shall also be covered under any such plans and benefit programs to the extent that dependents of other employees are similarly provided for. Specifically, Jarvie will be made a participant in both the Company's existing incentive compensation plans, the short-term and the long-term, copies of which are appended as exhibits to this agreement. If requested, the Company will enter into agreements with Jarvie providing for the

deferral of all or part of any bonus payments payable to him under such plans.

9. *Reorganization.* If the Company shall at any time be merged or consolidated into or with any other corporation or entity or if substantially all of the assets of the Company are transferred to another corporation or entity, the provisions of this agreement shall survive any such transaction and shall be binding upon and inure to the benefit of the corporation resulting from such merger or consolidation or the corporation to which such assets will be transferred (and this provision shall apply in the event of any subsequent merger, consolidation or transfer), and the Company upon the occasion of any of the above-described transactions, shall include in the appropriate agreements the obligation that the payments herein agreed to be paid to or for the benefit of Jarvie, his beneficiaries or estate shall be paid, and that the provisions of this paragraph 9 be performed.

10. *Benefit.* This agreement shall inure to the benefit of and shall bind the parties hereto and their respective legal representatives, successors, heirs, descendants, assigns and personal representatives.

IN WITNESS WHEREOF, the Company and Jarvie have signed this agreement as of the date and year first set forth above.

DR PEPPER COMPANY

ATTEST:

By_____

_____
Alvin H. Lane, *Secretary*

W. W. CLEMENTS,
Chairman–Chief Executive Officer

By_____
CHARLES L. JARVIE

Contracts are often amended. One of the most basic amendments is a simple extension, like the following, dated June 25, 1982, which extended Mr. Jarvie's agreement with Dr Pepper for one year.

June 25, 1982

Mr. Charles L. Jarvie
President
Dr Pepper Company
Dallas, Texas

DEAR CHUCK:

In accordance with the action of the Board of Directors at its last meeting, I am pleased to submit this letter agreement amending and extending your employment Agreement of February 21, 1980 in the following particulars:

> The term of the Agreement and of your employment is extended for one year beyond the original three-year term, with the same effect as if the original agreement had been for a term of four years terminating in 1984, rather than for three years, terminating in 1983.

In all other respects, the 1980 Agreement shall continue in full force and effect as originally written.

If this is in accordance with your understanding, please indicate in the place provided below and return one copy to me.

Sincerely,
DR PEPPER COMPANY

By_____

AGREED:

_____
CHARLES L. JARVIE

We might note that Mr. Jarvie resigned on November 24, 1982. When an agreement is terminated there may be negotiated trade-offs. For example, Mr. Jarvie gave up his rights under the company's supplemental pension plan. In return Dr Pepper agreed to pay him $100,000.

Here is another contract, signed by Aeronca, Inc., and Vice-President Richard W. Sappenfield in April 1980. The agreement covers essentially the same ground as that in the contract between Mr. Jarvie and Dr Pepper. However, there are a couple of points not featured in the Dr Pepper pact. Section IV of Mr. Sappenfield's contract spells out the bases for termination, including "serious misconduct on the part of the Employee or other good cause." Section VI provides for arbitration of disputes with respect to the agreement.

EMPLOYMENT AGREEMENT.

THIS AGREEMENT, entered into at Pineville, North Carolina, as of this 14th day of April, 1980 by and between AERONCA, INC., an Ohio corporation, with its principal executive offices located at 200 Rodney Street, Pineville, North Carolina (hereinafter called the "Company"), and RICHARD W. SAPPENFIELD of Michigan (hereinafter called the "Employee").

WITNESSETH

In consideration of the mutual covenants herein contained and other good and valuable considerations, the parties hereto agree as follows:

SECTION I—TERM OF EMPLOYMENT AND DUTIES

1.0 The Company employs the Employee upon an active full-time basis, as Vice President and General Manager of the Company's Aerospace Division, subject to the order, supervision and direction of the Board of Directors of the Company and any officer senior to him, and the Employee has accepted and agrees to remain in the employ of the Company in the aforesaid capacity upon the terms, conditions and provisions herein stated from the effective date hereof (April 14, 1980) thru April 30, 1983.

1.1 During the term of his employment the Employee agrees to devote his full business time, attention, skill and efforts to the business conducted by the Company and to continue to act as Vice President and General Manager as aforesaid from time to time (in each case, if elected) and faithfully to perform such executive, administrative and supervisory duties and to exercise such powers as specified in the Regulations of the Company from time to time and as the Board of Directors and officers senior to him may prescribe.

1.2 The Employee's duties shall be performed principally at the Company's plants located in Middletown, Ohio. It is intended that the Employee will move his principal residence to a home to be selected by him in the general area of Middletown, Ohio, by approximately the 30th day of June, 1980, at which place he and his family will reside.

1.3 There is attached hereto, and marked Exhibit A, a copy of Exhibit A to a letter dated March 7, 1980, executed by the Company and the Employee, setting out the general terms of the Employee's employment, the principal terms of which are incorporated herein. Reference is made to paragraph I.E., titled "Relocation Expenses," which shall apply to the change of location of the Employee's principal residence, required by the preceding paragraph 1.2.

SECTION II—COMPENSATION

2.0 The annual base salary of the Employee shall be the sum of $85,000 per annum, payable in equal semi-monthly installments.

2.1 The Board of Directors of the Company reserves the right to increase the compensation of the Employee, specified in this instrument, at any time or times hereafter and no such increase or adjustment shall operate as a cancellation of this Agreement, but merely as an amendment to this Section II, and all the other terms, provisions and conditions of this Agreement shall continue in force and effect as herein provided.

2.2 The Employee will be reimbursed for his reasonable travel and living expenses, incurred when traveling on the Company's business, pursuant to its established policies.

2.3 The Employee shall be a participant in the Company's 1980 Incentive Plan, pursuant to which it is possible for him to earn a bonus of not to exceed 50% of his annual base salary, provided the prescribed target profits and objectives set out in the Plan are achieved, as well as in subsequent plans (if any) which may hereafter be adopted.

2.4 The Company will, during the term of this Agreement, maintain at its expense, term insurance upon the life of the Employee in the face amount of $200,000, payable to such beneficiary as the Employee shall designate from time to time in writing to the Company and, in the absence of such designation, to his estate. Such insurance shall be in addition to such group term life insurance as the Company maintains for the benefit of salaried employees generally of the rank and status of the Employee.

2.5 The Company will grant to the Employee, effective upon his entering into the Company's employ on April 14, 1980, an option to purchase 7500 Common shares, par $1 per share, of the Company under and pursuant to the provisions of the Company's 1979 Stock Option Plan, the option price to equal 100% of the fair market value of the optioned shares on the effective day of the grant.

SECTION III—NON COMPETITION AND SECRECY

3.0 So long as this Agreement is in effect, the Employee shall not directly or indirectly become or serve as an officer or employee of an individual, partnership or corporation or owner or part owner or shareholder of any business, or member of any partnership, which conducts a business which, in the reasonable judgment of the Board of Directors of this corporation, competes in a material manner with the Company, unless the Employee shall have first obtained the written consent of the Board of Directors of the corporation.

3.1 At all times, both during and after the termination of his employment, the Employee shall keep and retain in confidence and shall not disclose to any persons, firm or corporation (except with the written consent of the Company first obtained) any of the proprietary, confidential or secret information or trade secrets of the Company.

SECTION IV—TERMINATION

4.0 Nothing herein is intended to prohibit the Company from terminating this Agreement for serious misconduct on the part of the Employee or other good cause; provided, that in the event that the Employee's employment is terminated rightfully by the Company, nevertheless the Employee shall be entitled to receive such benefits under the Company's employee benefit plans, in which he is a participant, as are provided by the terms thereof applicable to the termination of participants generally.

4.1 If the Employee shall become totally and permanently disabled (as said term is defined in the group long term disability insurance now being carried by the Company) the Company may not terminate this Agreement on account of such disability unless and until the waiting period (for payment of benefits) prescribed in such (or similar substituted) insurance then in force shall have expired during the continuance of such disability.

4.2 Any dispute or difference of opinion between the Employee and the Company as to the latter's right to terminate this Agreement shall be submitted to and determined by arbitration in accordance with the provisions of Section VI hereof set forth below.

SECTION V—OTHER RIGHTS AND PLANS

5.0 Nothing herein contained shall in any manner modify, imperil or affect existing or future rights or interests of the Employee to receive any employee benefits to which he would otherwise be entitled or as a participant in the present or any future incentive, profit-sharing or bonus plan of the Company providing for his participation, or in any present or future stock option plan of the Company or in the present or any future pension plan of the Company, to the extent such plans are applicable generally to salaried employees, it being understood and agreed that the rights and interests of the Employee to any employee benefits or as a participant or beneficiary in or under any or all said plans, respectively, shall not be adversely affected hereby.

SECTION VI—ARBITRATION

6.0 In the event of any difference of opinion or dispute between the Employee and the Company with respect to the construction or interpretation of this agreement or the alleged breach thereof, which cannot be settled amicably by agreement of the parties, then such dispute shall be submitted to and determined by arbitration by a single arbitrator in the City of Middletown, Ohio, in accordance with the Rules, then obtaining, of the AMERICAN ARBITRATION ASSOCIATION, and judgment upon the award rendered shall be final, binding and conclusive upon the parties and may be entered in the highest court, state or federal, having jurisdiction.

SECTION VII—ASSIGNEES BOUND

7.0 THIS AGREEMENT shall be binding upon and inure to the benefit of any successor of the Company and any such successor shall be deemed substituted for the Company under the terms of this contract. The term "successor" as used herein shall indicate any person, firm, corporation or other business entity which at any time, by merger, consolidation, purchase or otherwise, acquires all or substantially all the assets or business of the Company.

7.1 Neither this Agreement nor any of his rights or duties hereunder may be assigned by the Employee without the written consent of the Company.

SECTION VIII—MISCELLANEOUS

8.0 This Employment Agreement shall become effective April 14, 1980.

8.1 The headings or captions of sections or paragraphs are used for convenience of reference merely and shall be ignored in the construction or interpretation hereof.

8.2 As used herein, terms such as "herein," "hereof," "hereto" and similar language shall be construed to refer to this entire instrument and not merely the paragraph or sentence in which they appear, unless so limited by express language.

8.3 This is an Ohio agreement and the same shall be construed and the rights of the parties determined in accordance with the laws of Ohio.

IN WITNESS WHEREOF, the Company has caused this Employment Agreement to be executed by its duly authorized officer, and RICHARD W. SAPPENFIELD has affixed his signature hereto, as of the day and year first above mentioned.

AERONCA, INC.

By: _____

President

_____

Richard W. Sappenfield

EXHIBIT A

I.   Three year contract, on following major terms:
- A. Salary $85,000 per year.
- B. Potential Bonus of up to 50% of salary based on profitability and objectives under Incentive Bonus Plan.
- C. Additional Term Life Insurance Policy for $200,000 payable to whomever he chooses.
- D. Stock Options for 7,500 Common Shares under the 1979 Stock Option Plan. Option price determined by the mean between high and low sales on American Stock Exchange on first day of employment.
- E. Relocation Expenses
    1. Use of Transamerica Relocation Service.
        a. Price set by Transamerica to be based on average of three appraisals on present value of house. Price to sell in 60 days and close 30 days later.
    2. Closing cost of new home in Ohio.
    3. Moving Expenses
        a. Packing and moving of household items.
        b. Up to 30 days temporary living expenses for family in Middletown.
        c. Mileage for cars from Detroit to Middletown.
        d. Three trips for wife to look for new home in Middletown.

>   e. Miscellaneous other costs of actual moving family from Detroit to Middletown.
>
>   4. Interest differential for three years.
>
>   a. Aeronca will reimburse you for the difference between the interest on the present balance (approximately $90,000) on your home in Detroit and the interest on a mortgage of equal size on a new home in Middletown. This will be paid on a monthly basis for 36 months.
>
>   5. To whatever extent the above items are taxable Aeronca will "gross up" to provide you with these costs on a tax free basis.
>
> F. Directors reserve the right to increase salary.
>
> G. Usual non-competition and secrecy convenants.
>
> H. Arbitration clause.
>
> II. Executive Medical Plan
>
> III. Company Car
>
> IV. Country Club in Middletown

AERONCA, INC.

ACCEPTED:

By:_____
       John R. Stewart, Treasurer

_____

Richard W. Sappenfield

_____

Date

In the following contract excerpt between Senior VP K. O. Johnson and Coastal Corporation, a number of termination possibilities are spelled out, with severance pay limited to one month in each case.

3. TERMINATION, EFFECT OF TERMINATION AND NOTICE OF TERMINATION

a. *Termination.* This Agreement shall terminate on the occurrence of any one of the following events:

    (i) the death of the Executive;

    (ii) termination by the Company due to the permanent

disability of Executive. For the purpose of this Agreement, Executive shall be deemed to have permanently become disabled if at any year during the term hereof, because of ill health, physical or mental disability, or for other causes beyond his control, he shall have been continuously unable or unwilling or have failed to perform his duties hereunder for 120 consecutive days, or if, during any year of the term hereof, he shall have been unable or unwilling or have failed to perform his duties for a total period of 180 days either consecutive or not. For the purpose hereof, the term "any year of the term hereof" is defined to mean any period of 12 consecutive months during the Period of Employment:

(iii) termination at any time after two (2) years from the date hereof by the Company at its sole right and election or by the Executive at his sole right and election, subject in either case to the party who has elected to terminate the contract giving Notice of Termination as provided under Section 3.c. below one year prior to the date of any such termination.

(iv) termination by the Company for willful breach of duty by the Executive which is materially detrimental to the Company;

(v) termination by the Executive for Good Reason. As used in this section, Good Reason shall be the willful breach by the Company of any of the obligations imposed on it under this Agreement.

b. *Effect of Termination.* In the event of termination of this Agreement for any reason prior to the completion of the Employment Period the Executive shall be entitled to compensation earned by him prior to the date of termination as provided in this Agreement, computed pro rata up to and including such date, plus an additional sum equal to the Executive's base salary for a one month period.

c. *Notice of Termination.* Any termination by the Company or by the Executive shall be communicated by written Notice of Termination to the other party hereto. For purposes of this Agreement, a "Notice of Termination" shall mean a notice which shall indicate the specific termination provisions in this Agreement relied upon and shall set forth in detail the facts and circumstances claimed to provide a basis for termination

of the Executive's employment under the provision so indicated.

Some agreements are self-renewing in the absence of action to
terminate by either party. Such a provision is a feature of this pact
between Del E. Webb Corporation and Philip J. Dion. The contract
runs twenty-four months from the date of the agreement (August
1, 1982) and is then extended from year to year, subject to twelve
months' notice.

3. *Term*. The term of this Agreement shall be twenty-four (24)
months commencing on August 1, 1982, and ending on (and
including) July 31, 1984, and shall be extended from year to
year thereafter, subject to termination by either party at the
end of the twenty-fourth month, or any subsequent year by
giving twelve (12) months advance written notice. In the event
this Agreement should terminate by reason of the death of the
Employee, the Employee's widow will be paid applicable death
benefits to which she may be entitled under any then existing
benefit plans of the Company, plus six (6) months salary at
the Employee's then salary rate.

   In the event of termination of this Agreement at the end of
the twenty-fourth month or any subsequent anniversary upon
twelve (12) months advance written notice as provided in paragraph 3 hereof, the Employee shall continue to be employed
and he shall be entitled to the continuation of his then base
salary as well as all the employee benefits referred to in paragraphs 4 (b), including automobile, club memberships, life,
health and long term disability benefits, pension and profit
sharing benefits, until the date of termination resulting from
such notice.

Executive compensation and benefit plans, particularly those at
least partially designed to serve as Golden Handcuffs deterring the
executive from moving elsewhere, are sometimes so complex that
the employee who goes to another company does not know for some

time how much money he has coming from the previous employer. When this happens the employee may attempt to arrange for the new employer to indemnify him against loss.

In 1982, RCA hired Robert R. Frederick as president and chief operating officer. Frederick moved over to RCA from General Electric. A considerable portion of the agreement Frederick signed with RCA in October 1982 is devoted to coverage of losses he might suffer in his anticipated compensation from GE.

... In the event you do not receive an incentive bonus from the General Electric Company ("GE") for 1982 of at least the level of the award from GE for 1981, RCA will pay you an amount equal to the difference between the award, if any, you receive from GE for 1982 and your 1981 award from GE, less $60,000.

4. Promptly following execution of this agreement, RCA shall pay you the sum of $132,139 in recognition of the fact that termination of your employment with GE entails the loss to you of certain valuable employee stock options. You have advised us that you understand that such termination and your acceptance of employment with RCA will not result in the forfeiture by you of certain deferred incentive bonuses theretofore awarded you by GE. Nevertheless, RCA agrees that if any such payments should be forfeited it will pay you an amount equal to the amount forfeited on the date when such payment otherwise would have been made to you. You agree to furnish RCA with satisfactory proof of each amount forfeited.

5. You are presently entitled to certain retirement benefits under GE's retirement benefit program and have spent 34 years and 2 months in its employ. Upon your termination of service with RCA and its subsidiaries, RCA will calculate your retirement benefits under its retirement program as if your years and months of service with GE were years and months of service with RCA and, if the benefits so calculated exceed the sum of (a) the benefits to which you are entitled under such RCA programs based on your actual service with RCA and (b) the benefits to which you became or will become entitled under

GE's retirement benefit programs, RCA will pay the difference to you out of its general funds. Such payment shall be made in any form then permitted under the RCA Retirement Plan that you may select.

6. You are presently entitled to certain life insurance and disability benefits under GE's life insurance and disability benefit programs. RCA agrees to continue to provide throughout the term of this agreement, either through its group life insurance and disability programs or by supplemental life or disability insurance, benefits substantially equal to those to which you were entitled under GE's life insurance and disability benefit programs to the extent such GE benefits are forfeited.

One strong version of Golden Handcuffs is the completion bonus. This is not deferred compensation or stock. It is a flat sum to be paid the employee—in addition to all other payments under the contract—simply for staying with the company for the term of the contract. When such provisions are used they may be combined with extensive no-compete and secrecy clauses, since the employer not only wants to retain the services of the executive, but may be even more desirous of keeping the employee from working for a competitor or starting his own competitive business.

In 1982, NICOR Inc., an Illinois-based utility, acquired Birdsall, Inc., and signed Birdsall's principal shareholder, John H. Birdsall III, to a five-year contract. The agreement calls for a salary of $250,000 per year. In addition, if Birdsall stays the course, he gets a completion bonus of $250,000. The pact contains some tough-sounding secrecy and no-compete language, exemplified by the sentence "It is the desire, intent and agreement of Employee and Employer that the restrictions placed on Employee by this Section 6 be enforced to the fullest extent permissible under the law and public policy applied by any jurisdiction in which enforcement is sought."

5.3 In addition to any other compensation payable to Employee hereunder, and provided that his employment under this Agreement is not sooner terminated pursuant hereto, Employer will pay Employee, as a completion bonus, the sum of $250,000 on July 6, 1987, provided, that, said completion bonus of $250,000 shall be payable to the personal representative of Employee in the event of his death during his employment hereunder unless Employer shall have provided Employee with an equivalent amount of life insurance which shall then be in effect.

SECTION 6. ADDITIONAL COVENANTS OF EMPLOYEE:

6.1 During the term of this Agreement or during the term of his employment with Employer, Employee will not directly or indirectly engage in any business, whether as a proprietor, partner, joint venturer, employer, agent, employee, consultant, officer, or beneficial or record owner of more than one percent (1%) of the stock of any corporation or association, which is competitive to the business conducted by Employer, any subsidiary of Employer or any other affiliate of NICOR.

6.2 During the term of this Agreement or during the term of his employment with Employer, Employee will not divulge or appropriate to his own use or to the use of others, any trade secrets or confidential information of or confidential knowledge pertaining in any way to, the business of Employer, any subsidiary of Employer or any other affiliate of NICOR during such period.

6.3 In the event Employee breaches this Agreement by terminating his employment prior to the expiration of the term provided in Subsection 3.1 above, or if Employee is terminated by Employer pursuant to Subsection 7.1 below, Employee separately agrees, being fully aware that the performance of this Agreement is important to preserve the present value of the property and business of Employer, that for twelve (12) calendar months following the date of such termination, or until July 6, 1987, whichever shall be the earlier date, he shall not directly or indirectly engage in any business, whether as proprietor, partner, joint venturer, employer, agent, employee, consultant, officer or beneficial or record owner of more than one percent (1%) of the stock of any corporation or association, which is competitive to the business conducted by Employer, any subsidiary of Employer or any other affiliate of NICOR in the current geographical service area of Employer or in any geographical area served by Employer during the term of Employee's employment with Employer. Likewise, within such areas and during such period Employee shall not solicit nor do business competitive to the business conducted by Employer, any subsidiary of Employer or any other affiliate of NICOR, with any customers, partners or associates of Employer, any subsidiary of Employer or any other affiliate of NICOR.

6.4 Employee agrees that the breach by him of any of the foregoing covenants contained in Subsections 6.1, 6.2 or 6.3 hereinabove is likely to result in irreparable harm, directly or indirectly, to Employer and NICOR, and Employee therefore consents and agrees that if he violates any of such obligations Employer shall be entitled, among and in addition to any other rights or remedies available hereunder or otherwise, to temporary and permanent injunctive relief to prevent Employee from committing or continuing a breach of such obligations.

6.5 It is the desire, intent and agreement of Employee and Employer that the restrictions placed on Employee by this Section 6 be enforced to the fullest extent permissible under the law and public policy applied by any jurisdiction in which enforcement is sought. Accordingly, if, and to the extent that, any portion of this Section 6 shall be adjudicated to be unenforceable, such portion shall be deemed amended to delete therefrom or to reform the portion thus adjudicated to be invalid or unenforceable; such deletion or reformation to apply only with respect to the operation of such portion in the particular jurisdiction in which such adjudication is made.

LETTERS OF AGREEMENT

The letter of agreement is a contract. It may be worded in formal legal language, exactly like a contract, or it may be somewhat more informal.

The following are two examples. It might be noted that the salary of $1,200,000 which Phibro-Salomon Inc. agrees to pay Mr. Thomas D. O'Malley is surely an exceptionally high salary figure. Of course there are senior executives with considerably higher annual compensation, but ordinarily the bonus component is larger. Mr. O'Malley is not required just to scrape along on the $1.2 million, either. The contract calls for him to receive 39,000 shares of stock each year for the three years 1982–84, or an amount equivalent to the market value of shares not delivered to him.

Note that this agreement designates a part of the salary— $400,000—as defined compensation for the purpose of calculating the executive's pension.

This three-year agreement, scheduled to expire at the end of 1984, says that if Mr. O'Malley is fired as president but remains as an employee, his $1,200,000 salary continues. If he resigns because of "significant changes in management policy unacceptable to you," or because of unacceptable personnel changes, he gets $600,000 per year through 1984. The same is true if he is disabled or fired. If he dies his estate receives $600,000 per year. He also receives, if he is fired, the benefits of his stock deal.

It might be noted in passing that this agreement did not put Mr. O'Malley among the top five earners at Phibro-Salomon in fiscal '82. For example, John H. Gutfreund, co-chairman of Salomon Brothers, the investment banking firm acquired by the firm, received a salary of $300,000 with a bonus of $2,200,000.

May 21, 1982

Mr. Thomas D. O'Malley
1 Sea Gate Road
Riverside, Conn. 06878

DEAR TOM:

In view of the fact that you have assumed the responsibility of the Presidency of Philipp Brothers, Inc., I am pleased to confirm your employment agreement as follows:

Your employment with Phibro-Salomon Inc. is to continue for a period of three years which commenced January 1, 1982, and which will end December 31, 1984, during which, effective March 1, 1982, and for the balance of the term of this agreement, you are to serve as President of Philipp Brothers, Inc. You are to be paid as of January 1, 1982, $1,200,000 per year in equal monthly installments. $400,000 of such annual compensation will be includable in the calculation of your pension benefits under the Phibro Retirement Income Plan.

However:

(a) If you are removed from the presidency of Philipp Brothers, Inc. but remain as an employee of Phibro-Salomon Inc. or an affiliated company of Phibro-Salomon Inc., your salary will continue at the rate of $1,200,000 per year as provided above.

(b) If:

    (1) You are discharged from employment for any reason except malfeasance or other willful misconduct, or

    (2) are unable to work by reason of disability, or

    (3) after discussion and review of the matter with senior management of the company you resign as an employee because of significant changes in management policy unacceptable to you or because of significant changes in management personnel not acceptable to you, you will be paid at the rate of $600,000 per annum commencing with date of such discharge, disability or resignation instead of $1,200,000 per annum.

If you die during the term of the agreement your estate will be paid at the rate of $600,000 per annum commencing with date of death for the balance of the term of the agreement. The management will recommend to the Committee on Stock Options and Stock Bonuses and the Board of Directors of Phibro-Salomon Inc. while you are President of Philipp Brothers, Inc. that you are awarded pursuant to the Phibro Key Employee Stock Bonus Plan in each of the years 1982, 1983 and 1984, 39,000 shares of stock of Phibro-Salomon

Inc., but if such award is not made in full or in part in any of those years while you are President of Philipp Brothers, Inc., in lieu of such award you will receive payments at the end of each of the years 1982, 1983 and 1984 in an amount equal to the market value of the shares not awarded (based on their market value averaged for the month of December of each year) (discounted at 12% per annum from the normal vesting date had the shares been awarded on December 1 of each year). Additionally, if you are discharged from employment or resign from employment for any of the reasons set forth above you will also receive a payment in an amount equal to the market value (discounted at 12% per annum from normal vesting date) on date of discharge of the unvested shares awarded to you pursuant to the Phibro Key Employee Stock Bonus Plan which would have vested had you remained as an employee on the 5th anniversary of the last award.

In addition to the salary, stock options and stock bonuses referred to above, the Board of Directors may award to you such incentive compensation as it deems appropriate.

In the event that you are discharged or resign from employment, in consideration of the payments referred to above, you may not until January 1, 1985, engage in any other employment or business activity competitive with the business of Phibro-Salomon Inc. or its present subsidiaries.

You agree that at such time as you leave the employment of Philipp Brothers either during or subsequent to the term of this agreement you will maintain the confidentiality of all information regarding the company which you have, or will have received as an employee, officer or director and that you will not make any disclosure thereof to anyone else except as to matters which have been the subject of public announcement or disclosure or that are generally known in the trade or except as required by law.

This agreement is subject to the approval of the Committee on Compensation and Employee Benefits and the Board of Directors of Phibro-Salomon Inc.

Kindly sign and return a copy of this agreement in confirmation of the foregoing.

Very truly yours,

DAVID TENDLER
Co-Chairman
and
Chief Executive Officer

CONFIRMED:

_____

The letter of agreement between Chris Craft Industries and Evan Thompson keys bonus compensation to the earnings of TV stations.

LETTER OF AGREEMENT

AGREEMENT made as of the 1st day of September, 1982, between Chris Craft Industries, Inc., a Delaware Corporation with offices at 600 Madison Avenue, New York, New York (hereinafter called "Company"), and Evan Thompson residing at 16341 Sloan Drive, Los Angeles, California 90049 (hereinafter called "Thompson").

WHEREAS, the Company is desirous of assuring itself of the services of Thompson as President of the Television Broadcasting Division of Chris Craft Industries, Inc., for the period and on the terms and conditions hereinafter set forth.

NOW, THEREFORE, in consideration of the premises and their several and mutual convenants herein contained the parties hereto do hereby agree as follows:

1. The Company shall cause its wholly owned subsidiary, KCOP Television, Inc., Los Angeles, California (hereinafter called "KCOP"), to employ Thompson and Thompson agrees to serve KCOP for a period commencing September 1, 1982,

and ending August 31, 1985, at an annual base salary of $200,000 per year, payable in equal installments on the 7th and 22nd of each month, and incentive compensation, payable annually as hereinafter provided, equal to 1½% of the net operation income (before federal income tax) in excess of $5,000,000 of KCOP for each full fiscal year of the Company during the term hereof, and prorated for any partial fiscal year of the Company during the term hereof, computed in accordance with generally accepted accounting principles and as provided herein. The amount of KCOP's portion of such operating income as calculated for and included in the Chris Craft Industries, Inc. Annual Report to Shareholders shall be binding and conclusive on the parties hereto: *provided, however,* that KCOP shall be charged with interest income and expense for funds borrowed by and allocable to it, and *provided further* that there shall not be any charge against KCOP for Corporate Office expenses, whether or not the Company commences allocating such expenses to KCOP for reporting in its Annual Report.

Thompson shall receive hereunder as additional incentive compensation, payable annually as hereinafter provided, an amount equal to 1% of the net operating income (before federal income tax) in excess of $1,500,000 of the Company's wholly owned subsidiary, Oregon Television, Inc., licensee of television station KPTV, Portland, Oregon (hereinafter called "KPTV"), for each fiscal year of the Company during the term hereof, and prorated for any partial fiscal year of the Company during the term hereof, such income to be computed in accordance with the provisions hereof applicable to KCOP. Such additional incentive compensation from KPTV shall have no effect upon the base salary to be paid to Thompson hereunder.

Payment to Thompson of amounts earned hereunder as incentive compensation shall be payable on the first working day of January 1984, 1985 and 1986, based upon the net operating income of KCOP and/or KPTV for the most recently ended fiscal year of the Company prior to such date. Such salary and compensation shall be in addition to participation in any insurance, bonus, pension, stock option, stock purchase, profit sharing or other benefit plans of the Company in which Thompson may be eligible to participate under the Company's policies with respect to such plans.

The Company, KCOP and KPTV shall, by action of their respective board of directors, agree to perform all provisions hereof, on their part to be performed, during the period of this Agreement.

2. Thompson shall exercise all of the executive and administrative responsibilities of President of the Television Broadcasting Division of the Company, subject to its By-Laws and the supervision of the Board of Directors of the Company. Thompson shall devote all of his time during ordinary business hours to the interest and business of the Company and shall serve the Company faithfully, diligently and to the best of his ability. In connection with such employment Thompson shall (without additional compensation therefor) (i) perform such executive services and duties as may be required of him during ordinary business hours for any other broadcasting facility now or hereafter owned by the Company and (ii) serve as a director and officer of the Company and any of its subsidiaries if elected by the Board of Directors or stockholders of the Company or any such subsidiary.

3. Thompson shall be entitled to annual vacation time with full pay in accordance with the Company's vacation policies.

4. In the event that Thompson is wholly or partially "disabled" (as that term is hereinafter defined) for a period of six consecutive months, the Company shall have the right to terminate this Agreement by written notice thereof to Thompson. During such six month period, the Company shall pay to Thompson the base salary payable to him hereunder, and Thompson shall be entitled to the incentive compensation applicable to such six month period, payable in accordance with Paragraph 1 hereof. In addition, Thompson, his executors, heirs or assigns shall be entitled to the incentive compensation applicable to the balance of the fiscal year of the Company (ending during the term of this Agreement), if any, in which Thompson becomes disabled. "Disabled" as used herein shall mean a state of physical or mental incapacity or

inability which prevents Thompson from rendering fully the services required hereunder.

5. KCOP shall reimburse Thompson for all reasonable items of traveling, entertainment and miscellaneous out-of-pocket expenses incurred by him on behalf of KCOP or KPTV, payment to be made against vouchers signed by Thompson for such expenditures.

6. This Agreement shall inure to the benefit of, and shall be binding upon, the successors and assigns of the Company. None of its provisions may be waived, changed, modified, extended or discharged except in writing signed by the parties against whom the enforcement of any waiver, change, modification, extension or discharge is sought.

7. This Agreement shall be governed by the laws of the State of California.

IN WITNESS WHEREOF, the parties hereto have executed this Agreement as of the date and year first above written.

CHRIS CRAFT INDUSTRIES, INC.

By_____
LAWRENCE R. BARNETT
Executive Vice President

By_____
EVAN C. THOMPSON

WHEN A COMPANY IS ACQUIRED

Hughes Supply Company acquired the Marbut Company. The following contract is in essence a consulting agreement between Hughes and Marbut's chairman and chief executive officer, John W. Marbut, Jr. The agreement contains a detailed noncompete provision.

A few months after this agreement Hughes liquidated the Marbut

Company. Mr. Marbut, whose agreement provided that he could collect his compensation without providing any services, was able to continue to receive payments.

CONSULTING AGREEMENT

THIS AGREEMENT entered into by and among JOHN W. MAR-BUT, JR., a resident of Bibb County, Georgia (hereinafter referred to as "Consultant"); MARBUT COMPANY, a corporation organized under the laws of the State of Florida (hereinafter referred to as "Marbut"); and HUGHES SUPPLY, INC., a corporation organized under the laws of the State of Florida (hereinafter referred to as "Hughes").

WITNESSETH:

WHEREAS, Consultant has for many years been Chairman of the Board of Directors and Chief Executive Officer of Marbut and its predecessor Marbut Company, a Georgia corporation, and at the present time is continuing in such capacity under an employment agreement dated February 19, 1981; and

WHEREAS, Consultant desires to retire as an employee of Marbut; and

WHEREAS, Marbut and Hughes are agreeable for Consultant to retire, but desire to retain Consultant as an independent consultant and general advisor to Marbut Company and to extend the anti-competitive provisions of the employment agreement dated February 19, 1981; and

WHEREAS, the parties have agreed on the terms of the Consultant's future relationship with Marbut and Hughes and all desire to reduce the terms to writing;

NOW, THEREFORE, in consideration of the premises and the mutual covenants herein set forth, the parties agree as follows:

1. *Modification of Agreement.* This agreement shall replace the agreement among the parties dated February 19, 1981, relating to the employment of Consultant as Chief Executive Officer of Marbut.

2. *Terms and Duties.* Marbut and Hughes hereby engage

Consultant for a period beginning April 1, 1982, and ending May 31, 1988, as a general advisor and consultant to the management of Marbut on all matters pertaining to the business of Marbut, a wholly owned subsidiary of Hughes, and to render such additional services as are pertinent thereto. If so elected by the shareholder and Board of Directors of Marbut, Consultant shall act as a member and Chairman of the Board of Directors of Marbut during the term of this agreement. Consultant shall report and be responsible only to the Board of Directors of Marbut, and shall devote his best effort and such time as shall be necessary to perform his duties and to advance the interest of Marbut. Consultant shall not be an employee of Marbut and/or Hughes, but shall be a consultant to render general advice and consultation to the management of Marbut.

3. *Compensation.* As full compensation for any and all services which Consultant may render to Marbut, Marbut shall pay to Consultant the sum of $5,135.13, which shall be payable not later than the last day of each month during the term of this agreement.

4. *Disability Waiver.* Marbut recognizes that Consultant's association with Marbut Company during the past years has created goodwill of unique value to Marbut. Marbut desires to retain the services of Consultant and prevent them from being availed of by its competitors, even though Consultant may become disabled or incapacitated. Accordingly, it is expressly understood that the inability of Consultant to render services to Marbut by reason of absences, or temporary or permanent able cause, shall not constitute a failure by him to perform his obligations hereunder and shall not be deemed a breach or default by him hereunder.

5. *Death Benefit.* In the event of Consultant's death during the term of this agreement Marbut shall continue to pay to Consultant's legal representatives the sum of $5,135.13, which shall be payable not later than the last day of each month during the then remaining period of this agreement.

6. *Restrictive Covenants.* Consultant agrees and binds himself during the term of this agreement to not, directly or indirectly, own, manage, operate, join, control, be employed

by or participate in the ownership, management, operation, or control of, or be connected in any manner or otherwise engage in any business which is in direct or indirect competition to the business of Marbut and Hughes or any of their subsidiaries. For the term of this agreement, Consultant agrees not to engage directly or indirectly in any capacity, whether as an employee, officer, director or 10% owner or stockholder in any business in the wholesale plumbing, heating, electrical supply or other business engaged in by Hughes, Marbut, or any of their subsidiaries in the states of Florida, Georgia, Alabama, South Carolina and any states which adjoin these named states. The parties hereto also acknowledge and agree that the services to be rendered by Consultant under this agreement are of a unique and original character entitling Marbut and Hughes to enforcement of this agreement by injunction or other equitable relief. Enforcement of this agreement by Consultant shall be limited to liquidated damages as hereinafter set forth. In the event any portion of this restrictive covenant is determined by a court of competent jurisdiction to be unenforceable because of the scope of activities restricted, the extent of geographical territory to which the restrictions are applicable or the duration of such restrictions, the parties hereto agree to be bound by and to enforcement of such provision, to refrain from competing with Hughes, Marbut or any of their subsidiaries with respect to such activities, for such period of time and in such territory as such court shall determine to be enforceable. The rights of Marbut and Hughes to equitable relief in the enforcement of this agreement shall be in addition to any and all other remedies available through an action in law.

Marbut and Hughes agree and understand that Consultant may continue as a director of Macon Prestressed Concrete Co. and Cornell-Young Co. and this restrictive covenant shall not in any way affect his performance of his duties as a director of either or both of these companies.

7. *Expenses.* Consultant shall be entitled to receive reimbursement for all reasonable expenses incurred by him in connection with the performance of his duties. Consultant shall be entitled to continue using the Marbut automobile which

he is now using to provide transportation in connection with the performance of his duties.

8. *Relationship of Parties.* Upon the effective date of this agreement, the employer–employee relationship of Consultant with Marbut shall be considered terminated and the sole relationship between Consultant and Marbut will be one of an independent contractor. Marbut and Hughes are interested only in the results to be achieved and the conduct and control of Consultant's services shall lie solely with Consultant. Consultant shall not participate in any of the employee benefit plans offered by Marbut to its employees. Consultant shall be entitled to be a participant in the Marbut health insurance program, at his own expense. Because the common law employer–employee relationship is terminated, Marbut shall not withhold from the payments made to the Consultant under this agreement any state or federal taxes. All parties agree that upon execution of this agreement, Consultant shall not be considered an agent or employee of Marbut and/or Hughes for any purpose including, without limitation, employee benefit plans maintained by Marbut and/or Hughes, such as the Marbut Profit Sharing Plan and the Hughes Employee Stock Ownership Plan. Marbut and Hughes agree that Consultant may withdraw any benefits to which he may be entitled pursuant to the terms of such plans as soon as practical upon his request.

9. *Cancellation.* Hughes and Marbut may terminate this agreement only under the following conditions:

(a) Because of Consultant's fraud, misappropriation, embezzlement, willful misconduct or the like.

(b) Because Consultant violates any provision of this agreement.

Notwithstanding termination for cause, Consultant shall continue to be bound by the covenants in Paragraph 6.

10. *Liquidation Damages.* In the event Hughes or Marbut terminates Consultant's employment in breach of this agreement, as liquidated damages Consultant shall be entitled to continue to receive the basic compensation set out in Paragraph 3 for the term of this agreement. In the event of such a termination, Marbut and Hughes shall be entitled to en-

forcement of the terms of this agreement as set forth in Paragraph 6 hereof.

11. *Entire Agreement.* This instrument contains the entire agreement between the parties. It may not be changed orally but only by agreement in writing signed by the party against whom enforcement of any waiver, change, modification, or discharge is sought.

12. *Governing Law and Venue.* This agreement and performance hereunder shall be construed in accordance with the laws of the State of Florida. In any action, special proceeding, or other proceeding that may be brought arising out of, in connection with, or by reason of this agreement, the laws of the State of Florida shall be applicable and shall govern to the exclusion of the law of any other forum. All such actions or proceedings, whether instituted by Marbut, Hughes or Consultant, shall, at the option of Marbut or Hughes, be brought in a court of competent jurisdiction, either federal or state, located in Orange County, Florida, and Consultant consents to the jurisdiction of such courts and waives any applicable venue provisions inconsistent herewith.

13. *Personal Agreement.* None of the parties to this agreement shall transfer or assign this agreement or any part hereof without prior written consent of the other parties hereto.

14. *Enforcement.* If it shall be necessary for Marbut or Hughes to place this agreement in the hands of an attorney for enforcement of any of the provisions of Paragraph 6 hereof, Consultant shall be liable to Marbut and/or Hughes for all costs, expenses, and reasonable attorneys' fees incurred in connection therewith, irrespective of whether suit shall be commenced. The costs, expenses and attorneys' fees recoverable by Marbut and Hughes hereunder shall include, but not be limited to, costs, expenses, and attorneys' fees incurred on appeal or in administrative proceedings.

15. *Binding Effect.* This agreement shall be binding upon and inure to the benefit of any successor or successors of Marbut and Hughes and the personal representatives of Consultant.

IN WITNESS WHEREOF, each of the parties hereto has hereunto signed this agreement or caused this agreement to be

signed in its corporate name by its officers thereunto duly
authorized, this *1st* day of *April*, 1982.

HUGHES SUPPLY INC.

By:_____
                    President

Attest: _____
                    Secretary

MARBUT COMPANY

By:_____
                    President

Attest:_____
                    Secretary

"CONSULTANT"

_____
JOHN W. MARBUT, JR.

3

INITIATING THE REQUEST FOR A CONTRACT

When do you ask for a contract?

The most logical time is at the beginning of your association with a new employer.

You're negotiating with a company that is likely to make you an offer. You want a written contract. While you're not sure, you suspect that you may be the first executive who has made such a request. Your considerations:

- When to make your request.
- How to make your request.
- How to respond to the employer's question "Why?"

Why indeed? Rethink your reasons for wanting a written agreement. Essentially you want the arrangement to be on paper so that there can be no ambiguity about terms. You're not impugning anyone's integrity, nor are you trying to pull a fast one. The contract is simply a document that records the agreement in an orderly way, much like a purchase order.

When do you bring up the subject of a contract? Certainly it shouldn't be the first request you make. To broach the topic of a written pact within five minutes of shaking hands places far too much emphasis on the *fact* of the contract. Your mission at this stage is to determine whether you want to work for the company and to work out a good relationship that gives you what you want in money, perks and power.

So it's probably best to wait until the bargaining is well along before saying you want it in writing. Work out the general guidelines on compensation, authority, job title, and reporting relationship. Then talk contract when it's appropriate.

How do you bring up the subject of a contract? It's best not to introduce your desire for a written agreement as if it were of the same order as your requests in the areas of money and power. For example, if an executive, asked to say what he wants, should reply, "I want a total package amounting to $200,000 per year, with about half of that in base salary and half contingent on five percent better earnings for the unit. My title would be president, reporting directly to you as CEO. I'd need a completely free hand on hiring and firing. *And I want all this in writing, in an employment contract.*"

Possibly the last sentence will shake up the employer considerably. It changes the whole tenor of the proceeding. The implications are: "I don't trust you," and "I'm more interested in the job itself than what I can do for the company."

Let's pause at this point to consider these implications. Is your wish for a contract driven primarily by mistrust or self-interest or a combination of the two? If so, you have to ask yourself if you really want the job. A management position should mean more than a favorable agreement that is recorded in ironclad terms. Pervasive mistrust of the employer is not a healthy basis on which to begin the relationship.

However, in the real world career considerations sometimes make it necessary for a person to work for an employer whose integrity— or at least reputation—is less than that, say, of George Washington. Sometimes the money is so good that it can't be turned down. These are situations in which the contract is important.

But obviously you can't say that to the employer. So how do you raise the subject?

One approach is the "of course" method. This can be useful if

- you know that the employer has used employment contracts with managers;
- you had a contract on your previous job;
- contracts are reasonably well known in the industry.

Here's how it works. You're discussing some aspect—not necessarily a major one—of the relationship, and you say, "That's no problem. I suggest the contract should read this way: 'If the Executive's salary is increased during the term of the agreement the increased amount shall be considered the base salary for the remainder of the agreement.'"

You've introduced the idea of a contract as a subordinate point. The employer can stop and say, "What contract?" (If he doesn't you continue to assume that a written contract will eventuate.) You respond that you're assuming they'll have a written agreement. Just that. You don't explain why you assume that, or begin to make your arguments for a contract. That may not be necessary. The employer may not feel that the point is a big deal worth having a discussion about.

However, the employer may either question or object. The question, whatever its wording, is, "Why do you want a written contract?" Your answer must avoid particularization. There's nothing about *this* situation that impels you to wish to get it in writing. It's just that, in general, you have come to see a contract as an orderly way of concluding an agreement: "Because it's useful in clarifying points like the one we've just been discussing. Sometimes you overlook contradictions and omissions unless you put the thing into written form. You don't have to rely on human memory. You find it useful to get all sorts of agreements in writing, I'm sure."

Continue to the next point assuming that the matter of a written contract is settled. The employer asked why you want one. He didn't say he objects to one. If he is going to object, don't make it easy for him.

The employer may persist: "Oh, there's no need for a written contract. We always work on a handshake basis here." You agree heartily: "Of course. When we shake hands on this deal I'm committed and I know you are, too. Getting it in writing has nothing to do with commitment or trust. That's there already. The contract is for understanding of the details, so that there's something to refer to if any questions ever come up in the future. It's procedural, I know. That's why I want to get all the nuts and bolts out of the way so that they're all settled and we can concentrate on the important things."

If the employer continues to resist, you are surprised: "Do you have some objection to putting these arrangements into writing?"

Put the ball into the employer's court. Let the employer explain what's wrong with a written contract. This is a better position than your having to explain why you want one.

Since the employer cannot say the company does not want to be fenced in by a written agreement, the response is likely to be in general terms, citing precedent or policy or both: "We never have written contracts with executives. Never found that we needed them. We would not want to change our policy on that now."

One way to handle this kind of objection is the *intensification* approach. You restate the objection, making it stronger: "You mean you never put any kind of arrangement into writing? Option plans, pensions—nothing?"

Since it would be ridiculous to maintain that written agreements are never used, the employer is likely to say something like "We have various written arrangements, covering matters like options, and they are on file. What we don't do is make employment contracts with executives. We have a contract with the rank and file, and we don't make contracts with executives."

This position prevails with a number of managements. They view an employment contract as something that covers what personnel jargon calls the "nonexempt" ranks, the wage-and-hour workers. This contract is hammered out (some chief executives feel it is extorted) by collective bargaining. Since the word "contract" is linked to the collective-bargaining process, there is something unseemly about a manager asking for one, rather as if he came to work in grease-stained dungarees and a hard hat.

You can't change feelings by logical argument, but you can bypass feelings as an obstacle unless they are very strong. Just say, "This is nothing like the rank-and-file contract. It's just a memorandum, or letter of agreement if you like, that puts our arrangement into writing. Surely there's no objection to that."

Keep pressing for the contract on the basis that the employer has no serious objection to it, and that references to precedent and policy are relatively slight, pro forma obstacles. Finally the employer will have to tacitly agree to some kind of contract by saying something like "I see no reason not to cover a few of those points in writing if you wish, and if we come to an agreement. But I wouldn't think we need a formal contract."

That's all the agreement you need. Once the employer agrees that "something in writing" is okay, you can proceed to work out a deal with the reasonable assurance that you'll wind up with a contract.

But the employer may respond with emotion: "Why do you insist on a contract? Don't you trust me?"

Your tactic is total surprise: "That never crossed my mind. I'm sure if we didn't each think the other was trustworthy we wouldn't be sitting here. But, of course, everybody uses written agreements all the time, on sales, with consulting arrangements, all kinds of relationships. I want to make an arrangement that pleases both of us, get it down on paper so that we can both see there's no misunderstanding, put it away in a drawer and forget about it. Unless there is some serious reason why that would be a problem, can't we just assume that there's no reason not to put it in writing?"

If the employer is adamant and insists there be no written contract, and will not be budged from that position, you must decide whether to get what you can in compensation and perks to make up for the lack of a contract, or to withdraw. Withdrawal may seem pretty extreme, but then so does refusal by the employer to even consider a contract. If you decide to continue bargaining, ask again for an explanation. If it's nonresponsive—a repeated lame story about tradition, for example—try to infer the real reason. If the company feels that giving you a contract would open the floodgates to a multitude of similar demands, and if that is viewed as a very bad thing, then perhaps you should go ahead and take the job. One senior executive faced with this dilemma did just that. He negotiated an agreement, shook hands on the deal, and then made a little pitch: "I'm not reopening the subject of a contract for me. We settled that. But I'd like you to know that I am going to ask for a review of the no-contract policy. If I'm going to recruit the best available talent, I am going to have to get people who've been working abroad, where contracts are much more usual, and I am going to have to attract executives who will insist on a contract. It's so important to attract the best possible talent that I owe it to the corporation to do that."

He got the policy modified after a year or so—and ultimately did get a contract for himself.

We have been discussing employer resistance to the *idea* of a contract, not its provisions. We've based some of these observations and recommendations on the proposition that contracts are not unknown in the industry.

If your request for a contract is truly a pioneering venture, however, your sell will be somewhat different. One way to introduce the request is immediately following a major concession by you. Here's one way it might go. You insist that you are taking a great risk in making the move, and so you must be insured by an extremely handsome severance arrangement, one that is much larger than they will agree to. You bargain hard for it. Finally you concede, "All right, then, I can see you mean business on this. I do, too, but there are a lot of reasons that I want this job. So I'll back off. You'll agree to twice the last yearly base salary? Okay. You're willing to put that in writing, I suppose. . . ."

Inasmuch as the employer can hardly refuse to put in writing what he just agreed to, build on that foundation. Make the first addition a provision that is ostensibly for the employer's protection: "You'll want to put something in there to the effect that the agreed-on severance will not be paid if I'm caught embezzling, or something like that."

You don't have to continue to refer to a written contract as you negotiate each point. Finish the bargaining and then say, "How shall we work this? Shall I draw something up and submit it? Or do you want to talk to Legal? I don't understand all the ins and outs of the formal language of one of these agreements. . . ."

For this employer, you'll need to prepare an answer to the question "Why?" that is crisp, convincing, and does not arouse suspicion: "You hear and read more about the use of contracts for managers these days. I think it's a good idea. Practically every other relationship is dignified by being formalized on paper. Why not a relationship as important as this one? The provisions of this contract give us a set of reference points in case there is ever any question. No misunderstandings, no ambiguities—and no hidden resentments. I'm enthusiastic about the concept, and I intend to make use of contracts in recruiting the kind of executives we need in the operation that I will be running."

At first use the "of course" approach: take the contract for granted. If the idea is resisted, ask for an explanation. Justify the request by citing the regularity and precision offered by a contract, without in any way implying that there is a lack of personal trust in the relationship.

ASKING FOR A CONTRACT FROM YOUR PRESENT COMPANY

When you initiate the idea of a contract with your present employer, be ready for the "Are you crazy?" stare. You can also be sure that you'll encounter the "Don't you trust us?" and "Why rock the boat?" responses.

Contracts for managers are a relatively new idea. The resistance it arouses is expressed in objections that are used over and over again. The first class of objection has to do with the very idea of a written agreement. "We have never used contracts here!"

There are at least two types of answers. One is to broaden the definition of "contract": "Well, that may be true in the strict sense of the word. But we're not talking here about the kinds of contracts they give movie stars or athletes [although there is no fundamental difference], but just about written agreements covering certain areas like compensation. You must use written agreements on stock options, for instance." Work along the line that the *written agreement* is nothing new, that like any well-run company they use it frequently, etc.

A second approach is what might be called "safety in numbers." Help the employer overcome the idea that this is a radically novel departure from the norm. Cite statistics: e.g., the 1982 Ward Howell survey showing that more than 40 percent of *Fortune*'s 1000 use contracts for managers; the September 1983 *INC.* magazine showing that 95 of the *INC.* 100 make stock options available to top managers, and option plans involve written agreements, etc.

At this stage it's best to avoid the topic of Golden Parachutes. GPs are apt to be touchy and controversial. If you are not a senior executive the employer may feel that you are being pushy in demanding the same kind of protection given to the top brass. There are good answers to this argument, but this is not the stage to get into it if it can be avoided.

But maybe it can't be avoided. The employer may maintain that stock options are one thing; you're asking for a contract that covers much more ground: compensation, severance pay, job description, and so on. Such things are covered only in Golden Parachutes, which are given only to the very highest-level people because of their vulnerability in case of a takeover, etc.

It's best to still try to stay out of a discussion that seems to get into the ethics of GPs or the levels of the organization to which they extend. You might make the case something like this:

"And those are perfectly justified. Senior executives need to protect themselves against situations that can't be foreseen; situations in which they can get hurt because of circumstances that have nothing to do with their performance. I'm happy you accept that principle. It's fair and it makes sense. All I'm looking for is an orderly agreement, on paper, that offers the same kind of protection, at a different level. Certainly there's no foreseeable reason why this contract would ever have to be taken out of the drawer and looked at again. But since you agree with the idea that things can happen that penalize managers unjustly, then surely there's no objection to putting these thoughts in writing."

Your approach is to move the discussion past the resistance to the *idea* of a contract for a manager and onto the specific provisions of the contract as quickly as possible and with as little fuss as possible. Once the employer is focused on issues, the general objection to the contract itself is not likely to recur.

You can help to spur the negotiation onto the next plateau by using a tactic like this: "We seem to agree that the general proposition of written agreements with executives is not taboo. So I'm wondering if there is some particular area that you don't like to put in writing. For instance, you're not bothered by the idea of a severance paragraph, are you? Isn't it more businesslike to have this in writing?"

If the employer says, "We have no objection to putting this in writing, but the terms you're asking for are out of the question," then you can move on to discussion of the issue.

MAKING A CONTRACT WITH A FOREIGN EMPLOYER

Business knows no national boundaries today. The company you work for may be based in Tokyo, Stuttgart or Bahrain. The American firm you've been with for years may tomorrow become the subsidiary of an organization based in Paris or Montreal.

At the beginning of the 1980s more than a thousand firms operating primarily within the borders of the United States were under the controlling interests of foreign owners. These firms employed more than 1.6 million people. Many more Americans work for the more than thirty thousand establishments maintained in the U.S. by foreign-based firms. The foreign presence in the U.S. had doubled in the three years before 1980. The increase of foreign involvement in American business since 1980, while not yet quantified, has been even more dramatic.

People who grow up within a certain culture take a great many things for granted, things that seem outlandish to people from other parts of the world. This applies to business as well as to social customs. When you go to work for a foreign firm you may make certain assumptions based on your American experience and tradition; your employers are making certain assumptions growing out of their own backgrounds. As Frank Canny, chief of executive recruiting for Golightly-Harbridge House International, a worldwide consulting firm, points out, "This can be a prescription for disaster."

The contract you make with a foreign employer should spell out:

- job title and nature and scope of the job;
- precise times and periods relating to performance clauses;
- dollar amounts on all compensation, with payment to be in dollars (not foreign currency) and the method of payment specified;
- exact severance arrangements;
- and, in general, all contingency arrangements.

If the job requires you to spend substantial amounts of time abroad, you will want to consider arrangements for bringing your spouse or companion along for a specified amount of time per year, with arrangements for living accommodations. You may want to make arrangements for children to live at least part time in the foreign country, with provisions for schooling and travel expenses to and from the United States.

4

WHEN THE EMPLOYER
SUGGESTS A CONTRACT

There was a time when employers asked employees to sign contracts strictly for protection against the loss of trade secrets or competition. While the need for protection is still a powerful motivation, particularly in industries where secret information is all-important, companies are moving toward the use of written agreements for other reasons.

The company's motive is practically always self-protection, but today protection is being viewed in a broader sense. With the growth of human resources as a corporate planning function, greater emphasis has been placed on assuring the supply of executive talent for years ahead. Deferred compensation and other forms of Golden Handcuffs are designed to help assure this supply. Written contracts are yet another method.

Sometimes executives are surprised when the idea of a written contract is introduced. Typically a manager has had several interviews, worked out the questions of money and status, and feels that it's all over but the handshake. Then comes the "mere formality." The contract is offered almost as an afterthought, a custom so meaningless that the employer practically forgot to mention it.

If you are really sold on the job, your first instinct may be to grab a pen and sign, because that will officially close the deal. A swift second thought should caution you that you'd better read the document.

But that can be awkward. You're sitting in the employer's office. The two of you have practically had a love feast. You really feel that you're joining an organization that not only pays well and offers a fine opportunity, but gives you the chance to join forces with a great bunch of guys. Even to imply that you want to look over the contract before signing it might send the signal that you don't altogether trust your new friends.

However, the onus is on your new friends to understand your feelings. The boss ought to say, "You'll want to look this over thoroughly before signing it. Why don't you take it along with you?"

The new employer may not say that, however. He may just sit there. You can hastily glance at the agreement and sign it. You may settle yourself more comfortably in your chair and go over the contract carefully, clause by clause, while the employer watches. You may ask questions about various provisions, even ask for changes.

You *may* do that, but it's pretty awkward. The best thing is to get the hell out of there and give yourself the opportunity to look over the paper at leisure, getting legal help if there is the slightest question.

Here's a graceful way to do that. *Assume* that the final interview is over and that you've been hired. Assume also that *of course* the employer would never expect you to sign a contract without reading it. (After all, he'll expect you to look documents over carefully on the job.) Take it for granted that you'll take the contract along with you. Say something like "Thank you. I'm delighted that we're all set, and I look forward to getting started. How about three weeks from Monday, September twenty-fourth? That will give me time to wrap up everything with my present company. There are several important matters hanging, but I think if I really push I can handle everything by the twenty-fourth. Meanwhile, of course, I'll look this over and bring it in with me on the twenty-fourth. Or would you prefer that I mail it or drop it off before then? Whatever's most convenient."

If the contract has been offered as a formality, the employer has little choice but to agree. But if he insists that you sign right away, you're entitled to ask "Why?" And you'll do well to ask yourself why your would-be bosses are so anxious to have you sign a contract that they spring it on you when you're least likely to be able to take the time to consider it.

One way to get into a discussion of the need for the contract is to say, "A contract is somewhat unusual, isn't it? I haven't heard about contracts before in our industry. I guess some businesses use them to keep executives from working for competitors. Is that why they're used here?"

Give the employer a chance to explain why the written contract is so important. Ask, "Am I right in assuming that all employees have written contracts? Oh. I see. All managers? Not all managers? Which people do you like to have contracts with?"

Meanwhile you're glancing over the document. No doubt it will contain the standard sections covering conditions of employment, compensation, and termination. Don't try to scrutinize these in detail. Look for the less common section—a noncompete clause, for example. Keep asking questions: "I guess what I'm most curious about is why you use contracts with executives like me. Since I expect to be here a long time, and no doubt I'll be hiring people, it will help me to hear your philosophy about it."

If the employer sticks to the story that it's a formality, of modest importance, he cannot very well resist your casually taking it with you. If he insists, he has to give you a good reason. And, whatever reason he gives, you owe it to yourself to check the agreement out with special care. You have *not* yet got the job. There is probably something in the contract that will present a problem. Never agree to an unfavorable or dubious clause because you have been seduced by all the other aspects of the job. If this contract is a necessity, then there is something about the job that you don't know.

"DO YOU MIND IF MY LAWYER LOOKS IT OVER?"

Under ordinary circumstances no sane person would sign a contract that has a profound effect on his life without consulting a lawyer. But a great many employment contracts are signed this way. There are a number of reasons for this.

"Don't look a gift horse in the mouth!" The company offers a fantastic salary, bonuses, perks. The employee has been shown a seductive vision of status, power, and money. When the question of signing a contract is raised, it seems foolish and ungrateful even to read the provisions carefully, let alone ask that a lawyer look it over.

"What are you accusing us of?" The employer reacts with shock when the employee intimates that there might be some reason to get a legal opinion on the agreement. Does this mean a lack of trust? The surprise and indignation may be genuine or simulated; the employee can't tell. But it's an uncomfortable position. Nobody likes to accuse others of evil intentions on insufficient evidence. Besides, it will be necessary to retain the good opinion of the bosses. Much as the employee longs to have the contract looked over, it seems too touchy an issue.

"It's just a formality." Some people have no difficulty in doing what they want rather than what is expected or dictated by convention. Others must have very good reasons for getting out of step. If the contract is a standard form, and everybody signs it, what's the big deal?

"Maybe they'll change their minds." Often a person who has set what seems like a very high goal in a negotiation feels that its attainment will be resisted to the death, and that the objective can be reached only by a combination of luck and maximum effort. When the desired provision is offered, the employee feels that the adversary cannot really understand what is being given away, and so it had better be grabbed right away. This phenomenon also works in favor of the fellows who sell expensive merchandise off the backs of trucks. The employee is only too glad to get the whole thing wrapped up via a signature on a contract.

"I'll worry about that later." The mind has a remarkable capacity for minimizing drawbacks to a strongly desired course of action. Executives have spotted clauses that quite clearly hold the potential for future trouble, but the drive to accomplish the immediate ob-

jective takes precedence. The manager is confident that the agreement holds nothing that cannot be handled in due course. Negotiations can be reopened at a later date, perhaps, and the offending language stricken. Maybe the clause is not enforceable; the executive has heard that the courts will not uphold some of the things that are placed in contracts. The employee, who is after all not a lawyer, thinks that the threat cannot be as bad as it seemed. And whatever it says on paper, anything can be straightened out by discussion.

The pressures against the employee asking permission to show the document to a lawyer are of course particularly heavy when the occasion for signing a contract is a promotion. The manager who is being recruited from another firm is more likely to put a hold on things while he gets a legal opinion. But the individual who is being given a bigger job can fall prey to all of the pressures for immediate signature listed at the beginning of this section.

NEGOTIATE—BUT GET LEGAL ADVICE

The provisions of employment contracts are negotiated by employees. They don't have lawyers representing them in the negotiation. That situation will not change. The discussion is not a pure negotiation. Employer and employee are talking about the job, the pay, and the contingencies, matters of substance that cannot be resolved through third parties.

So the only way a lawyer is going to get into the act on the side of the employee is by commenting on the language in the agreement after the negotiation but before the signing.

Awkward though it may be, managers should try to obtain professional advice. The employer undoubtedly prepared his contract with the guidance of his legal staff. If the contract is truly a form that has been around for years and that "everybody" signs, that is all the more reason to take a fresh look at it.

But all the pressures to forgo that step remain.

None of the reasons for doing without a lawyer's opinion is logical. An employer is not going to have second thoughts and snatch a legitimate offer off the table. If this happens the employee had better reconsider the whole deal. Suggesting that an attorney have a look at the paper is not an insult. Rational employers do not hold grudges against people who are careful enough to get legal advice before signing an important document. Deferring potentially troublesome questions instead of resolving them when they should be resolved is no better a tactic in a contract negotiation than it is in any other circumstance.

When there is the possibility that the employer will require a written contract, the executive must first of all anticipate such an eventuality and think it through. There may be reasons for having difficulty with the situation, but there is no excuse for being surprised. The same holds true for the employee who has taken the lead in suggesting a contract. The employer produces a contract at the pivotal moment and says, "Okay. You asked for it. Everything you wanted is in here. Sign it and we'll get the show on the road." The employee who has not anticipated this reaction may be a little confused. This, after all, is what was requested. Does it make sense to say, "I won't sign it until I've talked to my lawyer"?

Of course it makes sense, but that doesn't make it any easier to say.

GETTING TIME TO CHECK WITH YOUR LAWYER

The first and most important point about obtaining legal advice is determining to do so. Frequently executives who have nerved themselves up to say, "May I have my lawyer look at this?" are surprised to find no resistance at all. The employer responds, "Of course. Take your time."

But perhaps the employer will ask, "Why?" The answer is, "I make it a point to always have a lawyer look over any legal document." Since this is a logical position, it may well be accepted without further discussion.

However, the employer may reply, "It's all right. Our counsel has looked at it." Their counsel has *prepared* it. But it might seem ungracious to say so. Instead, the manager might answer, "Of course.

And while I could ask if I might waste his time with a lot of nitpicking questions, that doesn't seem fair. Let me take this along. I'll get back to you tomorrow—or later this afternoon, if you like."

Have another topic to discuss. Treat the contract like an unimportant detail: "Once this is out of the way, we'll want to settle on just how my coming on board is going to be announced. Since that might be a little tricky, I'd like to make some suggestions. . . ." Talk about noncontractual matters. Get off the subject of the contract. If the employer says, "Can't we get this settled? Why don't you sign the agreement?," ask in reply, without putting too much emphasis on it, "Is there that much urgency on this? After all, it's pretty much a formality. We don't have to lose any time. We can work out a lot of details in the meantime. . . ."

Continued pressure by the employer should be a warning. Why the rush? Nevertheless, the employee may, for various reasons, want to sign. If so, at least he should request a few moments alone in an empty office to look it over.

Look for the potential trouble spots; for example:

- an overly broad termination clause;
- crippling noncompete provisions;
- bonuses dependent on extraordinary performance or top-management discretion.

If a problem is spotted, then what? For example, the termination section includes as "cause" any action which is "detrimental to the image of the company." That is a dangerous provision to sign. But the trade-offs may be so attractive, and the danger of lousing up the deal may appear so real, that the employee wants to sign as quickly as possible. Rather than try to modify this passage, the employee may want to put in other language that will mitigate the provision. In this case the employee might observe, matter-of-factly, "There's just one change I'd like to make. This is pretty broad. I suppose a lawyer would tell me it's okay, but to my unprofessional eye it looks as if it could cover just about anything. Since, as you say, there's no reason for us to worry about this termination part anyway, let's just take it out?"

The employer insists that it stay in, perhaps saying, as many employers say with varying degrees of sincerity, "I don't know much about these things, either. That's why I have to stick with what our attorney drew up." The employee then observes, "Okay. I know a quick way to resolve the uncertainties both of us might have. The vague language here has to do with who makes the decision about certain things—for example, who makes the decision about what constitutes an action 'detrimental to the image of the company.' Things like this come up in many kinds of agreements. The standard way of settling the ambiguity is to provide that in any difference of opinion the matter can be decided by the American Arbitration Association. Let's put that in. You can check it with *your* lawyer at your convenience...."

A number of executives, heading into a critical negotiation, have made arrangements beforehand with their lawyers for telephone consultation. The lawyer is not thrilled at handling a matter this way, but it is better than no consultation at all. The employee does not argue each point as it comes up. Instead he asks questions, makes notes, and then asks for a few minutes alone. There is no reason not to say exactly what he is doing. Surely he is demonstrating the kind of prudence the firm would expect if he were conducting company business. The lawyer may make suggestions for wording changes, provide definitions and interpretations of various provisions, and, if necessary, raise the red flag: "Do *not* sign the contract with that paragraph in it. Here's why and here's what to say."

Legal review of the employment contract should be as complete as possible. If there is difficulty in getting the time to have a lawyer look it over—for whatever reason—then the employee should use his skills to overcome the difficulty and persuade the employer to agree. Sometimes one must negotiate the right of legal review. It is as important to negotiate this right successfully as to negotiate many other points of the bargaining session.

5

HOW TO NEGOTIATE
A FAVORABLE
CONTRACT

A negotiation is an adversarial proceeding. No matter how nice the other party may be over lunch, a drink, or during the ordinary course of business, his role is changed when you sit down to face him across the table. A friendly or cordial relationship with the other party can be a deterrent to effective bargaining. You may not press as hard at crucial points as you might if the relationship were more impersonal. The other party may, if only inadvertently, use the friendship to get you to go easy.

The first point, therefore, in understanding the psychological environment within which the negotiation will take place is to view the other person as an *adversary*. You are not deadly enemies, you are not literally going to cut each other's throat, but you are definitely in conflict. Professional tennis players or high-stakes poker players may be the best of friends away from the court or the table, but when the game starts they give no quarter. Purge your mind of any tendency to "go easy" because of an existing friendship or because you don't enjoy being tough with nice people or "rocking the boat." A solid, mature relationship is not damaged by a hard-boiled negotiation conducted fairly but toughly. If anything, respect is enhanced and you are valued more highly.

It's wise to assume that your opponent has had considerably more experience in negotiation than you. This experience is likely to reveal itself at a critical stage; the adversary's instinct, developed by experience, will enable him to spot your weaknesses and exploit them. Experience also confers patience. To some extent, success in negotiating depends on outlasting the other guy.

You can compensate for the other person's edge in experience by doing a good job of pre-negotiation analysis. You need not probe to the innermost recesses of your antagonist's psyche, but you have to think about certain questions.

WHAT ARE THE PRESSURES ON YOUR ADVERSARY?

The other party in the negotiation wants, in general, the same things you do: money, recognition, security, a good self-image. Since the other party in a contract negotiation is usually your senior, he has more to lose. Furthermore, he has to think about precedent: whatever is given to you may have to be given to others.

Your opponent is apt to have two agendas. One is official, one is private. The official agenda covers such priorities as controlling costs, getting and keeping the best available talent for the firm, locking you into the company on terms that are advantageous to the employer and make you happy at the same time.

The private agenda involves *image*: self-image or public image. Is the adversary a person who likes to think of himself as a good guy? Fair, understanding, insightful? Is he a person who is careful about how he looks to others? How does he want to be perceived— as a nice person or as a hard-hitting battler? Does he get a kick out of the cut-and-thrust of a hard bargaining session? Does he want to win, in big things and small ones, no matter what? Some people are so competitive that they go all out for victory in everything, even when it is not to their advantage to do so, or when the prize to be gained is trivial to the point of being ridiculous. These are the high-rollers who argue with waitresses over a dime or who become ecstatic at a win on the golf course. Such negotiators are vulnerable. Their lust for victory can be turned to advantage by an adroit opponent, as can the lunging strength of a powerful but unpolished adversary in a judo match.

Who is looking over your adversary's shoulder? Just about everyone is accountable to somebody. How long has he been in his job? Who is his boss? If he reports to a board of directors, how active is that board? Is it questioning or complacent? How secure is your opponent's position and what does he have to do to make himself more secure?

To what degree will your adversary's resistance be stiffened by the fear of having to make similar concessions to others? This is an important thing to know. As we shall discuss, the objection "It's not our policy to sign contracts covering such provisions" is a common enough ploy. Sometimes it is merely a screening objection concealing the real problem, namely that the employer just does not want to give you what you want. Sometimes the "policy" objection is real: the stumbling block is not so much your particular demand as the establishment of precedent. (Your opponent will negotiate on the assumption that whatever concessions you win will become known to others in the company—*and he will be right*. It's neither effective nor perceptive to try to win agreement on the assumption that what is given to you can be kept a secret.)

What are the policies and precedents that will affect the negotiation? Does the company have a hard-and-fast rule against employment contracts? If you will be negotiating for money, does the company adhere to salary ranges in setting compensation? Whenever you seem to come up against a hard-and-fast rule, even one which is spelled out in writing, assume that there have been exceptions and look for them.

The present condition of the company and its industry are sometimes important factors, and can affect the climate in which the negotiation is conducted. Of course, your adversary is likely to cite tough times even if they don't exist, or even if they have no particular effect upon your position. Your ability to handle this ploy depends almost entirely on whether you feel the other party is really driven by it or just using it.

Have people gotten contracts similar to the one you're trying for? It's useful to know how well those deals have worked out, whether the contracted executives are still with the firm, whether the company has reason to believe that it made a good deal. If the company

contracted for certain provisions with Smith and got burned, it may
not be logical for the company to feel that the same thing is likely
to happen with Jones, but logic is by no means everything in a
negotiation.

And of course it is quite important to know whether the person
you are negotiating with is under an employment contract himself,
or ever has been.

You may not be able to answer all of these questions, but they
should be asked nevertheless. Even if you lack definitive information, you should think about the likely answers. Studying your
opponent is essential in any contest, and the negotiation of a job
contract may be one of the most important contests of your life.

Your opposite number in the negotiation has an official position
and an unofficial position. His official position is that of senior
executive, representing the corporation. While wearing this hat he
expresses the company's point of view. The company, through its
representative, wants to secure your services at the best possible
terms while keeping you happy.

The unofficial or personal position of the company's negotiator—
whether he or she is CEO, a senior line manager, human-resources
director, or lawyer—often affects the bargaining in ways that are
not always easy to detect. A successful negotiation means something
to him. If he is not the chief executive of the company, then he
wants to look good to his boss. If he is the chief executive, he may
have a director or two who do not extend rubber-stamp approval to
everything.

How much does it mean to your adversary to sign you up? How
badly will he be hurt if he does not sign you? These are questions
which you're unlikely to be able to answer completely, but on which
you may be able to get some leads.

Ask the headhunter. If you've been brought into the situation by
a search consultant, remember that the consultant is representing
the company, not you. The headhunter's job is to deliver a good
candidate whom the company is able to hire.

But the headhunter also wants to make the negotiation go as
smoothly as possible. He will brief you on the company and your
negotiating adversary. Why are they recruiting? How many people

have held the job in the past five years? If the company's executive-recruiting setup resembles a revolving door, you may want to think twice about entering that door. But if you do want the job, the turnover rate may put more pressure on the employer to hire you, and give you more leverage at the bargaining table.

Read the business press. Find out what the industry observers are saying about the company. Learn how the money markets view the company's securities. If the firm is booming along they may feel that they enjoy a buyer's market, and be less flexible in negotiating. If there have been hints that the management ranks are shaky, the employer may be that much more eager to bring in a new executive with a good track record.

Listen to the gossip. A lot of what passes along the grapevine is exaggerated or untrue, but that does not make it unusable. The stock market reacts to gossip. So may the person you're negotiating with. That is particularly true if there's any hint that his position may be in jeopardy. Try to get a line on the importance to your adversary of a successful negotiation with you.

FIND OUT WHAT THE OTHER GUYS ARE BEING PAID

Senior executives who want to know what people in comparable jobs are being paid can find a wealth of interesting and useful information in *Executive Compensation Reports*, a newsletter that reports on executive compensation programs, policies, and practices at publicly held companies. The staff of *ECR* reviews the compensation programs at more than 1,500 companies with annual sales in excess of $75 million and reports newsworthy developments. The letter is packed with articles that disclose the compensation arrangements of corporate officers (who are named), innovative stock plans, severance arrangements, etc.

Executive Compensation Reports is published by DP Publications Company, P.O. Box 3141, Alexandria, VA 22302; (703) 370-3817. Corporate libraries or human-resource departments—at least in larger companies—are likely to receive it. While the information is of exceptional interest to compensation specialists and personnel executives, the stories, written in clear and nontechnical language, should prove absorbing to any executive.

MAKE YOUR OPPONENT LOOK GOOD

There will be times when your negotiating adversary will hold out stubbornly on a particular point, not because he has not been personally persuaded, and not because he lacks the authority to accede, but because he doesn't know how to explain his concession to his superiors. This is particularly true, of course, when you're bargaining with someone other than the CEO.

You frequently can't detect this reason for resistance. The other guy is not going to admit it. But when you can't think of a better reason for the opposition, it may be reasonable to assume that the other party fears his inability to justify the move up the line.

Provide your opposite number with ammunition that can be used in justification. Do it indirectly, without indicating why you're doing it. If, for example, the sticking point is a larger-than-usual stock option arrangement, you might remark, "From the company's point of view it seems to me that is the best kind of incentive compensation. You've done well in making me back off my original idea that I wanted a bigger base salary. After all, if I do a good job the stock is worth more, and vice versa. So I feel that I'm working toward the company's goal at the same time I'm working toward my own."

When you provide ammunition for selling the agreement, you never acknowledge that it is ammunition. Neither does your adversary. Nevertheless, he will see that he can use it, and if this is the big problem holding up his agreement, you will have overcome an obstacle.

Executives negotiating for favorable provisions sometimes lose, not on the merits of the issue, but because they lock the employer into a fixed position.

Often the stumbling block is emotional rather than procedural or financial. Here's how it happened in one case. The bone of contention was the "cause" provision, which stated, after the usual references to fraud and embezzlement, that the contract could be terminated for cause if the employee were to "violate company policy." This, of course, is a provision that should be eliminated if at all possible. Ambiguity in the "cause" paragraph is a land mine which threatens the future of the relationship. It can lie there for years, harmless, because there's no need to activate it; but if things get nasty for any reason, the employer just might activate it.

But there are good and bad ways of attacking the too comprehensive "cause" provision. In this case the manager said, "This will have to come out."

The CEO glanced at the language of the contract. He seemed surprised. He scanned it to try to find the problem.

"You mean the part that says you can be dismissed for violating company policy? What's wrong with it?"

"It's too broad."

"Broad? But all it says is... Why would anyone want to violate company policy?"

"That's not the point, Jeff. It's that it makes this broad reference to company policy without defining it."

"But any senior manager knows what company policy is. My God, he ought to. He helps to formulate it!"

"Company policy can change overnight."

"Well, Andy, I don't know about 'overnight,' but of course it can change. I hope we're not so inflexible that we would never think of modifying our approach. But so what? When it changes, a manager knows it. Or at least he should know it."

"It's not really a matter of knowing about company objectives, or policies, or plans, or broad strategies. The term 'policy' can be made to apply to very minute points."

"Like what?"

"I don't know. Like when a guy decides to eat lunch, or where, or whether he puts in an expense voucher for lunch."

"Our guidelines on entertainment are pretty broad, Andy. Are you suggesting they be changed? I don't get into that end of it much. What is there about it that bothers you? Do you do that much business at lunch that this should be a big thing?"

"No, Jeff. The thing is that if a problem ever came up, the clause could be interpreted to mean that some minor thing was really a violation of policy and therefore that it voided the contract."

"Interpreted by whom?"

And now Andy realized he'd gone too far. "Well, by anybody. There could be difficulties..."

"What kind of difficulties?"

"Differences of opinion. There are all kinds of things that could come up, you know that. Even though a guy is doing a good job, the company for some reason or other wants to get rid of him, and so the contract is terminated."

"And the fellow receives a good severance deal. That's what we just spent twenty minutes working out. But what you're saying is that we could welsh on our agreement by citing this clause. Andy, I'll tell you frankly, that's an imputation I don't like. I'm bothered by the fact that you would think of it. And I'm bothered by your objection to language that, to me, is reasonable."

Now what? Andy can back down. He can continue to fight, and fail to get the contract. Or, if Jeff wants him badly enough, Andy can bull his way through and get the clause changed, giving himself a favorable agreement, but also leaving a nasty impression that will substantially affect the relationship between him and the CEO.

The executive polarized the negotiation by backing his adversary into a corner out of which he could not emerge without losing face. Polarization factors can be factual or emotional, but the emotional types are the most difficult. An employer can compromise on money, conditions of work, or job title, but it's tough to compromise when doing so appears to admit that you are a liar or a scoundrel.

In this case the manager's first mistake was not planning how he would tackle the problem of the "for cause" provision. The second mistake was not looking at and listening to the reaction of the CEO when he brought it up. The employer really did not understand the problem. The notion that anyone would demur at language enforcing a regard for company policy was outlandish to him.

The third and biggest error was to imply that the employer would use dirty tricks to break a contract. Of course that sort of thing happens. Of course the idea of a contract is to keep it from happening to you. And of course a good many of the provisions of the contract need never come into plan as long as mutual respect and confidence remain between the parties. Provisions like the overly ambiguous "for cause" paragraph pose a danger to the employee *only* if the employer tries to screw him. Most employers can tacitly admit this without taking it personally. Some will treat the employee's request for protection as an insult.

When the employer resents the insertion or removal of contract language because he genuinely feels insulted, the problem is emotional. When the employer pretends to be insulted as a ploy to retain a provision he wants, the problem is tactical. The latter is easier to handle than the former.

Since one cannot predict with certainty how an employer may react to a request to strike "for cause" language, it's best to frame the request in a way that avoids personalities.

In the example cited, Andy might have said, "Now, here's a point that is fairly trivial, but I would like to clear it up. This says the contract can be terminated without severance pay if the employee is guilty of embezzlement, et cetera. That's fine. If I ever did anything like that I'd expect not only to get fired but to be prosecuted. But let's take out everything after that. It doesn't mean anything anyway. I'm sure that if you felt you had to get people to follow company policy by putting it in a contract you wouldn't give them responsible jobs. As long as people are dealing with absolute confidence and trust, as I am with you, and I hope you are with me, there's no need for a lot of the stuff that is put into pieces of paper like this. You would never use this language to avoid paying severance which was otherwise due. Since that's the logical meaning of that clause, the only way it could get used is if, God forbid, I were dealing with someone else besides you on the nuts and bolts of termination. That's not going to happen. But lawyers like to sneak these little things in. It keeps them in practice."

Blaming unwelcome provisions on "the lawyers" is sometimes an easy, joking way to bridge the awkwardness—however slight—that goes with objection to part of the agreement.

The basic rule in avoiding emotional polarization is to keep everything objective. Instead of saying, "Under this clause *you* could demote me without changing my title," say, "Under this clause an employee might be demoted even while he retained his title. I can see why you wouldn't see that; it would never cross your mind. But of course you don't want it in there."

Look and listen. You can tell when a negotiating adversary is unduly startled or angry. Back off. Find out what the problem is. You are trying to negotiate a favorable agreement, not win an argument or score points or make somebody mad.

If the discussion seems to be drifting toward polarization, it's a good idea to stop right there and try to get it back on course: "I seem to have said something stupid here. I didn't mean to. There's no personal implication in anything I say. What I'm talking about is my feeling about the actual language of the clause. You see, when I read this it seems to say..." And you bridge back into a discussion of the language rather than the motives or the potential actions of the human being with whom you're bargaining.

Sometimes when a negotiation becomes polarized it's best to break it off and resume talking a few days hence. Resume the discussion as if the polarization had never happened. Your adversary may be glad to meet you on those terms. The issue that would have involved personal humiliation or loss of face for him is forgotten and both parties concentrate on the objective fact of the contract.

The essence of "no lose" negotiation is to see that both parties come out feeling that something has been gained without anything vital being lost. You can win financially while feeling like a loser emotionally. The skillful negotiator does not back the other party into an emotional corner.

Occasionally you will come across an employer who views the negotiating table as a gladiatorial arena within which personal strengths are to be displayed and personal frustrations worked off. This person likes to humiliate opponents. He cares more about making the other person crawl than about negotiating favorable terms.

Such an individual is hard to take personally, but is vulnerable in bargaining. The first rule is never to be irritated by anything this party says. Even if the abuse seems to be directed at you personally it should be overlooked as irrelevant to the process. Because it is not aimed at you. The other party acts this way toward lots of people, including his "friends and loved ones." Your real concern with bullying behavior in a contract negotiation is whether you can stand the other person if you have to work with him. Talk to those who do work for him; away from the negotiation he may be perfectly affable—he just gets kicks out of hard bargaining.

As we have seen, misdirection is a useful tactic at times. You give the adversary the impression that you are most fearful of loss in an area which is actually of little concern to you. Uncle Remus's Brer Rabbit implored the fox not to throw him into the briar patch. The malevolent fox proceeded to do just that, enabling the wily rabbit to escape.

The emotional type of negotiator may be particularly susceptible to misdirection. For instance, the employer who likes to come on strong, show who's boss, win a battle, etc., gets the idea that a manager will under no circumstances accept a provision that calls for a substantial proportion of the incentive compensation to take the form of stock options. (The employer gets this idea because the manager has sold it to him.) Insisting that the stock options be a part of the deal, the employer does not bargain hard on other parts of the agreement (e.g., termination and severance) which are the manager's real concern. Getting what he wants in these areas, the manager "gives in" on the stock plan. Everybody is happy.

TRADE-OFFS

You are in a favorable negotiating position when

- the employer gives the highest priority to a particular clause;
- you are not as interested in that provision as in others;
- the employer is not aware of your priorities.

Sometimes a manager is placed in such a favorable position

because the employer feels obliged to include a certain provision because of precedent. Take for example the no-compete provisions, which began in the hi-tech area but which have spread to other industries where the protection of secrets is particularly important—fashion, for example.

The employer insists on a three-year no-compete agreement. It's standard. The company requires that the clause be included in all agreements. Any exception, the company feels, would open the gates to a flood of exceptions.

Whenever the employer insists unduly on a provision, not because it must be maintained as a norm, and not because it has particular relevance to you, you have a potential advantage. In most cases you should try to eliminate the noncompete clause, but let's say that in this case you don't feel strongly about it. You've decided that your next career move is to go into business on your own in a noncompeting field.

Your first tactic is to insist all the more forcefully that the no-compete clause be stricken because your most likely offers in the future would come from other companies in the industry, etc. (Do not refer to the dubious enforceability of such clauses. Lawyers disagree on just how binding such provisions may be. The extent to which they hold up in court varies from state to state. In the final analysis, should you decide to challenge this clause, you might well have a better chance of overturning it than you would other clauses. But it's best to file away such thoughts at the time of the negotiation. You will not enhance rapport and trust with the employer by intimating that the noncompete clause is not worth the paper it's written on.)

At the appropriate time, hint that you might be willing to consider retention of the clause—for a quid pro quo. The obvious benefit you can receive in return is a sweetened severance arrangement. There's an evident connection; should you have to leave the company, you need to be protected especially well to make up for the limitation on your subsequent money-making activities.

But the improved severance scheme may not be your highest priority. Perhaps you would like to get paid more in salary or bonuses. Here the connection is more tenuous. Logically there is not that much of a relationship between your on-the-job compensation and a noncompete agreement.

You can just ask for the improved compensation in exchange for leaving in the clause the employer insists on. But the negotiation—and perhaps the subsequent relationship—will be more smooth if you can link up the quid pro quo with what you're giving up. So, for example, you might say, "Frankly, what I am free to do if I should leave this company is not a big consideration. I intend to succeed here, not someplace else. You brought the subject up; that's why we're talking about this contingency. Are you thinking that I won't be around very long?" The employer will respond that, no, this is just a pro forma thing, they require it of everybody, but they do insist on it for their protection, and so forth.

"Well," your response might be, "nevertheless, it worries me a little. Maybe I ought to get you to give me a bigger severance deal, to protect *me* in case our relationship ends. But I'm not going to do that. So let's talk about the compensation numbers. If I'm so valuable that you want to keep me from working for anyone else, then I'm worth more in salary. Let's say another thirty thousand base salary."

The employer's most likely rejoinder is to repeat that the clause is standard, it has no special significance, etc. So you say, "If it's not a big deal, why don't we eliminate it? Let's strike it and get on to more important things."

Since the employer won't strike it, and since he is adamant about a substantial increase in base salary, you "settle" for what you wanted all along: "All right, then. But I'll have to ask that the percentages be a little more favorable on the bonus arrangement. After all, you can't really have any objection to that. . . ."

Sometimes employers feel that because there are standard clauses that are in all their contracts, the employee should accept them without question. And many employees do; they don't care that much about the provision, they know it's standard, they don't want to rock the boat, etc.

One of the principles of good negotiating is that you do not give up any potential advantage without trying to use it. You achieve your objective by adroit manipulation of trade-offs. And one of the prime opportunities for advantageous trading occurs when the employer is forced to insist on a provision that you don't care much about.

MEETING RESISTANCE WITH QUESTIONS

Questions have a number of uses in helping to overcome resistance. The most obvious purpose of a question is the obtaining of information. In a negotiation, information is received through a number of media. When you ask a "Why?" question, you receive input in a number of ways.

The *content* of the answer constitutes information. Beyond the content lies what S. I. Hayakawa has called the "metamessage"— the meaning behind the words. For example, the employer says, "Rather than tie a large proportion of executive compensation to annual earnings, we are now moving in the direction of keying the pay plans of unit managers to accomplishment of overall corporate goals." The meaning behind the words is, "When we reward people on an annual bottom-line performance basis, they find ways to come up with short-term results that pay off big for them but push the corporation toward obsolescence. From now on, corporate is going to set the goals and enforce desirable behavior by controlling the payments. You do what corporate wants or you lose money."

Yet another source of information is the method of delivery of an answer. Is the other person slightly uneasy? Embarrassed? Overly emphatic? Self-confident? Matter-of-fact? Questioning is a two-way process. You formulate and ask the question, and you switch on all your receivers to monitor and interpret the response.

The "Why" question is almost always a must when the employer objects to a request. You not only want to know as much as possible about the reasons for the resistance, you want to gauge the strength and depth of the resistance.

There are certain techniques, familiar to courtroom lawyers and experienced interviewers, which can be used to keep the other person talking and draw out more response. One is the *reflection* technique. You "reflect" back what the other person has said. For example, the employer says, "A five-year term is out of the question. Three years is as long a term as we'll go for." The executive says, "You won't consider five years?" The employer responds, "No, because in the fast-moving circumstances of this industry you just can't tie yourself down," etc., etc.

A variation of reflection is *magnification*. Here you echo the objection, but with a twist that gives it more force than was intended:

"Our policy is to restrict all severance arrangements to one year tops. Most are far less than that."

"I see. You have *never* given anybody more than a year's severance pay?" The "never" is untrue and the employer knows that the executive knows it.

"Well, there have been certain exceptions. But those were for very good reason."

"Can you tell me something about the reason?"

Once the exceptions are out in the open the "policy" of no-more-than-one-year may not be destroyed, but it is severely dented.

Sometimes the other person can be prodded to elaborate by *echoing*—simply repeating the last couple of words with a questioning inflection:

"You will have total control over staffing. Corporate will get into the act only on very rare occasions."

"Very rare occasions?"

"Well, of course if you were to want to discharge somebody who's been with the company for thirty years, is well liked and so forth, we would want to..."

In meeting resistance the "Why" question can sometimes be effectively followed by "What?"

"So you do make exceptions. Under what circumstances would you make an exception in this case?"

The answer is unlikely to provide total satisfaction, but it may well indicate the kind of trade-off the employer is looking for: "I don't know. The thing is, we seem to have to take all the risks if we buy your formula. If you hit your market-share target you clean up even though the company shows negative earnings...." A revised formula that would key some percentage of compensation to overall performance is what the employer wants.

At a certain point it is frequently useful to ask a "What's your answer?" question. You seem to be heading toward an impasse. You've suggested several formulas, all of which got turned down. But the employer keeps talking. So you put the ball into his court:

"How would you handle this?"

"You mean if I were calling the shots myself? Obviously I would want it to be done the way we've proposed."

"But as we've discussed, that's not acceptable to me. So let's make it hypothetical. If you were in my shoes, and you were absolutely compelled to get a better deal than this present language suggests, how would you go about it? What would you figure to be the best compromise you could expect?"

The other party may be surprised by being asked to prescribe tactics. But often such a challenge makes him think, and his answer can be helpful in pointing to the areas in which you can expect to win concessions.

Finally, a question can be used to trigger a conclusion. You feel that a point has been discussed enough, and that the time is ripe for agreement. You ask, "Is there any reason why we should talk about this anymore? Let's see if we can meet each other on some common ground."

A problem that has been debated for half an hour can be settled in thirty seconds if this question is asked at the right time.

WHEN TO KEEP QUIET

Mark Twain said, "The right word may be effective, but no word was ever as effective as a rightly timed pause." And the historian Will Durant observed, "Nothing is often a good thing to say, and always a clever thing to say."

Whatever the reasons, silence is not prized by the American culture. American business people negotiating with counterparts in the Orient often remark on the tendency of Japanese, Chinese and Koreans to sit through long pauses in the bargaining. This is frustrating to us. Silence is a vacuum into which we tend to rush. When nobody is talking in a negotiation we have a feeling that nothing is going on.

Patient silence is a useful negotiating tool. *Because* silence exerts the kind of pressure just described, the negotiator who uses it wisely can gain a tactical advantage.

There are several points at which you may do well to keep quiet. One is when your adversary has just thrown you a curve or introduced a surprising element into the discussion. Many inexperienced negotiators feel it's all-important to pretend *never* to be surprised. They respond with a rush of words which come out well ahead of the workings of the brain. The result is that the person says something foolish, or takes a position which should not be taken, or gives up a point too easily.

When the employer introduces a point you haven't thought of, *think* about it. Say what you're doing: "I'd like to think about that for a moment." (There's no need to say that you're surprised, or that you hadn't thought about it before; another quirk of inexperience is to overexplain.) There's no harm in showing that you occasionally think things over.

Hold your silence for a little longer than you feel like holding it. Then you can respond, if you think of a good response. Or you can say, "That's an interesting angle. I'd like to come back to that later, if I may." The big thing is not to shoot from the lip.

Another opportune moment to use silence comes when the adversary has made an unrealistic statement. For example, he says, "We have never made more than a two-year agreement." You know perfectly well that that's not true. You don't want to call him a liar, so you sit there looking at him, a little startled. The uncomfortable silence may prompt him to modify the previous statement: "Of course, that does not include the special agreements we've sometimes made with certain technical people," etc. etc. You both know that this negates the previous statement and you can go on as if nothing had been said at all.

A third time to keep quiet is at the point of closing. You've made your pitch, and the employer is thinking it over. Let him think. Don't fill the vacuum with some more talk. It's anticlimactic, it makes you sound a little weaker, and it distracts him. Just sit there. Let the weight of silence add to the pressure.

There is a solid force to the negotiator who is so secure that sitting quietly is as natural as breathing. Cultivate the virtue of keeping still.

KEEPING CONTROL

Effective negotiation goes beyond the objective strengths and weaknesses of the contending parties, just as good poker playing depends on more than just the cards that are dealt. Winning negotiators are always in control of the process. They dictate the pace of the bargaining. They never seem startled or unprepared. This is the case even though the good bargainer's position is by no means always the stronger.

BODY LANGUAGE

The polite and unacknowledged struggle for control begins the moment you walk into the employer's office. You shake hands and choose a seat without being asked, perhaps moving the chair into a position you like better. You sit upright but relaxed, legs crossed, hands folded loosely in your lap, eyes meeting the employer's eyes.

There has been a lot of nonsense written about "body language." Most of it has been written by people who view the body as a transmitter of unconscious signals which can be "read" by the observer who is in the know. The attractive person you've just met at a party sits with legs slightly apart, which means that anything goes! The employer of whom you've just asked a big raise fingers the lobe of his right ear, indicating that he feels guilty and will agree if you persist. And so forth.

You cannot make fine-tuned interpretations of physical movements any more than you can receive brain waves. The title of the old song "Every Little Movement Has a Meaning All Its Own" may be true, and one day we may find the Rosetta Stone that enables us to decipher each tic and twitch. But as it stands now the negotiator who tries to read too much into the opponent's expression or posture is making a mistake. The folding of the arms may not indicate a closed mind but rather a slight gas pain.

However, you can *send* signals with your face and body. Your comportment and posture at the start of the negotiation are likely to be received by the other party as indications of your confidence or lack of it. So relax and stay relaxed.

GETTING DOWN TO BUSINESS

In our corporate culture the individual who is most pressed for time often seems to be the most important. The guy with another appointment is taken to be a bigger shot than the guy who has all day to chat.

That's why it's not a bad idea at the beginning for the employee to reverse the usual order and move the conversation from the stage of opening chitchat into the actual business. Ordinarily it's the boss who does that. He's the person behind the desk; the tacit assumption is that he is calling the shots. He is the one who decides that the opening small talk is at an end and it's time to get down to brass tacks.

Anticipate. Say, "I'm sure time is as important to you as it is to me. Perhaps we'd better get on with it."

The employer will agree, of course. He may be faintly surprised.

ASK A GENERAL QUESTION

Adroit questioning is the key to retaining control of the bargaining process. The manner in which the bargaining actually begins is important. It sets the tone for the whole proceeding.

One conventional procedure would be for the employee or job candidate to take the reactive role from the start, responding to the employer's questions. Another familiar beginning is for the employee to make a statement of requirements and then try to defend it.

It's better to establish up front that this interview is pretty close to an exchange between equals. You have not come, hat in hand, to make some kind of outlandish request. In fact, the employer should be trying to sell *you*. Some people who are particularly skilled at employment interviews are so good at turning the situation around that an observer would not know who was hiring whom.

One way to get the employer talking is to refer to some major development that has recently come to light. If there is no such news item, the annual report can be combed for possibilities: "I note that practically all of the earnings growth you showed last year was in the machine tool area, in one company you acquired two years ago. How long do you expect the oil and gas industry to continue as flat as it has been?"

The employer might tell you to go to hell, that he's not there to explain the annual report. He probably won't. He will give an answer that is apt to be the party line for senior management. The wording of the answer is not as important as the fact that the employer is giving it and you are receiving it. The faint implication is that you are not altogether sure that this corporation is where you want to stake your future, and you are looking for more information.

Experienced negotiators of employment agreements like to use the annual report as a bridge into the actual bargaining because the report almost always takes an upbeat tone. You don't tell the capital markets that you are floundering and that the future does not look bright. So the conversation arising from this starting point is not going to help the employer to cry poverty when you make your compensation demands.

BRIDGE INTO YOUR NEGOTIATING POSITION

"I appreciate your being frank with me about your outlook. [You say this whether the employer has been frank or not.] It helps to establish the context for what we're discussing." And now you begin your pitch. If you are new to the company you recap your track record. If you've been around for a while you recap what you've done for them. You don't dwell on the past long, but rather move on to the future, outlining what you can do for the firm.

"I want to be able to take on this job with a totally clear mind. As few outside considerations as possible. That's why it's important to get all the details squared away now, so that there's no misunderstanding." Your bargaining position is then put forward.

WHEN YOU NEGOTIATE, YOU SELL

The bane of the sales manager's existence is the salesman who will not ask for the order. Sales forces are clogged with persons who understand the product, present its features intelligently, and display sensitivity to the customer's concerns; they establish rapport, they inspire trust; but when the time comes to close the sale, they *don't*. They are Sergeant Yorks who won't pull the trigger.

Sometimes this reluctance to close stems from fear of rejection. Sometimes it is the result of a feeling that to "put pressure" on the other party is somehow not nice. Sometimes the salesman doesn't know how to close.

When you negotiate an employment agreement you are involved in a sale. The product is you. This can make it tougher to press for agreement. By and large society conditions us to avoid blowing our own horns.

However, by far the biggest reason for the failure of executives to "close the sale" is that they do not see themselves in the role of salespersons.

This book takes for granted the "selling" nature of the bargaining process that leads to a job agreement. It adapts from the sales area techniques which can be used to deploy your strengths advantageously, use questions to smoke out the "customer's" real situation, overcome resistance, and close the sale.

In some ways you have a considerable edge over the typical salesman. The employer is interested, or else you would not be talking about an agreement. But you have problems in common with the salesman. Your price may be too high; or your conditions may not permit you to fit into the customer's plans.

No sale is 100 percent trouble-free. There is always some resistance, which the person doing the selling has to overcome by building up perception of value, minimizing risk, and so forth.

A successful negotiator does that as well.

THE CONCESSION CLOSE

During most negotiations you have to make concessions. The basic principle is to buy as much with your concession as you can. The optimum use of a concession is to "close the sale."

Early in the negotiation you may have located a no-give point— a position on which your adversary is adamant. The no-give point may not be of vital importance to you. It is of considerably more importance to the employer because he must be concerned with the demands and expectations of a number of executives, not just you.

Often the underlying factor in a no-give position is precedent. You are asking for a base salary which exceeds the range. If the employer were negotiating with just you in mind, he might compromise or altogether meet your demand. Since he is worried about tearing the fabric of his compensation structure, he cannot give.

By not giving in too early on anything, even on matters which are not of tremendous interest to you, you've given yourself time to spot the exploitable elements in the employer's position. By seeming to harden your stand on a point which he really cannot negotiate, you've put him on the spot. He may tell you why there is no give in his stance. Or he may be unwilling to admit that he does not have the authority to compromise.

Don't give in. Suggest instead that all the other aspects of the agreement be discussed. Work out reasonable terms on the length of the contract, conditions of employment, and severance. Now all that is left is base salary. You already suspect that the employer would like to sign you up but really cannot give in on this point.

The employer is also in no position to settle the salary question by allowing you to get the money you want in another way. But *you* can suggest it. It's best not to make your concession/close suggestion as an obvious means of circumventing the salary range. Instead, you can say something like "When I assumed I'd be able to get the salary I need to make this move, I was willing to take just enough up-front money to cover my moving expenses. The fact is that coming to work for you—which I still want very much to do—will cost me a great deal, directly and indirectly. It's not just a question of private schools for the kids and the cost-of-living differential. If I stay in my house for another year or so, there are developments afoot that will boost the market value of the place by about $150,000. I was willing to put that aside, but now, well, I don't know. And then there's the fact that my wife, who has been active in the local community, has a good chance of being elected to the Town Council. That's not a matter of money. But it means a great deal to her. She was willing to forgo the chance if this opportunity turned out to be everything we had hoped. It's turned out to be most of what we had hoped, but there's no way I can tell her it's exactly what we want. So maybe I should rethink the whole thing. . . ."

You're giving the employer a chance to suggest that your up-front bonus be substantially increased. If the employer does not do so, you can say, "I'll be frank. The only way I can back off that salary requirement is if I'm able to get more money at the time I join your firm. It wouldn't be enough to make up the difference, I'm sure of that, but it would help me to make the decision and justify it. . . ."

If there's a possibility at all, the employer will indicate that he's willing to discuss it. Now you have two objectives: bargain for the best up-front bonus you can get, and use the employer's agreement to close the sale.

6

HOW LONG SHOULD THE CONTRACT RUN?

The usual length of time covered by an employment contract is three to five years, commencing with the date of the contract (unless otherwise specified). The termination date should always be specified.

Here's a typical term-of-employment provision:

The Company has employed and now employs the Employee upon an active full-time basis, as President and Chief Operating Officer, subject to the order, supervision and direction of the Board of Directors of the Company and any officer senior to him, and the Employee has accepted and agrees to remain in the employ of the Company in the aforesaid capacity upon the terms, conditions and provisions herein stated from the effective date hereof (April 1, 1980) through March 31, 1983, unless sooner terminated as hereinafter provided.

Note that this clause also covers the employee's duties, and that it refers to the possibility of earlier termination under subsequent provisions of the contract. The language covering reasons for early termination is crucial and will be discussed thoroughly a little farther on in this book.

Some contracts are automatically renewed from year to year by language like this: "This agreement shall be extended for an additional year on June 30 of each year unless either party gives to the other written notice of termination."

If the contract is to run for a specified term, any proposed deviation from the usual three-to-five-year range raises some interesting questions.

If the employer presses for a shorter term, the manager may wonder how deeply the organization is committed to him. If the manager is in a strong negotiating position and is sure he wants to stay with the company, he will push for maximum term plus maximum compensation.

Salary continuation (i.e., severance) payments will usually be higher under a five-year contract than under a three-year contract. If the manager has some doubts about his tenure (because of possible changes in the company or takeover by another firm) he will prize the longer term more highly.

When the applicant wants the job, but does not feel he is in a good position to negotiation a strong agreement, he should try to keep the term as short as possible.

The relationship (or "trade-off") between term and compensation can be used as a negotiating tool; e.g., the manager can "concede" on a longer term (which he did not value highly anyway) in exchange for higher base salary.

When you think about the term of the contract you touch upon a variety of subjects:

- long-term career strategy;
- your self-confidence;
- the nature of the challenge to be faced;
- the immediate and long-range prospects for the company, etc.

Ordinarily the employer will suggest the term. This suggestion may be automatic, arising from the fact that the company always thinks of, say, five-year agreements; or it may be the result of some calculation. Whichever the case may be, the executive should not accept the suggested term as a given, but should, rather, think through the question beforehand.

WHY THE EMPLOYER MAY WANT A LONGER TERM

When a company asks for a longer term (five years or more) it's reasonable to assume that an extended relationship, free of renegotiation, is the object. The firm is saying that it has confidence in the manager. However, the firm is not necessarily saying it has big plans for the manager. For example, the corporation that plans to make an executive head of a subsidiary within two years may assume realistically that a new and more lucrative agreement will have to be made at that time. However, the company that wants to be sure that an important task is handled reliably may want to tie up the person who can perform that task for as long as possible. The company that suggests a long-term contract may be saying, "We have big plans for you." But it may also be saying, "Once we're sure that we'll have you doing your thing for a while we can think about other matters."

WHY THE EMPLOYER MAY WANT A SHORTER TERM

One overriding reason for the employer to push for a short-term agreement is unwillingness to make a commitment. The obvious factor in many cases is that the company is not sure about whether the manager will work out. A second factor may be impending change in the structure of the corporation which will make the manager's services less desirable. For instance, the job to be filled may be marketing director for the consumer-goods division. If the firm is considering going out of the consumer-goods field it will surely want to avoid a lengthy commitment to a marketing specialist.

Precedent is another reason for the company's preferring a shorter term. Even if the employer has every confidence in the manager, and big plans for his future, there is still the question "What will the other guys think?" The specter of hordes of managers demanding five-year contracts may tend to overshadow the commitment to the individual.

WHY THE EXECUTIVE MAY WANT A LONGER TERM

A manager who is in a strong bargaining position will want to push that advantage to the limit by securing the most favorable possible terms extending over the longest possible period. To assure the continuation of the manager's services the company may be willing to make some attractive long-range concessions.

The manager should also have in mind the size of the termination agreement. The longer the term of the contract, the longer the period over which termination payments will be made; at least that is the general rule.

WHY THE EXECUTIVE MAY WANT A SHORTER TERM

The manager may be confident that over two or three years he can accomplish a number of things that will put him in a stronger bargaining position. Right now he just cannot get the compensation he wants. So he keeps the term as short as possible.

Basically, the strategy when you are negotiating from strength is to get the best deal over the longest possible period. It is bad strategy to take a mediocre deal and lock oneself into it for five years.

NEGOTIATING POSTURE ON TERM OF CONTRACT

If the company wants to make a two- or three-year agreement, the manager's question is "Why?" If he wants a longer-term deal he can say, "I'm surprised that you want to come to an agreement for just a couple of years. I have to ask myself why. One reason could be that there's going to be a big change in the organization. Perhaps a takeover. You wouldn't want to make any long-term commitments if that were the case."

Here the bargaining assumption made by the executive is that the employer's reluctance to commit long-term is *general*, not confined to this particular instance. The employer's rejoinder is likely to be reassurance: "No, there are no big changes contemplated." Then the employer must offer a reason. One standard pretext is precedent: "We never sign more than a two-year agreement." Here again the manager's best tactic is to ask why. It's hard for an employer to make a convincing case for avoidance of an extended commitment. If the company wants to hire the manager, they are hardly likely to admit that they haven't got much confidence in him. Nor is it easy to stick to a position that nothing longer than two years can be considered without giving a better reason than "We've always done it that way."

Most employers will agree to a longer term or suggest that the discussion move on to other points, returning to the term of the contract later. The manager may be willing to do this. However, if the employer seems willing to sweeten other parts of the contract— compensation, for example (but not severance)—in exchange for the trade-off of a short term, an alarm bell should go off in the employee's head. There is a possibility that all this company wants is some short-term work.

Be wary of trading a shorter term for bigger pay. They don't have to pay you if they fire you—unless the severance agreement forces them to. So require a bigger severance pay:

"Okay, I'll buy the idea that you won't want to make a five-year contract because that's not the way you do business. But of course I'm taking a risk when I move into the job. So I'm sure you'll be willing to agree to a severance arrangement that is around what it would be on a five-year contract—since, as we agree, it's not likely to come into play."

If you are moving into the job, and the employer insists on a short term without offsetting it with a large severance deal, think twice about the implications. Try for an up-front lump-sum bonus that will compensate for you the greater risk; for the truth of it is, you are taking a chance. If you can't get either an up-front bonus or a good severance arrangement, you *must* ask yourself why, think through the answers, and make your decision on the job accordingly.

SETTING THE TONE FOR THE NEGOTIATION

In most contract negotiations the term is not likely to be the paramount issue. But even if the term offered is what you want, this
does not mean that you should accept it without question. If you
want a long-term arrangement and they offer five years (which is
long-term enough for you), think about asking for seven. They are
likely to resist. But your position may make the employer a little
more flexible on other points. It will at least let the employer know
that you have come to bargain seriously and that you intend to take
nothing for granted.

The same framework does not apply if you want a short term.
You must be ready to justify it. Even if you are able to force the
employer to agree to a shorter term, you may leave a residue of
suspicion that you are just using this job as a career pit-stop. Even
if that is the case, you would rather not give that impression. And
if it is not the case—you prefer the shorter term because you think
your performance will put you in a stronger bargaining position
next time—it's not a bad idea to say so: "Frankly, I think that the
job I do for you is going to make me more valuable to you, and
worth more to you. If I do an outstanding job I don't want to be
tied down to a contract that gives me less than I am worth. You
don't want that, either. And of course if I don't do the job you
certainly don't want to be stuck with me because of a piece of paper.
So doesn't it make sense for us to agree to a two-year deal, and then
take a fresh look at it when you've had a chance to see what I can
do?"

Winning a point in a contract negotiation is not everything. You
will have to live with the job and the company. If they are unex-
pectedly adamant about a particular term, be alert to the implications. But if other things are more important, don't make a major
issue out of it at the beginning. You can always return to it. Meanwhile, it makes sense to see how the employer bargains on the other
issues.

7

HOW YOUR JOB IS DEFINED IN THE CONTRACT

The "duties" section of the agreement can become very important if the employer claims that the employee has not been carrying out the duties called for, or if the employee claims that the company is assigning duties or meting out treatment which is at odds with the agreement.

A useful "duties" section describes, along with the job title, the duties of the job and the reporting relationships of the person holding the job. The following is from an agreement between Frederick S. Pierce and American Broadcasting Companies, Inc.

WITNESSETH

FIRST: The term of this Agreement shall be for a period commencing September 1, 1981, and ending August 31, 1985. The Corporation hereby employs Mr. Pierce during the term of this Agreement, subject to his election as such by the Board of Directors of the Corporation (herein called the "Board"), as Executive Vice President of the Corporation.

Mr. Pierce shall report to one or more of the persons holding the following offices, as shall be determined by the Corporation from time to time: (a) Chairman of the Board; (b) the President.

The office of Executive Vice President of the Corporation

shall have the responsibilities set forth in Paragraph (a) of this Article FIRST or such responsibilities as may be assigned to such office by the Board, and/or the Chairman of the Board, and/or the President of the Corporation, provided, however, that the responsibilities assigned to such office shall be of a character and dignity appropriate to a senior executive of the Corporation.

(b) Responsibility for all activities of the Television Division, including news and sports, the owned television stations, Video Enterprises and theatrical motion pictures. In the areas for which such position is responsible, no officer except the Chairman of the Board and/or the President shall be superior in authority to such position.

Mr. Pierce's principal office shall be at the Corporation's headquarters.

Most books on management practice insist that there should be a job description for every job. But the descriptions applied to executive positions, if they exist at all, are likely to be incomplete or misleading. This is probably no drawback whatever for the talented manager, particularly when his responsibilities are apt to be described in terms of bottom-line results. Today's emphasis on stating what an executive is supposed to accomplish without defining his authority, responsibility, or parameters of operation is a logical if somewhat skewed outgrowth of the great popularity of the concept of management by objectives.

Employment contracts that are oriented principally toward compensation will usually contain quantifiable criteria, sometimes stated in terms of results which can be obtained by the individual alone (usually not possible for anyone except a salesman), more often establishing numerical or percentage goals for the operation which the executive runs or is a key part of. A manager can live out an entire working life successfully without ever worrying much about how his job is defined except in terms of the results he is supposed to achieve.

Sometimes, however, the job description becomes important because the employer tries to change the nature of the job of a person who is covered by a contract. One situation is that in which the company, frustrated by the ironclad language of the contract in every other way, attempts to humiliate the manager by giving him the most ignominious and demeaning of tasks while continuing to pay him the amount specified by the agreement. The hope, of course, is that the executive will no longer be able to stand it and will quit.

A company may well try this sort of maneuver if the "duties" clause goes something like this:

Executive shall devote his or her full-time and best efforts to the company and to fulfillment of the duties called for by his or her position, which shall include such duties as may be from time to time assigned him or her by the company.

There is nothing in this language that would prevent the company from assigning to you the duties of coffee messenger or cleaner of washrooms. True, this would likely be going too far for even the most hard-boiled of employers, but the potential is there.

A little more protection is afforded by an addition which is found (whatever the specific wording) in a number of contracts. After the word "company" come the words "provided that such duties are reasonably consistent with Executive's education, experience and background."

All right. If you've graduated from St. Paul's, Yale and Wharton, if you have spent twenty years rising to the heights in your industry, and if you are acknowledged by one and all as a person of distinction, you won't be assigned to latrine duty. But the words "reasonably consistent" and the elasticity of the three criteria winding up the sentence provide a lot of leeway for the employer. The most obvious course for an employer who was determined to force you out would be demotion. From the lofty position of vice-president for marketing you are plummeted to sales manager, Northwest Region. This involves a very difficult move and an exceptional reduction in status, but you might have a tough time arguing that it is inconsistent with your "education, experience and background," particularly if the employer can show that people with similar backgrounds have occupied similar jobs.

To protect himself against such a contingency the executive might negotiate for a provision like the following: "The Company agrees to employ the Executive for [term] at the Executive's present management position or at a higher responsible management position." This is somewhat better, but it is far from being ironclad. The employer might still try a sideways move, or might create a position ("vice-president for contingency planning") which is not a demotion but is a nothing job. This is, of course, tougher on the company. Sales manager, Northwest Region, is, after all, a real job which someone has to do, and which can probably be handled well by the executive in question. In fact, when the contract permits the manager to be demoted, the manager is measurable by the standards of that job, which may be more exacting than those of a more exalted position.

Being kicked sideways or upstairs may involve just as many frustrations and humiliations as being demoted, but it is not so apparent to the world at large. One retains the status of a weighty title. Gossip within the industry is likely to convey the idea that the employer wants to get rid of the executive, but in terms of being of interest to another company this is a lot better than being demoted. You may hate having to take the empty position, but you can devote your time to trying to find another job, or you can just say the hell with it and collect your paychecks.

Companies sometimes harass managers who have contractual tenure by insisting on the most inconvenient kind of relocation: "torture by transfer." This is becoming less frequent as executives, much more insistent than in the past on the lifestyle aspects of the job, demand protection against unwelcome transfer. This is attained by inclusion in the contract of language like "The Company agrees to employ the Executive at its corporate headquarters [address] or another location acceptable to the Executive."

A further refinement of the contract may specify present and even future titles (vice-president, executive vice-president, president, etc.). While this would keep the employer from dreaming up a meaningless title, it does not assure that the manager can retain his present status and function. One tactic used to make it tough for the manager whose agreement gives him "title protection" is to change the reporting routine so that he can be told in effect to report to an assistant vice-president even if he is president.

This can be a particularly effective ploy because it attacks the target in a vulnerable spot—the innate sense of status. "Pecking order" is by no means confined to the barnyard. We may be ashamed of our impulse to seek status, but we are driven by it nevertheless. Status-seeking has been implicit in all cultures and societies. In a particular tribe of New Guinea aborigines the people wear no clothes. However, the men of the tribe wear sheaths the color and shape of carrots on their penises. The bigger the "carrot" the higher the status of the individual. In that part of the world the carrot takes the place of the corner office.

An executive who is under attack by the employer may be protected by contract in a great many respects. The company can't demote him in terms of his actual job. His title cannot be downgraded, nor can he be transferred to "Siberia." If he is instructed to report to someone with an inferior job title he still makes the money he was making before. To the outside observer his role has not changed. So what's his complaint? He has been relegated to a lower place in the pecking order. The fact that status may be somewhat less tangible than money does not make its diminution any less painful.

Job contracts will increasingly attempt to build in safeguards against status attack. In the particular instance we have cited, the manager might include in the contract a provision relating to the reporting channel or channels to which he will have access. The contract might state that he would report directly to the chief executive officer. While this would by no means insure that the CEO's door would be open to the executive who had fallen out of favor, it would at least severely limit the employer's ability to relegate the unpopular person to a lower rung on the ladder.

But of course this does not provide anything like a complete defense against attacks on status. The company may not be able to demote you or change your reporting relationship, but it can still try to diminish you by other means. For example, one approach available to the employer bent on making things uncomfortable for a subordinate is the task force. This is a positive and useful tool for bringing a diverse group together to work on a particular corporate problem. The members of a task force are people who would ordinarily not be working with one another and who, after the purposes of the task force are achieved, may never work with one another again. The strength of the approach is that it encourages the members of the group to interact without being confined by the regular reporting relationships called for in the organization chart.

An employer, particularly one who has used the task-force technique before and thus established a precedent, might use such a move to impose on a disliked executive a demotion in fact if not in form. The target is assigned to the group and told that he must report to someone who is inferior to him on the chart—and, perhaps, someone whose supervision might be particularly galling. Refusal to participate, particularly if the company has used the task-force approach before and if the task assigned to the force is of some importance, might even offer the employer grounds for breaking the contract and dismissing the individual.

The contract can provide protection on specifics like job title and location. It can provide a good measure of protection on somewhat broader and less precise matters as reporting channel and assigned tasks. It cannot really keep a determined employer from trying to humiliate and debase a targeted employee. However, a well-drawn contract can make the employer think at least twice before trying to drive the unwanted executive out by means of status amputation.

As the practice of negotiating employment contracts for executives becomes more common, it is likely that the contracts will contain more complete job descriptions. After all, a comprehensive job description, including title, reporting relationship, level within the organization, location, responsibilities and staff, is a strong defense against change of status which is intended to degrade and drive out. But as we mentioned, although the practice of drawing up job descriptions is usually given lip service by most senior managers and practically all human-resource people, in practice it doesn't happen so often. One reason frequently given for the tacit avoidance of job descriptions on paper is the fear that the description will set up parameters which will be constricting to an innovative executive. While it is true that this is a situation to be deplored, a well-written job description can be framed so that it defines the job without being restrictive.

In moving into a new job, the executive who wants to negotiate a favorable contract may want to create a job description. If he has been recruited by an executive-search firm—today's preferred means of hiring managers—the headhunter has probably been given, or has worked out with the client, a fairly comprehensive description of the position to be filled. For example, in his book *The Executive Job Market* (New York: McGraw-Hill, 1965), Auren Uris presents an "executive sketch" used by a search firm in its quest:

THE POSITION

Operations manager, reporting to the vice-president and general manager of the division. He will be directly responsible for the profitability of this division through his subordinate organization. This includes:

General sales manager
  Plant managers at branch plants
    Product engineers
His specific responsibilities include:
A. Production
    (1) Production, forecasting, deliveries
    (2) Inventory controls, purchasing
    (3) Manufacturing costs
    (4) Quality of products
B. Sales
    (1) Sales programs for automotive products in OEM and resale markets
    (2) Sales forecasts to permit plant scheduling and control
    (3) Advertising programs
    (4) Customer contacts

C. Profits
   (1) Profit forecasting
   (2) Pricing policy
D. Engineering
   Product improvement, modification and development
   through engineering research
E. Personnel
   (1) Constructive employee relations
   (2) Maintenance of adequately trained personnel to
       protect the company and permit advancement of
       qualified persons

QUALIFICATIONS

A degree in mechanical engineering or business administration
is preferred, although the equivalent in manufacturing experience will be considered. Although the man selected will have
charge of operations, the emphasis will be placed most heavily
on his manufacturing know-how. He must be a good manager
and be able to anticipate production problems with practical
solutions. He must be thoroughly familiar with the manufacture of small, low-unit-cost, high-volume products and be
conversant with the demands of automotive OEM sales as well
as aftermarket needs.

OPPORTUNITY

There will be ample opportunity for the man selected to demonstrate his ability to run this division in his own way and to
qualify for greater responsibility with the parent company.
Compensation is composed of an attractive salary plus profit-
sharing bonus.

There are pluses and minuses to the inclusion of a job description
in the contract. On the downside the manager might fear that
enumeration in detail of the specific responsibilities creates numerous loopholes through which the employer might try to escape
if he wants to break the agreement, e.g. by pointing to the provision

for "Constructive employee relations" and claiming that the manager, no matter what else he may have accomplished, has not fulfilled this somewhat vague specification. This objection can be resolved by the inclusion of language to the effect that "the foregoing describes areas of responsibility which are typical to the position. It is not to be interpreted as limiting in the sense that the responsibilities must be confined only to the areas described, nor is it to be interpreted as indicating standards for satisfactory performance." The standards for satisfactory performance, if they are to be included, will be described in terms of results rather than areas of activity.

But it is not suggested that the job description furnished to the headhunter, or any job description generated by the employer, simply be included without question in the job agreement. The executive, in preparing to negotiate a contract, will want to collect information on which he will base his strategy and tactics. The job description is a necessary piece of information. Furthermore, the existence of the job description is likely to be beneficial to employer and employee. Like other provisions that may be negotiated into the contract, it is a commonsense measure which is likely to facilitate better relations between the executive and the company without reference to the contract.

The positive benefit of incorporating a modified job description into the contract is that it offers protection against excessive change in the conditions of employment, for example that which might take place when a company tries to restrict severely the scope and authority of the manager.

If elements of a job description are included in the contract, then there must be provision for inclusion of a new description whenever the manager is promoted. Again, the definition of the nature of the new job is a commonsense procedure that should take place whether there is a contract or not. Untold numbers of executives have failed in their jobs because they had no clear understanding of what they were supposed to do or what was expected of them.

A safeguard against the ploy of demeaning the executive by assigning him to subordinate positions in task forces that may be created to study trivial subjects may be achieved by putting into the contract words which define in general terms the nature of such additional assignments that may from time to time be imposed. One provision might state that the executive cannot be assigned to report, even temporarily, to someone of inferior rank. (They're unlikely to promote a messenger to executive vice-president just to humiliate you.) Other provisions might refer to the proportion of time which the manager might reasonably be expected to spend on duties outside his formal position, and to the assurance that extra effort as part of a task force is in no way to mean that the executive can be shut off from the reporting channels which have been agreed on as part of his regular job.

Provisions of the contract which define the responsibilities, scope, title and reporting channels that go with the job—as distinct from those which cover the performance expected in the job—are provisions that you hope will never have to be referred to. They are essentially protective devices which close off at least some of the avenues of attack that might be used by an employer bent on driving an unwanted manager out by means of humiliation and harassment. As covered elsewhere, you can negotiate them into the contract under the "What possible objection could there be?" tactic. However, such safeguards should never be of primary importance. If a manager thinks he is in dire need of such protection, he should ask himself again if he really wants a job with this firm, contract or not.

PROTECTION AGAINST UNWANTED TRANSFERS

The agreement between ABC and Mr. Pierce also specifies that "Mr. Pierce's principal office shall be at the Corporation's headquarters."

At the time of signing, location of employment may not be a big issue to the manager. This is particularly true in the case of younger executives who have not begun families or put down roots. If anything, they may welcome the possibility of transfer to new fields, or at least be indifferent to it.

That situation may change, so it's worthwhile to give some thought to a restriction on the company's right to transfer. Of course, for those who want to stay put or at least retain the option to stay put, there is more urgency to the question of a "location of employment" section. Unlike other provisions that are likely to be in the contract and therefore must only be modified, the location language must be added.

Here is one fairly typical section:

> During the Employment Period it is understood that the Company expects to maintain its principal place of business in [location]. If the requirements of the Company, as determined by its Board of Directors, make it desirable to relocate the principal offices of the Company to another location during the Employment Period, the Executive will be consulted in advance of any such relocation.

If the provision were to end here, allowing only that the executive be "consulted in advance," it would be weak. A provision should carry something like the following to endow it with teeth:

> The Executive will not be required to render services hereunder outside the New York metropolitan area without his approval. *Whether or not such approval is given, the Executive shall be entitled to the compensation provided for in Paragraph 2 . . .*

A shorter way of putting it is contained in another contract:

> Unless the Executive otherwise consents, the principal place of the Executive's employment shall be within a 50-mile radius of Princeton, New Jersey . . .

MOONLIGHTING

You may want to give yourself the freedom to do some spare-time work—consulting, speaking, writing, etc. If so, make sure the employment agreement does not preclude outside activity.

The relevant language is found in the "Employment" or "Services" section. Here are two excerpts which could be interpreted as forbidding any outside activity:

> During the term of this agreement the Executive shall devote his full time and energy to the business and affairs of the company...

> The Executive hereby accepts such employment and agrees to devote his full working time and best efforts to the services of the company...

In order to allow certain kinds of outside activity the language should resemble these two excerpts:

> During the employment period the Executive agrees to devote *substantially all of his normal business time and attention* (reasonable vacations and periods of leave excepted) to the affairs of the Company and the promotion of its interests...

> Executive agrees that at all times during the term thereof, she will devote all of her undivided time *during customary business hours* to the business and interest of the company...

"Customary business hours" is a useful phrase to incorporate into this section.

These days a substantial number of executives moonlight. Most do it secretly, because they're afraid they'll be fired. But more and more of them are taking the chance, mostly because they need the money, but to some extent because they enjoy it.

Managerial moonlighting can include such activities as teaching, consulting, running a small business or mail-order firm, bookkeeping and financial and tax counseling, law practice (for corporate attorneys), programming (for computer experts), writing (for public-relations people), selling, etc. Often the free-lancer works in the underground economy, being paid in cash or kind via the barter system. If you can do tax returns and books for your doctor or dentist, or advertising for your grocery and liquor stores, you can save a lot of money.

An employment contract might attempt to preclude moonlighting by a typical "duties" paragraph like the following:

> Executive shall devote his or her *full-time and best* efforts to the Company and to fulfilling the duties of his or her position, said duties to be assigned to him or her by the Company...

The stopper for the would-be moonlighter, of course, is "full-time and best." If you want to free-lance, or think you may want to in the future, try to negotiate this wording out. The "full-time" must go; "best" might be kept, but you're better off if the entire phrase is eliminated.

Some companies are adamant about opposing all forms of moonlighting. Others may permit it—if only by ignoring the fact that it goes on—but want to retain the right to forbid certain kinds of free-lance work. Certainly few firms would be willing to simply eliminate the "full-time" requirement from a contract without a fight.

YOUR BARGAINING POSTURE

You have no current plans to free-lance. Success in your job is all-important, and you will be devoting great efforts to that end. You'll be working long hours, and working weekends, but you will not be working on the company's business twenty-four hours a day. You don't imagine that anyone in the company does that, nor do you think the company expects it.

The company will benefit if you are always sharp and at your best. Can that situation be best assured if you just sit around in your spare time, or would it be better if you keep your edge and develop your skills by exercising your mental muscles on other challenging tasks? A team benefits when an athlete works out on his own.

You would, of course, engage in no off-job activity that competes with the company or that in any way could damage the company's interests. Your free-lance work will be like ongoing training. The company doesn't have to pay for it; in fact, the company benefits in another way, because that additional income makes you more secure financially and able to tackle the challenges of your job with peace of mind. At the same time emphasize that the money you will earn in free-lance activities is minimal. You are doing it to keep busy in leisure time and to develop yourself. It's like a paid hobby. (It's important to play down the money end, because you don't want the employer to think you enjoy a substantial outside income.)

Be ready to point out the ways in which certain kinds of free-lance work would make you more valuable to the company—by helping you enhance particular skills, by giving you another string for your bow through the addition of new abilities, by widening your circle of contacts, etc. Some employers respond that volunteer community work is all right, but they don't want employees engaging in paid activities. To this you might say, "But getting paid is the test. It's not important how much I get paid. I want to test myself in the marketplace." The majority of employers may approve of community volunteerism as good public relations, but few have much respect for "do-gooding" as a real test of ability, so the "test myself in the marketplace" argument will be received with some sympathy.

EVIDENCE YOU CAN CITE

If you've been around the company any length of time you've probably learned about various people who moonlight. *Never name names.* It's enough, perhaps, to say, "Since other people in comparable jobs do free-lance work, I know the company has no policy that rules it out."

You might think of quoting Peter Drucker as an authority on the beneficial nature of free-lancing: "Business organizations should be more tolerant of the manager who develops an outside interest; indeed, they should encourage it." Drucker says that the manager benefits when he has "a genuine, true, major outside interest. Not a hobby, a genuine interest... It not only develops your strengths; it helps to protect you against the inevitable shocks."

YOUR TRADE-OFF

Your initial bargaining position is simply that the term "full-time" (or its equivalent) should be removed from the contract. Your agreement with the firm rests on your satisfactory fulfillment of what is expected of you, without any limitations. As for the question of precedent, you don't take seriously the proposition that moonlighting is unknown in the firm: "Do you mean that no one in this company engages in any outside activity for money? At all?" Since this is unlikely to be the case—your negotiating adversary may himself have some outside interests—the argument may shift to the question of outside activities that create a "conflict."

This is the ground you want to be on. At first you may insist that the nature of any free-lance work you do is up to you (and you don't acknowledge that you'll do any). Then you may finally give in and agree to limiting language something like this:

> The Executive will engage in no paid activity for any competitor of the Company or any organization in a related field.

At the proper moment you should be ready to "concede" and agree to such a provision, which you will suggest. The advantage of language like that just quoted is that by excluding certain kinds of activities, i.e. work for competitors, it by implication allows everything else. Be careful not to allow the employer to put in a "not limited to" phrase, which has the effect of making the forbidden activity only one among many, the rest unspecified. (Always avoid "not limited to" if possible.)

8

COMPENSATION: OPTIONS, BONUSES, DEFERRALS, COST-OF-LIVING ADJUSTMENTS, ETC.

Money is the centerpiece of the contract.

Sometimes the employment contract simply specifies the minimum salary, leaving bonus agreements, etc., to be described in separate documents.

Here's a typical section (from a contract dated August 1, 1982, between Del E. Webb Corporation and Philip J. Dion, a senior vice-president):

Compensation: (a) The Employee's minimum base salary shall be One Hundred and Twenty Thousand Dollars ($120,000) per annum, payable as nearly as possible, in equal semi-monthly installments (except to the extent that Employee may have elected to defer payment pursuant to the provisions of the Company's Executive Deferred Compensation Plan or such other deferred compensation plan of the Company as may be in effect from time to time) subject to adjustment (but not below the minimum base salary provided above) in accordance with the regular procedures established by the Company for salary adjustments.

(b) The Employee shall participate in any incentive compensation plan, pension or profit-sharing plan, stock purchase plan, annuity or group benefit plan, medical plan and other benefit plans maintained by the Company for its executive employees, in accordance with the terms and conditions thereof. In addition, the Company will provide the Employee with a suitable automobile and an active membership in a suitable country club of the Employee's choice.

The salary provision of course sets a minimum, not a maximum. While that is standard, it's nevertheless wise to make sure the language permits the salary to go up but not down.

The tacked-on perk line concerning the automobile and the country club is not an uncommon feature of executive job contracts. As this book discusses elsewhere, the wisdom of putting perks like these into the contract is open to question.

When the contract spells out the entire compensation arrangement, it is apt to get complicated. One may find an example in the following, quoted from an agreement between Esquire Inc. and Martin Winkler, dated December 12, 1978. Mr. Winkler was a vice-president of Esquire and president of Esquire's Belwin-Mills music-publishing subsidiary. A compensation section as convoluted as this underscores the importance of having a lawyer's advice and for arranging for arbitration in case of a dispute.

2. *Compensation.*

(a) As compensation for his services to Belwin under paragraph 1(a) of this Agreement during the Employment Period, Belwin will pay to Employee (i) basic compensation at the rate of $143,000 per annum plus (ii) additional compensation in respect of each full fiscal year of Belwin which commences within the Employment Period, beginning with the fiscal year which commences April 1, 1979, in an amount equal to the applicable percentages (as hereinafter defined) of the pretax net profits (as hereinafter defined) of Belwin for such fiscal year in excess of $1,400,000. Such basic compensation shall be paid in approximately equal weekly installments, and such additional compensation shall be paid within 30 days of receipt by Esquire of financial statements, certified by the independent public accountants at the time employed by Esquire, which include the results of operations of Belwin for the fiscal year in respect of which such additional compensation is payable. The amount of additional compensation in respect of any such fiscal year shall not be prorated if the Employment Period terminates during such fiscal year.

For purposes of this paragraph 2(a), the "pretax net profits" of Belwin for any fiscal year of Belwin shall mean the consolidated earnings before provisions for taxes on income of Belwin and its consolidated subsidiaries for such fiscal year remaining after deduction from gross revenues and other income of all normal cost and expense deductions determined in accordance with generally accepted accounting principles applied on a basis consistent with the 1977 Financial Statements (as defined in the Purchase Agreement) or as contemplated by the notes thereto, including, without limitation, after deduction of (i) an amount equal to the amount of basic compensation paid to Employee by Belwin during such fiscal year under this paragraph 2(a) and (ii) an amount equal to all state, local and franchise taxes accrued by Belwin and its subsidiaries during such fiscal year, but before (A) any deduction for any additional compensation paid or payable to Employee at any time under this Agreement, (B) any provision for any Federal or foreign income taxes in respect of such fiscal year and (C) any allocation or apportionment to Belwin of amounts representing general corporate overhead of Esquire (or its successors or assigns under paragraph 6 hereof) or charges relating to the allocation of the purchase price of Belwin in excess of its book value. The parties agree that "pretax net profits" shall not include the profit or loss, as the case may be, resulting from unusual and nonrecurring items which are not identifiable with, or do not result from, the usual or typical business operations of Belwin and its subsidiaries. The parties agree, however, that the "pretax net profits" of Belwin shall be increased or decreased, as the case may be, as provided in Exhibit A attached hereto. In case of any dispute between Employee and Belwin as to the amount of additional compensation payable to Employee in respect of any fiscal year, determination of the amount so payable by the independent public accountants at the time employed by Esquire, made at the request of any party, shall be binding and conclusive on all parties hereto. For purposes of this paragraph 2(a), the "fiscal year" of Belwin means the annual period for which Esquire files its Federal income tax returns.

For purposes of this paragraph 2(a), the "applicable percentages" shall be (i) 4% of the portion of the pretax net profits for such fiscal year of Belwin in excess of $1,400,000 but not more than $1,900,000, (ii) 5% of the portion of the pretax net profits for such fiscal year of Belwin in excess of $1,900,000 but not more than $2,400,000 and (iii) 6% of the portion of the pretax net profits for such fiscal year of Belwin in excess of $2,400,000.

Nothing herein shall prevent the basic compensation provided for in this paragraph 2(a) from being increased or decreased at any time in respect of future payments, or the other terms or provisions of this Agreement relating to the Employment Period from being modified or amended, by the written consent and agreement of Belwin and Employee, as approved by the Board of Directors of Esquire; and nothing herein shall prevent Employee from being entitled to receive any bonus or additional compensation which may be voted or approved by the Board of Directors of Belwin or Esquire. If any substantial entity shall be added to the Music Group of Esquire during the Employment Period pursuant to paragraph 1(b) hereof, then the parties hereto agree to negotiate in good faith to determine whether any further compensation to Employee is appropriate as a result of duties Employee undertakes on behalf of Esquire with respect to such entity.

(b) Whenever any of the following provisions of this Agreement shall require Belwin to pay any amount to Employee's beneficiary, such payment shall be made to such individual or individuals, and in such shares, as Employee shall last have designated by written notice delivered or mailed by first class mail addressed to the Secretary of Esquire or, in the absence of an effective designation, to his widow or, if she shall not then be living, to his children in equal shares or, if no such child shall then be living, to his descendants in equal shares *per stirpes*. If no such beneficiary shall be living when any such payment is required to be made, Belwin shall have no further obligations hereunder. Employee may, in the manner provided above, change any such designation from time to time, may designate successor beneficiaries and may make separate designations in respect of each provision of this Agreement under which any such payment may be made.

STOCK OPTIONS

These days incentive stock options (ISOs) are a staple of executive compensation. The Tax Reform Act of 1981 has made this device attractive to employees by reducing the tax rate on capital gains; by decreeing that no taxes need be paid until the stock has actually been sold; and by assuring capital-gains treatment if the shares are held for one year after they are bought. The recipient of the option must wait two years before exercising the option. The option cannot be exercised more than three months after the recipient ceases active employment with the company. If these provisions are not met the profit is taxable as ordinary income.

Companies may also offer employees "nonqualified" stock options. The plus is that the plan is free of the restrictions imposed by the Tax Reform Act. The minus is the loss of the capital-gains advantage.

WHY COMPANIES OFFER ISOs

The incentive stock option is an expensive perk from the company's point of view. With a nonqualified option plan the company can deduct an amount equal to the income the executive realizes upon exercising the option. There is no such deduction possible under the ISO, so the company forgoes a considerable tax break in order to give its employees a piece of the action and the tax-deferral advantages of the ISO.

So why do companies do it? By far the paramount reason is the competition to attract and keep good people. When other firms offer ISOs, the firm that does not is at a disadvantage in recruiting.

To strengthen recruiting efforts, companies have become ingenious in devising attractive compensation programs. Here are some examples:

Manufacturers Hanover has a stock plan with five options. Participants are offered ISOs, nonqualified options, and stock appreciation rights. In addition, the company offers restricted stock and restricted stock *units*. Those who take restricted stock grants have voting rights during the restricted period. At the end of the period the participant simply owns the shares. Restricted stock units carry no voting rights during the restricted period. At the end of the period the holder can choose to receive the current value of one share for each unit, cash or a combination. Both restricted stock and restricted stock units pay dividends during the restricted period.

EASCO Corporation offers ISOs, nonqualified options, and stock appreciation rights from a pool of about 5 percent of outstanding common. No more than one third of the pool may be issued as SARs. The nonqualified stock can be sold for up to 15 percent under fair market value. Vesting is one third immediately and one third each successive year.

Vesting is not always this rapid. Another manufacturing company has an ISO plan with a five-year term on each grant. The vesting schedule is 20 percent through the first four anniversaries with the last 20 percent vesting after fifty-four months.

In 1983 Doyle Dane Bernbach disclosed an agreement with President and Chief Operating Officer Neil Austrian under which Mr. Austrian receives 120,000 stock appreciation rights at book value. This bonus pays out if the company earns a total of $100 million after taxes over ten years. After five years Mr. Austrian is entitled to receive an amount equal to the five-year aggregate dividends on the SARs.

Fairchild Industries tends to give stock appreciation rights to officers and stock options to nonofficers. The SARs—the right to receive in stock or cash the gain in market value of stock—pay out half in stock and half in cash. The options available to nonofficers are generally ISOs.

SCOA Industries (retailing) offers participants in the stock purchase plan, who are selected by a committee of outside directors,
shares that are priced at book value on the day of the offer. Participants have thirty days to accept. The stock may be paid for by
payroll deduction, with no interest paid on the balance, or by any
other means acceptable to the committee.

Marshall & Ilsley Corp. (banking) offers executives an interesting
variety of stock plans: ISOs, nonqualified-stock options, tandem
stock appreciation rights, "purchase rights" to restricted shares, and
"cash equivalent rights" in connection with the purchase rights. The
pool of available shares is between 4 and 5 percent of outstanding
common. No more than half the pool may be handled as ISOs or
non-ISOs. Nonqualified options may be discounted as much as 15
percent of fair market value. "Purchase rights" make it possible to
purchase restricted shares at a price determined by the administering
committee. The cash equivalent rights may be very generous. The
holder of stock is entitled to receive in cash up to 100 percent of
the excess of fair market value when restrictions expire over the
purchase price of the shares. The committee may have pegged that
purchase price as low as par value—$1 per share. The company's
stock was around the 30 mark late in 1982.

TWO-PRICE STOCK PLANS

Beverly Enterprises, a health-care company, provides a two-way
stock plan. One is an ISO scheme which calls for the employee to
exercise options at fair market value, but which carries the capital-
gains advantage built into ISOs.

The company also has a plan offering nonqualified options at 85
percent of fair market value. The administering committee allocates
the pool, increased in 1983 to 900,000 shares, between options and
restricted grants. Restricted shares vest at 20 percent per year, with
participants able to receive dividends on (and vote) unvested shares.
A Golden Handcuff feature in this provision is that shares still
restricted are forfeited on termination unless the committee decides
otherwise. Options have a five-year life, with a vesting period of at

least one year. Payment of the discounted amount may be in cash, common or both.

This is an example of the growing trend toward offering more options in the "compensation cafeteria."

LOANS FOR STOCK PURCHASES

In 1983, American Express adopted a plan under which the company may offer loans to executives to finance purchases of the company's stock. The stock may be bought as part of an option plan, directly from the company, or on the open market. Maximum credit is limited by the individual's base salary. The interest rate was set initially at 9 percent. The administering committee can change the rate and is authorized to set rates below the market.

CAN YOU CHOOSE AN ISO PLAN?

Some companies give employees the chance to choose ISO treatment for their stock purchases as ISOs, thus realizing favorable tax treatment. (An ISO bestows the right to purchase company stock at an established price for ten years. The price must equal 100 percent of fair market value at grant. Options are limited to $100,000 per year plus unused carryovers. Shares held at least one year from purchase and two years from grant receive capital-gains treatment.)

Harris Corporation, an electronics firm employing more than 25,000 people, offers participants in the stock-purchase program the opportunity to treat their shares as ISOs. This program includes virtually all full-time nonunion employees, excluding officers, directors and key employees who have outstanding ISOs or options on more than 1,000 shares.

Each participant may use up to 10 percent of compensation to buy stock from a two-million-share pool. The price per share is set at fair market value at the beginning of plan year, with purchase allowed at the end of the year. Shares bought under the ISO (as opposed to the nonstatutory) plan are held in escrow for the required two years.

THE BENEFITS OF ISOs FOR EMPLOYEES

For the young manager the offer of stock options constitutes admission to the club. The company thinks enough of you to provide you with the same perk the top brass gets. There is considerable psychic satisfaction in the offer.

Viewed objectively, the ISO is by no means perfect. For one thing, the value of the company's stock must go up for the exercise of the options to be worthwhile. The price you agree to pay is fixed. If it's $30 a share, you can buy the stock (up to the $100,000-per-year limit) for that price after the specified time period has elapsed.

However, the "locked-in" aspect of the stock price takes some of the pressure off the executive. The stock may be drifting at about $35 when the two-year period ends, so the purchase does not appear wise. Then the stock market takes off and the shares go up to $55. Now the stock is a good buy at the locked-in $30.

But while the executive can exercise his right to buy when the price is high, he cannot sell for at least a year if he wants to get the full benefit of capital gains. Therefore the market must at least remain at its present level for the sale of the shares to really pay off. If it should drop back to $30 during that time, the executive is definitely not ahead of the game.

Furthermore, there is the question of getting the cash to exercise the option. By putting up the shares as collateral the employee can get a bank loan, but the interest on the loan may wipe out a considerable portion of the profit. The company may offer a lower-than-going-rate interest loan. (This is a practice more popular with banks than in other industries.) You are then, of course, more solidly locked into the company, which is now your creditor. There are pluses and minuses to taking a low-interest loan from the company as a perk (for one thing, the wisdom of the move may depend on provisions for complete or partial forgiveness at time of termination), which are discussed elsewhere. It is sufficient here to note that the company loan, if available, is not necessarily the answer to the manager's prayers when the time comes to get up the cash for the conversion of stock options.

This is not to suggest that ISOs are insignificant perks. They are potentially of great value, and their availability offers some bargaining room. But they should not be taken at face value as the ultimate in incentive compensation.

YOUR BARGAINING POSITION

Since the provisions of ISOs cost the company money, the company naturally thinks and acts as though the offer is incredibly generous and should be snapped up by the grateful employee without discussion or question.

The employee's position should be a little different. The ideal posture to try to achieve is one in which the stock option is an "of course" perk, as much to be expected as health insurance or a pension plan. (Things are moving in this direction. If and when changes in IRS rules make it less onerous for the company, stock options for executives are likely to become standard perks. Furthermore, their use may spread below the executive ranks. While the corporation may not be quite so eager to lock in a key-punch operator, enlightened human-resource experts say that everyone works better with a piece of the action.)

The manager, in negotiating, can begin his maneuvering for this perk by anticipating its mention by the employer, who may be saving it as the *pièce de résistance*: "I know you provide stock options here, and of course I'll expect the size of my option plan to be commensurate with the job." When the employer tries to argue that the ISO is anything but routine and is a fabulous concession, the manager can respond with points about the payoff depending on stock performance, adding, "But that's the risk someone in my position has to take. Since I expect my contribution to help to move those shares higher, I am certainly willing to take a part of the action." The executive can't get the employer to buy the idea that the employee is doing him a favor by taking the option plan, but the value of the ISO as a bargaining chip can be somewhat deflated.

TRY FOR MORE FAVORABLE OPTIONS

Once the principle of the stock plan has been established, the executive can negotiate for something better. One possibility is the junior stock plan, discussed below. There are other possibilities, all aimed at enabling the executive to obtain the optioned shares at less or no cost.

Appreciation grants credit the employee as the owner of a certain amount of stock as of a particular date. There is a termination date which closes out the period of "ownership." If the stock has gone up on the termination date, the employee can take the amount of the appreciation in either cash or stock.

Phantom options are more favorable to the employee than appreciation grants, because they carry no specific termination date, permitting the employee to decide during the applicable period— ordinarily three to five years—when to exercise the option.

Full-value grants are simply bonuses consisting of stock rather than cash. If certain criteria are met, the employee gets a certain amount of stock.

Besides bargaining to get the stock at a discount or at no cost, the manager may want to try to negotiate the criteria which determine the value of the stock options. Basically the criterion is the price per share at the time the option is exercised and at the time the stock is sold. Under this formula the executive's own abilities are likely to have little bearing on the bonus earned.

A way around this is the formula value approach. Here the value of the cash or stock paid out depends on certain agreed-on criteria— time with the company, departmental profit, share of market, return on investment, etc. The manager whose efforts are measurable, and whose self-confidence is solid, can try to get such a formula into his agreement: "This is to your advantage because the plan becomes a more direct incentive. I influence the payoff through my own efforts. . . ."

Overall, stock options are widely used and will figure importantly in most executive contracts. The executive benefits to the degree that the plan can be positioned as an "of course" perk, and to the extent that the cost of conversion of the options is reduced.

JUNIOR STOCK OPTIONS: BACK TO THE DRAWING BOARD?

Stock options are a dubious perk, to say the least, when the market goes down. And even when the market is bulling upward, traditional stock options may pose problems. The manager may not have the cash to exercise his right to buy. The company may be willing to provide a loan to facilitate the buying of the stock, but this becomes quite a rigid set of Golden Handcuffs, to be avoided if possible.

While companies have been willing to sell stock at a discount far below the market value, the rules governing incentive stock options do not permit this. Moreover, the $100,000-a-year limit on the value of ISO stock that can be bought by an individual has cramped the ability of many corporations to provide truly magnificent incentive compensation.

So a new approach was developed: the junior stock plan (JSP).

Under the JSP concept the company creates a new class of stock which can be given or sold only to employees. The special stock is aptly termed "junior," as it is subordinate to the company's primary common stock in liquidation, dividend, and voting rights. But at the same time, the junior stock can be sold to executives at considerably less than the value of regular common. The regular stock may be trading at $50 while junior stock is being sold for $25.

Early in 1984 the Federal Accounting Standards Board issued an interpretation which, while it in no way dimmed the luster of junior stock for the employee, made it considerably less attractive for the company. Under this interpretation, the company would be required to treat the differential as an expense on its annual report. Since this would substantially reduce net income on the report, the effect has been to practically bring to an end the issuance of junior stock options. However, as an official of the SEC remarked to the author, the concept of the junior stock option is so useful that employers will without doubt devise an equivalent.

This section reviews junior options in their original form, on the assumption that a similar approach will become available.

HOW JUNIOR GROWS UP

The key to the attractiveness of the JSP is that at a specified time the junior stock can be exchanged for regular common stock. Since there is a rule that exchange of two kinds of stock within a corporation is tax-free, there is no tax liability at the time of the swap.

Here's the way it works. The executive buys the junior stock at the bargain price of $25. He is liable for up to 50 percent tax on the difference between the $25 and the $50 value of the common stock at the time of his purchase—but after that the tax breaks flow in his direction, and he is enabled to buy far more stock than would have been possible under an ISO plan.

Time passes and the conditions necessary for the exchange of junior into common are met. By now the company's shares are trading at $100. The switch is made. When the executive sells his common stock he has a tax base of $50—the $25 paid for the junior stock plus the price differential at that time. So $50 per share is a capital gain, taxable at 20 percent.

WHY COMPANIES LIKE THE JSP

The company enjoys greater tax deductions under the JSP than with the ISO. But the most attractive feature is the company's latitude in setting the conditions that must be met before the junior stock can be converted. There are usually two conditions applied to the conversion of junior stock; one relates to tenure, the other to performance.

Tenure. The JSP specifies that the manager must remain with the company for a designated period, say five years. This require-ment is, of course, a staple of Golden Handcuff schemes.

Performance. The big plus for the company is its capacity to add performance elements that conform with overall company objectives to the more traditional requirements that key payments strictly to performance of the company's shares on the stock market. For example, *INC.* (September 1983) reports that Genentech's 1982 JSP specified that junior stock converts to common when the com-pany has enjoyed either after-tax income of at least $20 million for four successive quarters or after-tax income—when divided by the average number of outstanding common shares—of at least $2 per share for four consecutive quarters.

As the use of JSPs spreads, the choice of criteria to which the payoff is tied will grow. Companies can use earnings, sales, or other performance benchmarks as prerequisites for conversion. The con-cept makes compensation specialists salivate. At last, they exult, they have a mechanism with which to tie executive effort to cor-porate progress.

WHY MANAGERS LIKE THE JSP

The junior stock plan enables the manager to buy a lot more stock than he might have bought under an ISO. Furthermore, the plan permits the acquisition of more than $100,000 worth of stock in a year. The latter feature is of course applicable only to senior and highly paid managers. However, the "bargain price" aspect of the plan should be of interest to managers at all levels.

BUT WHAT IF THE MARKET GOES DOWN?

For the manager, JSPs have drawbacks in common with ISOs. You are locked in for a specified length of time before you can enjoy your advantages. And then there is the possibility that the market will lumber, bearlike, over a declining curve during the waiting period, a contingency that considerably reduces the value of the perk. Just as with an ISO, the executive must ask the question "What if the market is static or goes down?" Many people whose options proved less than golden because of the market slump of a few years ago were financially deprived and also emotionally damaged. They felt that they had locked themselves into tough situations for the promise of gains which proved illusory.

YOUR NEGOTIATING OBJECTIVE

What you want is a "no lose" situation, in which you can take advantage of your conversion privilege if the stock goes up in value, but be cushioned against a bear market. There is a variation of the JSP which offers this possibility. A corporation can issue convertible debentures instead of common stock. You buy the bonds at bargain rates, and when the requirements are fulfilled you have an option. You can convert if the value of the common stock makes this worthwhile, or you can hang on to your bonds.

Citicorp uses another variation. Managers can buy "book-value" junior shares. The book value is keyed to the profitability of the company, independent of the stock market. The executives can sell these shares back to the company or exchange them for common stock.

THE PITFALL OF THE OVERALL GOAL

JSPs share a common drawback with ISOs from the executive's point of view: winning the big prize depends on conditions which are, to a considerable extent, out of his or her control. If there is every likelihood that the company's profitability will go up more than enough to meet the requirements for conversion, then there is little to worry about. But, as is discussed elsewhere in this book, the manager who is negotiating a contract must examine all of the trade-offs involved in the question of individual versus group standards.

PHANTOM OPTIONS

The phantom stock option lists the employee as owning a certain number of shares, with the grants running from one year to ten years or more. The employee chooses the time for exercising the option and receives cash or company stock for whatever appreciation has occurred.

Many phantom plans offer discount prices. For example, under the Carolina Power & Light plan, deferred compensation is converted into phantom shares at a 3 percent discount off fair market value.

The following is a Martin Marietta agreement covering a phantom stock plan.

AGREEMENT AMENDING PHANTOM SHARE AGREEMENTS

Agreement, dated May 31, 1983, between Mathematica, Inc., a New Jersey corporation (the "Company"), and Tibor Fabian, an employee of the Company or one of its subsidiaries (the "Employee").

WITNESSETH

WHEREAS, the Employee as a key employee of the Company or one of its subsidiaries is a participant in the Company's Long-Term Incentive Compensation Plan (the "Plan") which calls for the making of certain payments to participants in consideration of services previously performed for the Company, all as more particularly described therein; and

WHEREAS, the Employee, pursuant to the Plan, has entered into one or more Phantom Share Agreements ("Phantom Share Agreements") with the Company; and

WHEREAS, the Company has entered into an Agreement in Principle with Martin Marietta Corporation ("MMC"), dated May 12, 1983, which contemplates the merger of the Company with a wholly-owned subsidiary of MMC, said merger (the "Merger") being a Reorganization Event as defined in the

Plan and in the Phantom Share Agreements; and

WHEREAS, the Committee as defined in the Plan acting pursuant to Section 12.(b) of the Plan has authorized, subject to the consummation of the Merger, certain payments to participants in the Plan in full and final settlement of any entitlements they may have thereunder; and

WHEREAS, the Board as defined in the Plan acting pursuant to authority conferred therein has terminated the Plan, contingent upon consummation of the Merger, and has approved, subject to said contingency, the full and final payments to participants authorized by the Committee, as aforesaid

NOW, THEREFORE, in consideration of the premises and the mutual convenants hereinafter set forth, it is agrees as follows:

1. Effective upon consummation of the Merger, the Phantom Share Agreements between the Company and the Employee are amended to read in their entirety as follows:

"(a) The Company agrees to pay the Employee as full and final settlement under the Plan the sum of $466,846.00, said sum to be paid as follows: an initial installment of 20% to be paid upon consummation of the Merger and the balance of 80% to be paid in four equal installments on the first through the fourth anniversary dates of such consummation. Each such installment shall be paid irrespective of whether or not the Employee is an employee of the Company or any of its subsidiaries on the date said installment becomes due. The Company hereby waives, and agrees not to assert, any right to set off the amount of any claims, liabilities, damages, or losses the Company may have against any amounts payable by the Company hereunder.

"(b) In the event of the Employee's death, any installment otherwise payable to the Employee pursuant to paragraph (a) hereof shall be paid to beneficiaries designated to the Company in writing, or in the absence of such designation, to the Employee's estate.

"(c) All payments under this Agreement shall be net of the amount sufficient to satisfy any federal, state, and local withholding tax requirements.

"(d) Any and all payments hereunder shall be paid in consideration of services performed for the Company or its subsidiaries or for their benefit by the Employee. All such payments shall constitute a special incentive payment to the Employee and shall not be taken into account in computing the amount of salary or regular compensation of the Employee for the purposes of determining any pension, retirement, death, or other benefits under (i) any pension, retirement, life insurance, or other benefit plan of the Company or any subsidiary thereof, or (ii) any agreement between the Company or any subsidiary thereof, on the one hand, and the Employee on the other hand. Nothing contained herein shall be deemed in any way to limit or restrict the Company, or any subsidiary thereof, from making any award or payment to the Employee under any other plan, agreement, arrangement or understanding, whether now existing or hereafter in effect.

"(e) No rights granted to the Employee under this Agreement shall be assignable or transferrable by the Employee, except by will or by the laws of descent and distribution. During the life of the Employee, all rights granted to the Employee hereunder shall be exercisable only by the Employee or by the Employee's guardian or legal representative."

2. The Employee, upon consummation of the Merger and receipt of the initial installment as above provided, irrevocably releases and forever discharges the Company and its affiliates, and their respective successors and assigns and the officers, agents and employees of all of them, from any and all liabilities, claims, demands and causes of actions whatsoever, at law or in equity, arising out of or in connection with the Phantom Share Agreements and/or with his participation in the Plan, and agrees that he shall have no further interest in the Plan or any award made thereunder except that said release shall not apply to claims or payments under the Phantom Share Agreements as amended pursuant to paragraph 1 above.

3. This Agreement shall be null and void in the event the Merger is not consummated.

4. This Agreement shall be governed in all respects by the internal laws of the State of New Jersey without giving effect to principles of conflict of laws.

IN WITNESS THEREOF, the parties have entered into this Agreement as of the date first above written.

MATHEMATICA, INC.

By _____

_____

Executive

GUARANTY

The undersigned, for value received, hereby guarantees to the employee who is a party to the above agreement (the "Agreement") the due and punctual payment of all amounts payable pursuant to the Phantom Share Agreements (as defined in the Agreement), as amended pursuant to paragraph 1 of the Agreement, when and as the same shall become due and payable, in accordance with the terms of the Phantom Share Agreements, as amended pursuant to paragraph 1 of the Agreement, and, in default of such payment, hereby convenants to pay such amount so due and payable upon demand of such employee made in writing and delivered personally or mailed, postage prepaid, by registered mail (air mail, where appropriate), return receipt requested, to the undersigned, at 6801 Rockledge Drive, Bethesda, Maryland 20817, Attention: William A. Snowden, or at such other address furnished for such purpose by the undersigned to such employee. The undersigned hereby waives, and agrees not to assert, any right to set off the amount of any claims, liabilities, damages or losses the undersigned may have against any amounts payable by the undersigned hereunder. This Guaranty shall be effective upon consummation of the Merger (as defined in the Agreement) and shall be null and void in the event the Merger is not consummated.

MARTIN MARIETTA
CORPORATION

By _____

DEFERRED COMPENSATION

"Salary reduction" or "deferred compensation" plans are fairly common for senior executives. The idea is to put the money you earn today into some kind of interest-bearing fund so that you can draw upon it after retirement, when your tax rates are lower. It's the same principle as that of the IRA or the Keogh.

The money is invested in a fixed-income fund, a stock and/or bond fund, company securities, etc. When you reach fifty-nine and a half you can withdraw the money, in a lump sum or in installments. If you leave the company before retirement age you get the money in a lump sum. At that time, you have the option of rolling it over into an IRA or into a similar plan offered by your new employer. Or you can take the money in a lump sum and pay taxes on it, using ten-year averaging.

If you die, the money becomes part of your estate.

You can borrow against the money in your deferred plan, just as you can borrow against an insurance policy. In case of hardship—extraordinary expenses—you can apply for permission to withdraw the money.

A simpler form of deferred compensation can be achieved when the company agrees to pay you a lesser salary for a specified number of years, that period stretching beyond your retirement from the company. In other words, instead of receiving, say, $120,000 a year for each of the five years leading to your retirement, you would receive $75,000 a year for eight years, thus providing a source of income in your retirement and reducing taxes overall. In its most basic form this arrangement has drawbacks. For one thing, the employee does not receive interest on the deferred amount (although the company may be able to put the deferred amount into accounts that earn interest for the firm). A second potential problem may be the question of whether the company will be able to continue to pay you years into the future. This may be circumvented by the purchase of an annuity.

THE PLUSES AND MINUSES

Simple deferral with little or no interest costs you money. At the least, a deferred-compensation arrangement should provide interest. Better yet, it should offer you some flexibility in taking advantage of investment opportunities. For instance, one useful feature of such a plan should be the opportunity to invest the deferred amounts in company stock.

Care should be taken to make sure that the deferred amounts are not subtracted from the amount on which your pension, insurance, and health benefits are calculated. This may not be automatic. The manager whose pension base is diminished by the amount deferred may lose more than he gains.

Some employers try to introduce Golden Handcuff provisions into deferred-compensation plans; for instance, forfeiture of interest or return on stock if the employee does not stay with the company for a specified period of time. Avoid any such provisions. If you decide that you want a deferred-compensation plan, it must bring you a full measure of interest and be without strings in the form of forfeiture provisions.

For the current relief from taxes offered by such a plan, you give up a considerable measure of control over money you have earned. You are paying for the tax break; try to calculate just how much you will be paying. Unless the return on your deferred income is very favorable (at or above the prime rate), the net after-tax benefit may be not much better than what you'd make if you took the money now, paid taxes on it, and put it into one or more of the variety of investment opportunities available today. This factor may be offset to some extent if the deferral plan enables you to buy company stock.

YOUR NEGOTIATING POSTURE

Deferred compensation is not much of a perk. It's your money; the company merely provides a mechanism for you to defer part of what you earn. It doesn't cost the company anything, and may even earn money for the firm.

Don't allow deferred compensation to be considered in the same category as bonuses, stock option plans, etc. Even if you are quite interested in a deferral arrangement, it is best to make it an afterthought. A manager who chooses compensation deferral as a dominant point is not in the strongest possible position in the negotiation.

Negotiate first on the things that actually cost the company something, in money or commitment. Get what you can on these fronts. Then bring up deferral as an "of course" benefit; if they don't have a plan for it, why not? It's a simple thing to arrange.

HOW MUCH CAN YOU DEFER?

E. F. Hutton has a deferred-compensation savings plan for which an administering committee sets the maximum contribution, up to $500,000 per year. The participant can shelter all cash earnings except defined compensation under the pension plan and overtime pay, as well as 10 percent of after-tax earnings and any qualifying rollover from another retirement vehicle. Those eligible for this plan include "certain employees including officers."

RETIREMENT BENEFITS FOR EXECUTIVE AND SPOUSE

Perkin-Elmer Corporation of Norwalk, Connecticut, made the following arrangement with Chief Executive Officer and Chairman Robert H. Sorensen: If Mr. Sorensen remains in the employ of the company until disability or retirement age (he was sixty-two when the agreement was announced in 1983), he receives annual payments of $100,000 after disability or retirement. Should Harriet K. Sorensen, Mr. Sorensen's wife, survive him, she receives $50,000 per year for life. This same arrangement would be activated by a change in control.

WHAT WILL YOUR DEFERRED DOLLARS BE WORTH?

Golden Handcuff agreements usually rest heavily on some form of deferred compensation. The perceived advantage to you is that it transfers a substantial portion of earnings from high-bracket to low-bracket years.

However, inflation could make that deferred after-tax net significantly less than it would be if you took the money now and invested it.

If you are attracted by a deferred-compensation arrangement, consider (a) keying what you will receive to the prime rate at the time you will receive it; (b) giving yourself the opportunity to have the deferred amount invested in company stock if the stock is doing well.

RECEIVING DEFERRED COMPENSATION BEFORE RETIREMENT

Executives at Standard Oil of Ohio may opt to begin receiving payout of deferred compensation before retirement. The decision is irrevocable; the executive cannot switch back to full deferral. The individual who chooses to receive deferred compensation while still employed forfeits the unpaid amounts in case of firing for cause or resignation without company consent.

The decision to start receiving deferral payout before retirement is a major one. The availability of the option to do so is not a valuable perk for most executives.

DEFERRAL FOR DIRECTORS

National Service Industries gives each nonemployee director an annual retainer of $4,800 plus $400 for every meeting attended. (Officer directors receive $100 per meeting.) Directors may defer part or all of these payments until service on the board is terminated. Then they have the option of being paid in a lump sum or in ten annual installments.

The deferred money earns semiannual interest at the prime rate, discounted 1–3 percent as the prime increases.

Under an interesting feature of the plan, the company matches the deferred amount by up to $5,000 per year, adding this incentive to the executive's account.

BONUSES

The bonus, in all of its various forms, is a staple of executive compensation. The questions and examples on the following pages suggest the kinds of bonuses that might be available, as well as some of the issues and potential problems that should be considered.

When a manager is told that the bonus plan is lucrative, one logical question is, "Compared to what?" A glance at some of the various disclosure documents the company issues can provide an idea of the scope and balance of a bonus arrangement.

For example, an electronics corporation (annual revenue $1.7 billion) rewarded its five most senior executives in fiscal year 1982 with bonuses ranging from 62 to 84 percent of salary, with the average being 70 percent. The chairman and CEO got a salary of $332,500 plus a bonus of $222,492. (This was supplemented by $162,381 in company contributions under profit-sharing and deferred-income-savings plans, deferred bonus portions, and accrued supplemental retirement contributions.)

Fifteen other officers received only an average of about 30 percent of salary.

If a manager discerns a significant difference in size of bonus percentage between senior managers and others, he may have some questions. If senior management receives a certain proportion in bonus, why is the same degree of incentive not extended to lower management ranks? Conversely, if the bonus percentage for those below the top rung was significantly higher, the executive might have questions about the commitment of senior management or the prospects of the company.

EARNINGS BONUS UNITS

At Exxon Corporation, participants in the incentive program can receive bonus payments in cash, shares, or "earnings bonus units" which convey the right to receive cash equivalent to earnings per share. These units have a life of five years, with payout earlier if the limit is reached.

ENCOURAGING MANAGERS TO TAKE STOCK

To encourage executives to take bonuses in stock rather than cash, the Mayflower Corporation offers stock with a cash value of 150 percent of the value of the bonus. The value of the stock is computed on fair market value the last day of the year.

MINIMUM BONUSES

While moving in the direction of tying bonuses to increase of shareholder value, some companies have found payouts reduced sharply.

Newmont Mining Corporation established a formula limiting bonuses to 2 percent of the amount by which pretax income exceeds 8 percent of stockholder equity, or 2 percent of cash dividends on voting stock, whichever is smaller. No bonuses were paid. The firm then set up a minimum fund of $500,000 for funding bonuses.

KEYING BONUSES TO COMPANY PERFORMANCE

Incentive bonuses may be paid in a form that constitutes a further incentive. The recipient may find the bonus for the current year tied in with how the company does for the next several years.

Under one such plan, annual bonuses may be in the form of immediate cash payment or performance shares vesting three years later according to the company's earnings over that period. At the time of vesting the executive may receive up to half the value in equivalent cash. The rest is paid in stock.

One of the interesting things about such plans is that the choices made by executives may be viewed as indicative of their faith or lack of faith in the company or their commitment to long tenure. The manager who seeks the maximum in cash can be deemed to be a doubting Thomas.

BONUSES BASED ON UNIT PERFORMANCE

The incentive plan at Goodyear Tire & Rubber was once based on sharing of a corporate pool. The plan was amended in 1982 to authorize the chairman and chief operating officer to tie some payouts to divisional or other operating profit and return-on-investment (ROI) goals. An executive's share may be increased 30 percent if the target is exceeded. The executive's allotment may be reduced by 30 percent if the goal is not met.

LONG-TERM AWARDS

Borden Inc. instituted a 1984 management incentive plan which states that any money left in the fund after annual bonuses are paid may be carried forward, but can be used only for "long-term performance improvement award allocations..."

LONG-TERM BONUSES

Merck & Company Inc. has superimposed "strategic" long-term bonuses onto the existing bonus plan for some senior executives.

The existing plan is based on an annual pool determined by nonmanagement members of the board's compensation and benefits committee. The pool cannot exceed either 100 percent of participants' total salaries or 12 percent of incentive earnings, whichever is lower. Incentive earnings are calculated on the basis of net income in excess of 10 percent of average net capital or preferred stock dividends plus $2.60, multiplied by the number of common shares outstanding.

The plan pays off in annual cash bonuses and deferred awards.

The new "strategic performance awards" operate on five-year cycles. Payout is based on achievement of performance objectives and "other factors relevant to the strategic health of the Company."

BONUSES DESPITE POOR PERFORMANCE

A company with revenues at around the $3 billion mark had an executive bonus plan that included more than a thousand executives and was based on attainment of financial and personal performance goals. The firm had a lackluster year, with sales and profits dropping off.

Under the bonus plan there could be no bonuses for officers. Therefore, "special" bonus payments were made, with the awards amounting to half of the fund that would have existed if objectives had been met.

To forestall a recurrence of this unhappy situation the board scrapped the old plan and put in a new one applying to about 250 managers. The new plan is based "solely upon the company's reported earnings," with great latitude being exercised by the compensation committee in determining the pool and making individual awards.

Examples like this underscore what has happened to many executive compensation plans. They have come to be relied on as definite sources of payout, just like salary. While there are variations in the payout, the variations have little to do with individual accomplishment. The compensation committee simply passes out the money. When bad years result in sharply reduced earnings, the bonuses must be paid anyway.

HOW SENSITIVE IS THE BONUS PLAN TO SLIGHT DECLINES?

Some compensation plans make bonuses highly vulnerable to relatively slight downturns. Kimberly-Clark saw profits dip less than 5 percent below the level of the previous year. Overall company performance was, however, better than it had been two years before. This shortfall had a devastating effect on the incentive compensation plan. Whereas two years before, eighteen officers had shared $1.1 million, now twenty-three officers shared less than $250,000.

In judging an incentive plan, particularly a new one or one that has not been tested by a bad year, the executive will do well to try to calculate the effects of various degrees of change in the company's results.

EXERCISING OPTIONS WITH BONUSES

Motorola's executive incentive plan calls for awards to be made by the compensation committee. The annual amounts may be paid immediately, paid in installments, or deferred. An interesting feature is that if an award is more than 50 percent of base salary, the amount exceeding 40 percent of base salary must be used to exercise a stock option.

PRODUCTIVITY IMPROVEMENT

Here's how a Southern utility is trying to improve managerial performance by keying compensation more closely to results. Executives may qualify for two bonuses, one based on corporate performance and one on an individual performance. There is no payout for either unless return on equity (ROE) meets established criteria. Each award is a percentage of the midpoint of the executive's salary range. Awards range from zero to 20 percent, depending on achievement of individual and corporate goals.

The *zero* payoff used to be rare in executive compensation plans. Even the most indifferent performer could be comfortably sure of a nice bonus in the older and clubbier days.

SUPERBONUSES

When you own the ball you can dictate how the game is played. By most standards a bonus that is 100 percent of salary is considered high. In fiscal year 1982 Leon Levine, chairman of Family Dollar Stores, Inc., received a salary of $110,000 and a total bonus of $606,787, making Mr. Levine's bonus 549 percent of salary. This gave Mr. Levine four times what was paid to the next-highest-paid officer, President Lewis E. Levine, who was paid $175,000. Lewis Levine's salary was $145,000, or $35,000 more than the chairman's, but he garnered a mere $30,000 in bonuses.

Leon Levine held 42.2 percent of the common stock of Family Dollar Stores.

WHAT HAPPENS TO YOUR BONUS IF YOU LEAVE?

Under the terms of the agreement, the employer terminates the manager with three months left to go in the fiscal year. The manager counts on getting at least three quarters of the annual bonus that has been part of his compensation package. However, he finds that the agreement calls for total forfeiture.

Annual bonus awards usually require employment through the fiscal year in order to qualify for payment. Pro rata payout of long-term incentives such as stock plans is more common. However, the manager should never assume that he will receive any part of an incentive bonus unless it is spelled out in the contract.

When the manager voluntarily defers an annual bonus he is almost always fully vested in it. However, even here there is reason for caution. Interest or earnings on the deferred amounts may be forfeited through termination of the job unless the contract specifies otherwise.

INTEREST-FREE LOANS AND GUARANTEED BONUSES

When Robert H. Nassau joined American Hoist & Derrick Company, he signed a contract guaranteeing a salary of at least $150,000 and bonus of at least $30,000 per year. In addition Mr. Nassau got an interest-free loan of $200,000 to cover relocation costs including the purchase of a home. Annual repayment of the loan consists of up to half of the bonus payout for the previous year.

If Mr. Nassau's agreement is terminated the loan is repayable in full within 180 days—unless the termination takes place following a change in control. In that case Mr. Nassau's Golden Parachute provides that 75 percent of the unpaid balance will be forgiven.

Mr. Nassau, who had come to American Hoist as president and COO, was designated as the company's next CEO in November 1983.

LOANS FOR MANAGERS

Texaco offers a designated group of executives (about 260) the opportunity to borrow up to three times annual salary. Loan requests are individually considered and granted only if the loan "may reasonably be expected to benefit" Texaco. Interest is the same as that paid to Texaco employees under the "fixed income fund option" of the employee savings plan, or the New York Fed discount rate plus one percent, whichever is lower.

AMENDMENTS

As the need arises, contracts may be amended. The following example shows how American Standard Inc. revised its compensation agreement with Chairman-President-CEO William A. Marquard.

March 7, 1984

Mr. William A. Marquard
Chairman & Chief Executive Officer
American Standard Inc.

DEAR MR. MARQUARD:

Your employment agreement dated February 10, 1978 (the "Agreement") provides ((Section 3(a)) that you will not receive stock options in conjunction with contingent cash awards under the Long-Term Plan of the Incentive Program but will receive additional cash instead. As you know, by action of the Board of Directors, the Long-Term Plan was suspended in May 1982, with the understanding that long-term incentive awards for the foreseeable future would be composed of stock options and restricted stock. In November 1982, executives participating in the Long-Term Plan were awarded options and restricted stock, and you participated in those awards in accordance with the formula applicable to all participants.

This letter will serve to confirm your understanding with the company as follows:

1. Until such time as the Company reinstates the Long-Term Plan or a similar compensation arrangement providing for long-term incentive awards in the form of cash, Section 3(a) of the Agreement referred to above shall be considered inoperative, and you will receive and accept incentive awards in the same form as those granted to other senior executives.

2. The provisions of Section 5(b) of the Agreement will apply to any awards to you of restricted stock made before the start of the Consulting Period, so that awards with maturity dates after termination of the Employment Period shall not be

prorated and the shares covered by such awards shall not be forfeited so long as the Consulting Period continues.

If the above is correct, please sign a copy of this letter in the space provided below and return it to the undersigned.

Very truly yours,

AMERICAN STANDARD INC.

By:_____
    Keith D. Bunnel
    Vice Chairman,
    Administration

_____

Richard A. Lenon
Chairman, Management
Development Committee

Confirmed and agreed to as
of the date first above
written:

_____

William A. Marquard

SHOULD PERKS BE INCLUDED?

Most senior management jobs carry with them what might be called "first-cabin" perks, privileges that enable the manager to live and work in a more comfortable style than subordinates. Such benefits include first-class air travel, company cars, club memberships, chauffeured limousines, resort facilities, yachts, overseas trips, etc. A lot of executives see these things as being necessary to their performance. A lot of nonexecutives deem them wild abuses, worse than the infamous three-martini lunch.

Occasionally, perks like these are written into contracts:

Company Automobile. The Executive shall be provided with a company automobile under arrangements at least equivalent to those currently in effect with respect to other Company Senior Executives.

Country Club Membership. The Company will reimburse the Executive for his initial membership fee and monthly dues (during the period of employment) for one country club membership to be approved by the Company. Upon conclusion of the period of employment, the Executive's right to such membership shall terminate with all rights thereunder reverting to the Company; if requested to do so, the Executive shall execute such assignments as necessary to accomplish this result.

Without knowing the precise circumstances it is not altogether clear how such provisions get into a management employment contract. From time to time the inclusion has been suggested by the employer. Such a suggestion may be a useful negotiating ploy. The manager, pleased by the unrequested offering of these perks, may relax in his pursuit of some other aim. The perks themselves are no different from those given as a matter of course to all senior managers.

When the manager specifically requests the inclusion of country club membership, special hotel accommodations, etc., the reason is sometimes more emotional than logical. The executive has come to think of these and similar perks as signifying the achievement of life's dreams. In *The Final Days* (New York: Simon and Schuster, 1976), Bob Woodward and Carl Bernstein tell of the embattled Richard Nixon standing with his lawyer, James D. St. Clair, at the bow of the presidential yacht *Sequoia* while eight bells toll, the crew stands at attention, and the national anthem is played. The President turns to St. Clair and (as "members of the crew looked away in embarrassed silence") says, "They pay you nickels and dimes, but this is what makes it worth it."

Or, the manager may insist on the inclusion of the perks because of suspicion that they will be reduced or eliminated. During the most recent economic downturn quite a few companies initiated at least modest measures of austerity for managers, cutting out chauffeured limousines, first-class accommodations, etc. Some executives are particularly rankled by such moves. In one conglomerate, during the most disastrous four quarters of the company's history the senior financial officer, while preaching the gospel of cost-cutting, insisted on continuing to travel to London via the Concorde when all others had been relegated to tourist class on slower aircraft.

But in the last few years first-cabin perks have come to be looked upon as something more than privileges of rank designed to make things more pleasant. They are regarded by many as tax shelters. In *The Book of Perks*, by James R. Baehler (New York: St. Martin's Press, 1983), the chapter heading "Finessing the Tax Man" introduces advice like the following: ". . . there are many everyday costs that can be shifted to your company. The goal is. . . to transfer some of your living expenses. In that way, you are not spending after-tax dollars for some of your living costs and the company gets a tax deduction for its expenses on your behalf. Everybody benefits but the tax man. . ." The reader is then advised about having the corporation pay for home entertaining, cars, clubs, tickets to football games, etc.

Surely executives and companies could not have imagined that the escalation of perks into the equivalent of tax-free compensation would altogether escape the notice of the outside world, including politicians. For years legislators have been aware that the growth of "statutory" fringes like health- and life-insurance premiums, pensions, and day care have created a sizable amount of untaxed income in this country. Efforts to subject these benefits to some measure of taxation have fallen victim to fierce and massive opposition. The survival of the country's health care system may depend in part on taxing employee health plans, but the number of politicians willing to stand up in favor of such taxation is understandably skimpy.

But when we come to the "nonstatutory" fringes, ah, there's a different story. In the *New York Times* of September 18, 1983, Representative Fortney H. Stark, Democrat of California, gave the rationale for his bill to curb tax perks: "Tax-free benefits, needless to say, are of considerably more value to an executive in a high bracket than to a line worker in a low to middle bracket. Thus it's not surprising that tax-free benefits accrue disproportionately to those with higher incomes—putting a significant kink in the progressivity of the income tax system. In an ever-shrinking tax base, the salaried worker bears a heavier burden on his compensation. He pays for his car and his greens fees with after-tax dollars."

Representative Stark goes on to contrast this burdened wage earner with the "chief executive officer of a major company who drives a company car to the airport where the company jet is waiting to take him to a get-away weekend at the company's midtown hotel suite. On his return he spends the afternoon at the country club whose membership comes with his title. All that without paying a dime in personal income tax."

The Congressman's assertion that the growth of fringe benefits as substitutes for taxable wages "extracts billions from the tax base" is hotly disputed. Michael J. Romig of the U.S. Chamber of Commerce says, "Common sense tells us that the fringes we and our neighbors enjoy as the fruits of our labors do not amount to a hill of beans when matched against our taxable salaries. . . . Nontaxable fringes represent less than 5 percent of our compensation..."

But this is not an issue in which logic is apt to predominate. The objective facts about untaxed fringes are likely to be engulfed by gut feelings. Country club memberships and the like are a conspicuous and easy target for legislators. It may not be possible to put a dent in the huge budget deficit by raising taxes or cutting costs, and the great bulk of employee fringes may be invulnerable to efforts to impose some taxation, but at least the fat-cat executive can be made to pay his own bills at the club. Never mind the argument that these amenities are legitimate business expenses. The issue as perceived by large numbers of the public is likely to be *fairness*. Can you imagine yourself impaled by Mike Wallace's microphone while you try to explain on camera why the company should foot the bill for your country club membership while the rank-and-file worker foots his own bill at the Elks?

High-level fringes as a significant means of avoiding taxes are a dubious bet. They will come under increasing scrutiny and attack. And this is a very good reason to avoid having such perks spelled out in employment contracts.

For one thing, the contract may become a public document (as have many of the agreements quoted in this book). Consider a situation in which your contract becomes a disclosure document filed with the Securities and Exchange Commission. Would you want to have it contain the provision that you and a companion must enjoy a one-month trip abroad with four-star accommodations guaranteed at all stops?

Company cars, clubs, etc., are likely to be provided to all executives of a certain rank if they are provided to any, so insisting that they be included in the contract is like insisting on the privilege of eating in the executive dining room. You don't need a contractual guarantee. In fact, if the company offers the unsolicited inclusion of such perks, it might be a shrewd tactic to turn them down politely, asking in return that you be given a better deal on options or severance.

And, except for the most extraordinary circumstances, it is not good strategy to make perks like these part of your bargaining position. You are likely to get them anyway, if they are gettable. If they are so tough to get that they must be made part of a contract, then the winning them may do more harm than good, since they are unlikely to stimulate the warmth and goodwill of colleagues and subordinates. By winning the inclusion of such doubtful prizes you may at the same time be giving up things of far greater importance.

Let your negotiating eye remain focused on the important aspects of the agreement—the job, the money, the conditions of termination, the severance deal. Bypass the small perks. They are dead ends.

NEEDLESS PROVISIONS

Here's an entry in a job contract:

> *Vacations:* During each year of the term of this Agreement, Mr._____may take vacations at the standard number of days set by the Company's policy, or such longer period as the

Board may authorize, during which time his compensation shall be paid in full and he shall continue to participate in all other rights and benefits.

Here's another:

Expenses: The Company will reimburse the Executive for all reasonable and necessary expenses incurred by him for or on behalf or for the benefit of the Company in the performance of his duties. . . . The Company will pay, or reimburse the Executive for the payment of, all traveling and living expenses incurred by him while on the business of the Company away from his place of residence.

Obviously, these provisions would be regarded under most circumstances as routine matters, standard company policy. It is conceivable that the vacation clause might be inserted on behalf of an executive who planned to take long vacations and knew that the board would approve them. The expense clause is somewhat more mysterious.

Unless there is a specific reason for inclusion of language covering routine matters that are covered by ordinary company policy, don't clutter up the negotiation or the contract with them. They may be a part of the "boilerplate" of the contract form, in which case it is well to read them carefully to see if there is something unusual; otherwise, leave such things as vacations and expenses to general policy.

AUTOMOBILE ALLOWANCE OR CASH

Sometimes the wording of the perk gives the cash equivalent, as in this agreement between the Coastal Corporation and Senior Vice-President K. O. Johnson:

> *Automobile Allowance:* The Executive shall, in lieu of being furnished with a company automobile, receive a monthly automobile allowance of Three Hundred Fifty Dollars ($350.00).

CADILLAC ONLY

The make of the car provided by the company is not often specified. As one exception, Phibro Corporation's consulting agreement with Milton Rosenthal, an outside director, specifies, along with annual compensation of $300,000, that Phibro will

> (b) Provide you with a chauffeur-driven Cadillac automobile or equivalent and a representative office and a secretary in our New York headquarters.

9

PROVISIONS FOR
TERMINATION

People about to marry rarely contemplate in great detail the eventuality of divorce. There are, of course, exceptions, as exemplified by prenuptial agreements.

The contractual provision for severance pay is the "prenuptial agreement" of the job relationship. Both parties hope the relationship will be a long and happy one. But if the employer becomes disenchanted, the employee needs protection. That protection is provided by the agreement in writing that the company will pay the money which would be paid over the entire life of the contract or for a substantial portion of it.

The following, from a contract dated February 23, 1983, between Financial Corporation of Santa Barbara and David L. Tilton, is a termination section covering various circumstances leading to termination: termination by the employer, by the employee, because of death or disability, and change of control. (The change-of-control provision is not, however, a Golden Parachute. It does not offer Mr. Tilton any particular severance benefits in the case of a takeover or merger.) This agreement also covers certain possibilities peculiar to the industry (the employer is a savings-and-loan association), for example termination for regulatory reasons.

The "termination for cause" provision here is representative of such clauses. It lays out the circumstances that would lead to termination "for cause." It also calls for written notice, which is not a feature for all "cause" provisions.

6. *Termination by Officer.* (a) If, during the term of this Agreement, the Company's Board elects a person other than Mr. Tilton to all of the positions currently held by Mr. Tilton at the Company or the Association's Board elects a person other than him to all of the positions currently held by him at the Association, Mr. Tilton shall have the right to retire from full-time service to the Company and its subsidiaries and to render only such consulting and advisory services as the Company or the Association may request. Any such services and the conditions under which they shall be performed shall be fully in keeping with the position or positions Mr. Tilton held under this Agreement. In the event of such retirement, unless such other person is elected following a finding of disability pursuant to Section 7(a), Mr. Tilton shall continue to be entitled to receive the compensation provided for in Section 5 until February 22, 1986.

(b) If the Company becomes a party to any merger in which it is not the surviving company, or if the company sells all or substantially all of its assets, or if there should occur a change in control of the Company by virtue of a change or changes in the ownership of its outstanding voting securities (whether as an incident of a reorganization or otherwise), then Mr. Tilton, without limitation on any other rights he may have hereunder, may, within ninety (90) days after receiving notice of any such event, terminate his employment hereunder as of a specified date not less than ten (10) nor more than thirty (30) days after delivering written notice of such termination to the Company. The compensation provided for in Section 5 shall be terminated as of such specified date.

For purposes of the foregoing provisions, a change of control shall be deemed to include the holding or acquisition by any person or entity (or group of affiliated persons or entities) of more than twenty (20) percent of the Company's outstanding voting securities.

7. *Termination by the Company.* The compensation pro-

vided for in Section 5 and Mr. Tilton's employment by the Company and the Association may be terminated by the Company or the Association prior to expiration of the term set forth in Section 2 only as provided for below:

(a) *Disability*. In the event that Mr. Tilton shall fail, because of illness or injury, to render services under this Agreement for six (6) consecutive calendar months or for shorter periods aggregating one hundred thirty (130) or more business days in any twelve (12)-month period, the compensation provided for in Section 5 and his employment by the Company and the Association may be terminated as of six (6) months after the end of such six (6)-month or one hundred thirty (130)-day period, as the case may be, or until February 22, 1986, whichever occurs first. The Company and the Association shall offset against payments of Mr. Tilton's salary any payments received by him as a result of such illness or injury pursuant to any federal or state program or any salary continuation or similar program established by the Company or the Association except payments intended as reimbursement for past or anticipated medical and other expenses.

(b) *Death*. The salary provided for Mr. Tilton in Section 5 and any Additional Benefits which do not by their provisions (applicable to all eligible employees similarly situated) end or become payable at his death shall continue to be paid, for a period of six (6) months following the date of death or until February 22, 1986, whichever occurs first or in accordance with the provisions of such Additional Benefits, to his Beneficiary or Beneficiaries (as designated pursuant to Section 8). If Mr. Tilton's death occurs while he is receiving compensation payable under Section 7(a), such compensation shall cease, and his compensation payable under this Section 7(b) shall begin and continue for the full six (6)-month period provided for in this Section 7(b) or until February 22, 1986, whichever occurs first.

(c) *For Cause*. The compensation provided for in Section 5 and Mr. Tilton's employment by the Company and the Association shall be terminated upon the expiration of thirty (30) days after written notice of a termination for cause has been given to Mr. Tilton by either Board. A "termination for cause" is a termination by reason of either Board's good faith determination that Mr. Tilton (i) acted dishonestly or incompetently or engaged in willful misconduct in the performance of his duties, (ii) breached a fiduciary duty for personal profit to himself, (iii) intentionally failed to perform reasonably assigned duties, (iv) willfully violated any law, rule or regulation (other than traffic violations or similar offenses) or any final cease-and-desist order, or (v) materially breached this Agreement.

(d) *At Will.* Each of the Boards may terminate Mr. Tilton's employment by the corporation whose Board so acts at any time without cause but such termination shall be without prejudice to Mr. Tilton's rights to receive the compensation provided for in Section 5 until February 22, 1986.

(e) *For Regulatory Reasons.* Mr. Tilton's employment by the Company and the Association and the compensation provided for in Section 5 shall be terminated upon Mr. Tilton's being removed from office or permanently prohibited from participating in the conduct of the affairs of the Association pursuant to any order duly issued by the Federal Home Loan Bank Board or the Federal Savings and Loan Insurance Corporation or the California Savings and Loan Commissioner, which order has become final. Mr. Tilton's employment by the Company and the Association and the compensation provided for in Section 5 shall be suspended upon the entry of any order referred to above or Mr. Tilton's being suspended from office or temporarily prohibited from participating in the conduct of the affairs of the Association pursuant to a notice duly served by the Federal Home Loan Bank Board or the Federal Savings and Loan Insurance Corporation or the California Savings and Loan Commissioner, as of the date of such entry or service, unless stayed by appropriate proceedings; provided, however, that in the event the charges specified in any such notice are dismissed, the Company or the Association may in their discretion pay all or any part of the compensation withheld from Mr. Tilton pursuant to such suspension and reinstate any or all (in whole or in part) of the obligations so suspended.

(f) *Upon "Default."* Mr. Tilton's employment by the Company and the Association and the compensation provided for in Section 5 shall be terminated upon the occurrence of a "default" as defined in Section 401(d) of the National Housing Act, as amended.

(g) *Upon Determination That the Association is in an "Unsafe or Unsound Condition."* Mr. Tilton's employment by the Company and the Association and the compensation provided for in Section 5 shall be terminated at any time that (i) the Federal Savings and Loan Insurance Corporation enters into an agreement to provide assistance to or on behalf of the Association under the authority contained in Section 406(d) of the National Housing Act, as amended; (ii) the Federal Home Loan Bank Board or the Association's Principal Supervisory Agent approves a supervisory merger to resolve problems related to operation of the Association; or (iii) the Federal Home Loan Bank Board determines that the Association is in an unsafe or unsound condition, unless the Federal Savings and Loan Insurance Corporation, the Federal Home Loan Bank Board or the Principal Supervisory Agent determines that the continuation of this Agreement is necessary for the continued operation of the Association.

The definition of "cause" can be the key provision in case of a dispute over severance. There are two problems with language that gives the employer wide latitude in deciding that the employee has given sufficient "cause" to be dismissed without getting the severance arrangement for which the contract provides. Problem one is that a court may indeed uphold the company's contention. Problem two is that the ambiguity of the language may add to the company's leverage when a compromise is suggested: "You can fight this thing in court if you want. Maybe you'll win, maybe you'll lose. It will probably take two years just to get on the calendar, and five years to trial. Can you afford the legal fees? No problem for us; we have the lawyers on retainer anyway. What do you say we settle this thing? We're willing to make some severance arrangement, but of course not anything like what the contract calls for. . . ."

A vague "cause" section can heighten the pressure on a manager who is already worried about what a dispute and a court case will do to his bank balance and his image in the industry.

Here's a typical "cause" paragraph that might conceivably be used against the manager:

For Cause: Executive's employment with the Company may be terminated for cause if the Executive is determined to (1) have acted incompetently or dishonestly or engaged in deliberate misconduct; (2) breached a fiduciary trust for the purpose of gaining personal profit; (3) neglected to perform assigned duties; (4) violated any law, rule or regulation.

The inclusion of the word "incompetently" in clause (1) broadens the clause considerably and can also give it another meaning. Dishonesty is something that can be judged against accepted standards, as can "misconduct." Incompetence is a vaguer concept. If the CEO of the company decides that the manager, fulfilling the prophecy of the Peter Principle, has been promoted to his "level of incompetence," is the company entitled to invoke this clause? If one raised the possibility at the time of negotiation one would be told that the very thought is ridiculous. The company would do no such thing. And no doubt there would not be a thought of using the provision in that way. But it would be there, available if circumstances and feelings were to change so radically that someone wanted to use it two years hence. If "incompetently" does not have the meaning that many would assign it, what is it doing there? Delete it.

The language under clause (4) is fairly broad. After all, a locality may have quite a few laws covering all sorts of trivial matters. A dispute with a neighbor over a piece of property may result in technical violation of a statute. If the thrust of the agreement is to confine "cause" to serious crimes, then the contract should say "convicted of commission of a felony."

The biggest problem is clause (3), "neglected to perform assigned duties." This language would seem to give the employer a free hand in deciding whether or not the manager can be dismissed for cause.

On this language the manager should take a negotiating stand. "Neglected to perform" is the sticking point. What constitutes neglect? Who decides on it? Might any performance short of superhuman be construed as constituting neglect? Again, the employer will of course be at pains to say "Perish the thought." But that is not enough. Nobody is perfect. Human lack of perfection is the main reason for laws and contracts. Therefore, a contract provision that might be violated by a lapse from perfection does not belong. If an employer were to insist upon it, the reason might be a desire to keep a bargaining chip for the future.

As noted elsewhere, you should include an arbitration clause. But the inclusion of arbitration does not bestow immunity from harm. Help any potential case you may have before a panel of arbitrators by eliminating all contract language that might be used against you unfairly.

The inclusion or deletion of a word or phrase in the language defining "cause" can be decisive. For example: "[Cause shall mean] the Executive's failure to perform the customary duties of her position." There is too much latitude here. If the line cannot be deleted entirely, then it should be lengthened by one word: "... the Executive's *gross* failure to perform the customary duties of her position." "Gross" is not specific, but its inclusion shifts the center of balance of the provision toward a point at which it requires major dereliction on the executive's part to nullify the agreement.

It is vital that the employee examine the "for cause" provision carefully, track its references to other provisions of the contract, and anticipate the possible ways in which any of the language could be used to try to reduce or eliminate the severance pay called for in the agreement.

This can happen. For example, a manager negotiates a contract that looks very favorable; looks, in fact, like a "dream" agreement. The money and status are all there. The contract runs for five years: "Executive's employment shall continue until June 30, 19 , subject to the provisions of paragraph 4." Paragraph 4 has three provisions. The company or the employee may terminate "without cause" on sixty days' written notice. If the employee terminates without cause, the contract is voided. If the company terminates without cause, the employee gets two years' severance pay. In case of death or disability (disability being illness or incapacity for a continuous period of six months), there are generous provisions for the employee or the employee's estate.

So far so good. The third item in Paragraph 4 says that the employer may terminate immediately for "cause," which is described as "including without limitation" fraud, misrepresentation, embezzlement, intentional "violations of the law or company policies or a breach of the provisions of this agreement, including specifically the failure to perform the duties of employment specified in paragraph 2."

There are dangers here. Let's look at them.

The gaping pitfall in this agreement for the executive is the "for cause" provision. Such provisions are sometimes overlooked or given insufficient attention by managers who are intent on winning the best possible severance terms. The employee instead bargains adroitly and stubbornly for a generous arrangement—two years' base salary, 100 percent of the last year-end bonus, etc.

This severance arrangement is substantial, and the manager is justifiably pleased at having gotten it into the contract. However, the severance pay is to be paid only if the company terminates the contract by giving written notice of termination "without cause." A stingy or vindictive top management could decide to cut way down on the severance pay or eliminate it altogether by terminating "for cause." Managers who are hit with such a blow protest that they have done nothing to bring on the "for cause" provision. They have looked at the words in the contract and seen terms like "fraud,'" "embezzlement," etc. The paragraph refers to violations of law or activities of such moral grossness that the offending party would have to be a master criminal. Since few of us see ourselves as lawbreakers or monsters, we never think that "for cause" provisions of this nature could possibly come into play.

But there are two jokers in the hand. The term "cause" is defined as "including without limitation" the items which follow. In other words, a good many other things might be construed as giving cause for termination. The field is wide open. Embezzlement, theft and so on are simply examples.

The paragraph is made immeasurably more dangerous by inclusion of the words "violations of... company policies or a breach of the provisions of this agreement, including specifically the failure to perform the duties of employment specified in paragraph 2."

The employee who has never "violated" *any* provision of company policy is a rare person indeed. Taking home a scratch pad or a pencil might be interpreted as being against company policy. But the violation need not consist of such a petty transgression. "Company policy" might include an innocuous-looking set of principles to which no one has paid any attention since they last appeared framed on the wall of the company founder's office a hundred years back. One of these pious principles might go something like this: "Everyone who works for this firm has a responsibility to keep his superior informed at all times of any potential problem that might adversely affect the firm's overall performance." In this day of profit centers, top management is quixotic if it thinks unit managers will provide an accurate and up-to-date flow of information, especially when times are tough. In *Harvard Business Review* (March–April 1977), Richard G. Hamermesh observes that details of divisional profit crises in diversified companies "reach top management very slowly because the organizational structure of most diversified companies tends to suppress bad news." If managers were fired for suppressing bad news, the white-collar unemployment rolls would be swelled considerably.

But the manager who, like his innumerable counterparts, sat on bad news for a few months might find when the crunch came that he had been in violation of company policy, and therefore the victim of a termination "with cause" which would deprive him of severance pay. Perhaps in the course of a long, painful, and expensive lawsuit the company position might be overturned. But the threat of having to go through such an agonizing process might be sufficient to compel the executive to settle for a lot less than the contract allows.

The other trap here is the inclusion, as a "cause," of "failure to perform the duties of employment specified in paragraph 2." When we turn to that paragraph we find this: "The Executive shall devote his or her best efforts to the performance of such duties as may from time to time be assigned by the Company..."

Here we are in *Catch-22* territory. The manager who signs a contract that defines the job as performing duties assigned by the company, and lets it go at that, is leaving a gaping hole in the protection that the contract is designed to afford. In the wording of the agreement being used as a sample, any effort, however sincere, that falls short of perfection might be taken as "cause" for denial of severance pay.

When the term "best efforts" is combined with the term "such duties as may from time to time be assigned by the company," the agreement contains a potentially lethal brew. Elsewhere we discuss the provision by which the company reserves the right to assign the employee to an unlimited range of tasks. That provision has proven in some cases to be a weak reed for management to lean upon. In a celebrated 1983 case a TV reporter, Christine Craft, was awarded $500,000 in damages in her suit against the owners of a Kansas City station that dropped her from the anchorperson job because she was "too old, unattractive and not deferential enough to men." Reports of the case focused on the station's defense contention that Ms. Craft was not magnetic enough, and that since TV news was show business, the ratings meant everything. Therefore the station had the right to take her out of the highly visible anchor spot on the nightly news.

Ms. Craft had a contract with the station, one paragraph of which gave the station the right to reassign her. The journalist acknowledged that she had not read that provision. It is, indeed, rather a standard part of such contracts. The station had not fired Ms. Craft. It had reassigned her to reporting duty, and was still paying her. Evidently the jury felt that this reassignment, permissible on paper, was unjust and damaging because of the reasoning (if it can be called that) which led to it. The case may have wider implications in that the finding, upheld by the judge, suggests significant limits on the company's right to reassign, let alone fire, employees.

But of course the social overtones of Ms. Craft's case, combined with some of the special features of her industry and the singular candor of her employers in stressing cosmetic values (participants in a focus group were asked, "Is she a mutt?"), make it unique. The person negotiating an employment contract must assume that the company's right to assign is relatively unlimited, that it is a powerful tool, and that the employer can indeed fire him for failing to perform assigned tasks, demeaning though they may be.

YOUR NEGOTIATING POSTURE

Your ideal accomplishment would be to eliminate altogether the provision for early termination by the employer. This being impractical, negotiate to limit the bases on which you may be fired without receiving the full severance pay called for in the contract.

Your first target is the line that says the company may terminate the agreement "for cause." Instead of allowing the word "cause" to be unlimited—with the contract simply including a few examples—work to limit "cause" to illegalities: fraud, theft, etc. If the employer insists that the provision must include other reasons for termination as well, insist that they be specified in the contract. Your position is that if you are *grossly* derelict in handling your legitimate responsibilities, the employer may have a right to fire you. But the dereliction must be big, it must be relevant to your rightful position (not a Mickey Mouse job cooked up in order to degrade you), it must be documented, and you must be warned about it. Here is the kind of provision that might offer reasonable protection against unilateral termination of a manager who is carrying out his duties:

> The Company may terminate this Agreement in the event of repeated and demonstrable failure on the part of the Executive to perform the material duties of Executive's management position (as described in Paragraph 2) in a competent manner and failure of the Executive to substantially remedy such failure within 30 days of receiving specific written notice of such failure from the Company.

Here is a "cause" provision with safeguards. The termination can be triggered only by really bad performance. It has to be demonstrable. The manager's performance is measured against the standards of his legitimate position (described in Paragraph 2). And perhaps best of all, the manager has to be warned in writing.

The inclusion of the written warning is one of the keys to a good contract. Senior management hates to put such things in writing. They may be the grounds for a lawsuit. More to the point, the written warning must document the specific areas in which the executive is not measuring up. Elsewhere this book discusses the importance for the manager of documenting satisfactory performance, e.g. maintaining a file containing letters and memos of commendation, laudatory comments in the house organ, PR releases to the trade press, and especially budgets, quotas, and objectives, with evidence that they have been met. When satisfactory performance is quantifiable it is particularly useful, but even the fluffiest of puffs in the house organ can have some value in court. (Cross-examining the employer, the plaintiff's lawyer asks, "If he was not doing a good job why did you say all these good things about him?" It's not all that easy for the employer to reply that it was a lot of baloney and meant nothing.)

Negotiate hard to get the "cause" limited and defined so that it is restricted to illegality or gross, repeated, and documented poor performance, with a warning in writing.

In the phrase "demonstrable failure... to perform the material duties..." the word "material" is important. You don't want to leave yourself open for dismissal in the case of failure to perform some trivial duty that has no meaning in terms of performance.

As for the other trap, failure to "perform such duties as may from time to time...," get the employer to state what this is supposed to mean. What it is likely to come down to is that you don't do what a superior tells you to do. If you cannot eliminate this provision altogether, negotiate to achieve wording like this:

> The Company may terminate the Agreement in the event of repeated and demonstrated failure... to carry out the reasonable instructions of Executive's superiors provided such instructions reasonably relate to and are not inconsistent with the Executive's management position, or any failure to carry

out a material instruction of the foregoing nature which is not remedied by Executive within ten (10) days of receiving written notice of such failure from the Company.

Here again the emphasis upon relevance, substantiality, and written warning provides protection against capricious or malicious firing.

Some contracts offer the executive a kind of counterbalance to the provision that allows the company to terminate for "cause." This provision says that the employee may terminate the contract for "good reason" and receive specified benefits. In a typical contract containing this provision, good reason is defined as including reduction in salary, failure by the company to continue benefits like life insurance or health insurance, and attempt by the company to fire the employee without providing a written bill of particulars. The definition continues: "[Good reason shall mean] without your express written consent, the assignment to you of any duties inconsistent with your positions, duties, responsibilities, and status with the Corporation..."

In our discussion of the "duties" clause we have emphasized the importance of spelling out reporting relationships and, in general, of preservation of status. On occasion employers have tried to drive employees to resign—or to accept significantly lower severance pay than called for in the contract—by such "humiliation ploys" as requiring the employee to report to inferiors or imposing demeaning requirements.

When this happens you can try to ride it out, but the emotional wear and tear are enormous. Furthermore, the imposition of such humiliations does not enhance one's image to other potential employers. (When a dispute leads to extremes like these, word gets around.)

You can assure a measure of self-protection if the contract goes beyond specifying the title (a president can still be told to clear everything with an assistant vice-president) to describe your reporting channel(s), for example that you will report directly to the chairman of the board.

Another precaution is to indicate the general standard of treatment that is to be accorded you. This can sometimes be done with one word. For example, note the use of the word "dignity" in this contract between ABC and its president/COO:

> Mr. Pierce may continue in the employ of the Corporation as an employee and perform such duties as the Board or the Chairman of the Board may assign to him, such duties to be of a character and dignity appropriate to a senior Executive of the Corporation...

WRITTEN NOTICE

The requirement that the company give you reasons, in writing, for firing may be one of your most powerful tools in forestalling the termination and in getting your full severance pay.

It's one thing to call in a manager and say, "We've decided to make a change," or "The chemistry isn't right," or "It's time for a whole new team," or "We're not happy with the job you've been doing," or "We've decided that you'll be happier somewhere else." It's quite another thing to document the reasons for the dismissal. Top management is usually very reluctant to put the reasons for firing a manager into writing. For one thing, there is the fear that the document can be used in a lawsuit. Certainly you want the written specifications because they will form the basis for your action against the company if you decide to take one.

Another reason that the requirement for a written notice will deter firing is that the person doing the firing may be hard pressed to produce specific infractions to put in the document. It has been customary to assume in American business that the manager is constantly involved in jungle warfare. The big money paid to executives helps to compensate them for the peril of being fired at any time for no good reason at all. That's changing. Some courts have held that there is an implicit contract between the company and the employee, and that there must therefore be a reason of some substance for the firing. And, apart from all the legalities, firing managers out of hand is just not something that can be done in as carefree a fashion as was once the case.

So when a senior executive sits down and tries to put on paper the reasons for terminating a subordinate, there may not be much of substance to write. The firing may be deferred or forgotten about altogether. A clause like the following is therefore useful:

> *Notice of termination.* Any termination by the Corporation or you shall be communicated by written notice to the other party. With respect to any termination by the Corporation for Cause, Retirement or Disability, the Notice of Termination shall set forth in reasonable detail the facts and circumstances claimed to provide a basis for such termination.

The above clause would be enhanced in power if the employer were obligated to provide it in *advance* of termination. As it stands now, the notice of termination is accompanied by the list of reasons. An advantageous alteration of this language would go something like this:

> *Notice of impending termination.* With respect to any termination by the Corporation for Cause, the nature of the Cause shall be communicated to the Executive in writing at least thirty (30) days before the termination for Cause is put into effect. The Executive shall be given the opportunity to correct or justify the Cause...

DOCUMENTING YOUR PERFORMANCE

Your contract will contain some kind of provision relating to performance. You will have negotiated to bring that provision into the real world by making it applicable to the broad, general performance of your material management duties.

Think ahead. Imagine the "worst case," in which the company claims that you have failed to fulfill your obligations under that provision, relieving the employer of his agreement to pay severance upon termination of the arrangement. Of course, this is unthinkable; you're doing a good job, you intend to continue to do a good job, your company values your contribution, the people you're dealing with are straight shooters, etc., etc. But think about the "unthinkable" anyway. Every provision written into a contract has the potential of being implemented.

How can you prepare for the contingency, remote though it might be, that the company may claim you have been doing an unsatisfactory job? By documenting your performance.

No doubt your files contain much of the documentation you need. The point is to put the material together in your own personal and confidential folder. Here you will include the quantifiable data; budget objectives for your unit, for example, along with actual performance against those objectives.

Amass material that puts your quantifiable performance in perspective. This will be particularly important if you fall short of objectives. Get the figures for other divisions and for the company as a whole. If you missed budget by 3 percent and nobody else came within 8 percent, this does not make you a paragon, but it shows that you did your job at least as well as anyone else. If your performance is better than that of competitors or than the industry average, your proof material is enhanced. While it is unlikely that you can put together complete figures, particularly for competitive firms, the idea is to get whatever you can. The file is for your benefit, so collect everything that seems relevant. If a particular fact cannot be made to support your case, you don't have to use it.

Collect data that help to explain any failure to reach objectives. For example, at budget time you may make certain requests on which you are turned down or for which you receive substantially less than you've asked. Make sure your request is in writing, with full support material, and do everything you can to get the turndown in writing as well.

Go beyond the numbers. Keep a file of correspondence that acknowledges your contribution, sheds light on your importance to the company, reflects top management's confidence in you, hints at bigger things in the future. Keep a file of performance-review reports if any. These are usually couched in complimentary if not fulsome terms for anyone who is not an absolute idiot, but a judge and a jury would not necessarily know that. Your bosses might find it hard to testify that the praise they gave you did not mean anything.

Court? Judge? Jury? Testify? Yes. The whole thrust of documentation of your performance against the standards established in the contract is to prepare for the "worst case," the possibility that you might have to sue to collect your full severance pay. Of course you don't think it will come to that, nobody ever does. Nevertheless the "unthinkable" does sometimes happen. People who thought they had practically been sanctified by the firm wind up battling for a postfiring settlement. Even if, as is altogether likely, the worst never happens, it's just as well to be prepared. There are whole industries based on preparing for what almost never happens.

In building your file, be comprehensive. Include items which may seem to you to be insignificant if not downright fluffy: puff pieces in the trade press, items in the company house organ, routine letters of commendation. Such items can contribute to the making of an impressive case in support of the proposition that you have indeed fulfilled the requirements of your management position.

While the chances are that you will never have to use this file in court, you are likely to find it valuable in negotiating your next agreement. Unfortunately, a lot of managers come to compensation negotiations woefully unprepared. A judicious selection of the material in your support file can serve as impressive proof material when you ask for more money or power.

WRITING CONFLICT-RESOLUTION METHODS INTO THE CONTRACT

Obviously, the basic strength of a contract lies in its legal enforceability. However, the principle of avoidance of litigation is an important one, one that the executive in particular should never lose sight of.

Corporations don't like lawsuits. However, the company's antipathy to going to court may be more a matter of image than of money. The money an employee might recover in an individual suit can often be written off in various ways and may be at least partially covered by insurance. The larger company's concern is apt to lie in the area of precedent. Paying one employee the disputed sum doesn't hurt much; having to pay more to five thousand employees as a result of the decision can hurt a lot.

But if the firm wants to go to the mat it is likely to have considerably more resources than the individual. The company has lawyers on staff and on retainer and of course is far better able than the lone manager to ride out the agonizingly long time required to get a final decision. As word gets around that the employee is suing the former employer, prospective new employers are apt to be scared off. Even if they can overcome the feeling that this person may be something of a hot potato, they will have doubts about whether the person involved in the suit can devote full time and attention to the job. Furthermore, things might come out in court or in pretrial hearings that embarrass the employee and perhaps the new employer as well.

Practically any section of a contract is subject to different interpretations under different circumstances. For example, the basis on which a bonus is computed may be pretty complicated (see pages 146–52). If there is a difference of opinion, both executive and employer would surely hope for a means of resolving the dispute short of going to court. Imagine, for example, a situation in which the vice-president of marketing is meeting daily with the CEO and senior executives at the same time his lawyers are wrangling with company counsel on the precise meaning of "pretax net profits."

It is to the advantage of both parties to build into the contract a provision for resolving complex financial issues relating to incentive compensation. As more companies initiate plans to fine-tune incentive compensation by tying it to various performance measures, such differences are likely to come up more frequently.

Here is a section embodying a method for settling differences in this area:

In case of any dispute between the Executive and the Company as to the amount of additional compensation payable to the Executive in respect of any fiscal year, determination of the amount so payable by the independent public accountants at the time employed by the Company, made at the request of any party, shall be binding and conclusive on all parties hereto.

Assuming that the corporation's accounting firm is a reputable organization, the executive should not be uncomfortable with a provision like this. The manager who is tempted to fight for the right to an independent audit is carrying suspicion—not to say truculence—to considerable lengths. If he can't trust the company's regular accounting firm he should not be working there.

Differences between employee and employer on matters other than the minutiae of the compensation plan must be settled in other ways. As Michael Roth of Gould & Shea, the New York law firm, remarks, one of the most frequent causes of the most bitter and savage controversy is the question of whether an executive terminates employment voluntarily or is forced out by the employer. On this question can ride hundreds of thousands or even millions of dollars.

Of course the conditions of termination—the causes, initiatives and legalities—can lead to lawsuits. Some companies will build into agreements provisions that try to discourage the employee who is tempted to seek legal remedies. Here is such a provision:

In the event that any action, suit or other proceeding in law or in equity is brought to enforce the provisions of this agreement, and such action results in the awarding of a judgment in favor of the Company, all expenses of the Company in conjunction with said action shall be payable by the Executive.

Such a sweeping provision should be resisted with the utmost vigor. To sign it is to place a severe and needless handicap upon yourself.

The likelihood of seeing this kind of language in a contract submitted to you is not great. Such provisions are, however, used in a more limited sense in connection with legal action relating to a confidentiality or noncompete clause.

THE ARBITRATION CLAUSE

Your contract should carry a provision for arbitration. The standard forum for argument and resolution is provided by the American Arbitration Association. This nonprofit organization maintains panels of arbitrators and administrative services for judging labor and commercial disputes. Here is a typical arbitration clause:

> Any controversy or claim arising under this Agreement shall be settled by arbitration in accordance with the Rules of the American Arbitration Association then in effect. The controversy or claim shall be submitted to three arbitrators, one of whom shall be chosen by the Company, one of whom shall be chosen by the Executive, and the third of whom shall be chosen by the two so selected. The party desiring arbitration shall give written notice to the other party of its desire to arbitrate the particular matter in question, naming the arbitrator selected by it. If the other party shall fail within a period of 15 days after such notice shall have been given to reply in writing naming the arbitrator selected by it, then the party not in default may apply to the American Arbitration Association for the appointment of the second arbitrator. If the two arbitrators chosen as above provided shall fail within 15 days after their selection to agree upon the third arbitrator, then either party may apply to the American Arbitration Association for the appointment of an arbitrator to fill the place so remaining vacant. The decision of any two of the arbitrators shall be final

and binding upon the parties hereto and shall be delivered in writing signed in triplicate by the concurring arbitrators to each of the parties hereto. Judgment upon the award rendered by the arbitrators may be entered in any court having jurisdiction thereof.

One of the messages of such a clause is, *"Read your mail."* Be aware of any notices sent to you in connection with a dispute. Typically, a contract may specify the notification procedure this way:

Any notice, request or other communication required or permitted pursuant to this Agreement shall be in writing and shall be deemed duly given when received by the party to whom it shall be given or three days after being mailed by certified, registered or express mail, postage prepaid, addressed as follows:

If to the Company:
  The Stonesong Press, Inc.
  319 East 52nd Street   Attention of
  New York, N.Y. 10022   the Secretary

If to the Executive:
  John J. Tarrant
  6789 Erdgeist Drive
  Anywhere, New York 00498

Any party may change the address to which communications are to be mailed by giving notice of such change in the manner provided above.

A general arbitration provision like the above is best. Some contracts more sharply delineate the areas to be submitted to arbitration:

> In the event the Company terminates the Executive by reason
> of permanent disability or for cause and the Executive disputes
> the accuracy of such finding of disability or cause, the accuracy
> of such findings shall be submitted to arbitration in accordance
> with the rules of the American Arbitration Association or its
> successor...

Arbitration makes sense. Occasionally a corporation with counsel
on staff or retainer will prefer to keep the arbitration clause out of
the contract, on the assumption that if the only recourse is legal
action the company is vastly better prepared for it than the employee.
Since this is likely to be the case, push for inclusion of a general
arbitration clause. Point to the fact that it is often included in
employment contracts, and place the burden of argument on the
employer to show why it should be left out.

INCLUDING BENEFITS IN THE SEVERANCE AGREEMENT

Continuation of benefits like health insurance can be very important
after termination of employment. For reasons of image and convenience, some executives also want to retain access to nonmonetary
perks that went with the job.

In 1983, Cadence Industries Corporation changed its severance
arrangements with several officers to provide all benefits, including
use of an automobile or automobile allowance, for twelve months
following termination. This provision is not contingent on a change
in control. If there is a takeover, executives terminated within two
years of the change (unless for cause) receive all severance payments
in a lump sum; automobile allowance in a lump sum; the right to
swap unexercised options for their spread in cash; and cash equal
to the spread on restricted awards under the stock incentive plan.

Cadence's employment contract with Chairman and President
Sheldon Feinberg specifies, in addition to base salary and incentive
compensation, death benefits of three times base salary and disability
benefits of 50 percent of base salary, payable until death or age

sixty-five. The company agrees to make fifteen annual payments of $42,500 to build a retirement fund. Up to half of each payment may be used to make related income tax payments. Feinberg or his beneficiary can receive the money on termination or death.

In addition to a Golden Parachute, the contract gives Feinberg the option to begin a five-year consultancy arrangement at the end of the five-year term of the agreement. This provision carries a noncompete proviso, but allows consultation on a nonexclusive basis for annual compensation of half the base salary in effect on December 31, 1990, with cost-of-living adjustments.

Medical insurance is expensive. Executives who have had company-paid plans all their working lives are often shocked at the size of the premiums when they're obliged to foot the bill themselves. Since the employer must of course maintain the plan anyway, the assurance of continuing health benefits to terminated employees (in certain cases) can be a relatively low-cost benefit.

However, it is frequently overlooked. You may someday welcome the inclusion of a paragraph like the following:

> Following termination of this agreement, and unless and until the Employee accepts full-time employment with another party, the Company shall provide and continue to provide to the Employee such insurance benefits (including medical and life insurance) as the Company generally provides for any group or class of employee of which the Employee would have been a member if his employment had continued.

If the extended coverage cannot be provided indefinitely, bargain to make it as long as possible. Certainly it should extend through the life of any post-termination payment schedule.

Agreements on stock plans and other compensation arrangements may carry extensive provisions on termination. Here, for example, is the relevant section of the Esquire Inc. 1979 stock award plan (as amended May 28, 1981) with President Bernard Krauss:

6. *Termination of Employment of Krauss.*

If Krauss ceases to be employed by the Company, his rights with respect to shares of Common Stock awarded or which may be awarded to him pursuant to this Plan shall be as follows:

(a) in the event of the death or the permanent disability of Krauss, then all 25,000 shares of Common Stock not theretofore awarded to Krauss under this Plan shall immediately vest in Krauss upon the occurrence of such event, and, subject to Paragraph 11 hereof, a certificate representing such shares shall be delivered promptly to Krauss or to his designated beneficiary or representative or, in the absence of such designation, as may be designated by Krauss's will or, if applicable, by the appropriate statute of descent and distribution;

(b) if Krauss (i) resigns or (ii) is discharged by the Board for cause prior to April 1, 1983, then, with respect to the fiscal year of the Company during which such event shall have occurred, Krauss shall promptly receive the number of shares (rounded to the nearest whole share) of Common Stock equal to the product of (x) 5,000 multiplied by (y) a fraction, the numerator of which is the number of whole months during such fiscal year of the Company served by Krauss prior to such resignation or discharge and the denominator is 12, and subject to Paragraph 11 hereof, a certificate representing such shares shall be delivered promptly to Krauss (and Krauss shall not have any right to receive, and shall not receive, any additional shares of Common Stock pursuant to this Plan with respect to such fiscal year or any subsequent fiscal year of the Company); and

(c) if for any reason (other than as a result of death or permanent disability referred to in clause (a) above or a discharge for cause referred to in clause (b) (ii) above) Krauss' employment by the Company is involuntarily terminated prior to April 1, 1983, then all 25,000 shares of Common Stock not theretofore awarded to Krauss under this Plan shall immediately vest in Krauss upon the occurrence of such termination, and, subject to Paragraph 11 hereof, a certificate representing such shares shall be delivered promptly to Krauss.

7. *Termination of Employment of Executives.*

If any Executive awarded shares of Common Stock pursuant to this Plan ceases to be employed by the Company and all subsidiaries of the Company, his rights with respect to shares of Common Stock awarded or which may be awarded to him pursuant to this Plan, and related cash payments, shall, subject to the provisions of paragraph 14 hereof, be as follows:

(a) in the event of the death or the permanent disability of such Executive prior to the fourth anniversary of any such initial award, then, with respect to the period of 12 months (commencing with the day and month of such initial award) during which such event shall have occurred, such Executive (or, in the event of his death, his designated beneficiary or representative or, in the absence of such designation, the person entitled to benefits under this paragraph 7 (a) pursuant to the provisions of such Executive's will or, if applicable, the appropriate statute of descent and distribution) shall promptly receive the number of shares (rounded to the nearest whole share) of Common Stock equal to the product of (x) the number of shares comprising such initial award to such Executive multiplied by (y) a fraction, the numerator of which is the number of whole months during such 12-month period served by such Executive prior to such event and the denominator of which is 12, and, subject to Paragraph 11 hereof, a certificate representing such shares shall be delivered promptly to such Executive (or, in the event of his death, to such beneficiary, heir or designated representative), together with an amount in cash equal to the market value of such shares, as determined by the committee, as of the date of such event (and neither such Executive nor his beneficiary, heir or designated representative shall have any right to receive, and shall not receive, any additional shares of Common Stock, or any additional related cash payment, pursuant to this Plan after the date of such event); and

(b) if such Executive (i) resigns or (ii) his employment by the Company and all its subsidiaries shall be terminated for any reason (other than his death or permanent disability) prior to the fourth anniversary of any such initial award, the Executive shall not have any right to receive, and shall not receive, any additional shares of Common Stock, or any additional related cash payment, pursuant to this Plan after the date of such event.

8. *Dilution and Other Adjustments.*

In the event of any change in the outstanding shares of Common Stock by reason of any stock dividend or split, recapitalization, merger, consolidation, split-up, split off, liquidation, combination, exchange of shares, distribution to holders of Common Stock other than cash dividends or other similar corporate change, Krauss and each Executive awarded shares under this Plan shall receive, on each day thereafter on which an award shall be made hereunder, the number and kind of shares which, if the shares of Common Stock (as authorized on March 28, 1979) to be awarded on such day had been awarded on March 28, 1979, and had not been disposed of, such person would be holding at the day such award is made as a result of such event or transaction.

Sometimes it is convenient for both parties to settle the agreement with lump-sum payments.

Fairchild Industries President John Dealy had a contract running through August 1983 providing for minimum annual compensation of $195,000. In 1981 he had been paid $366,212 in cash and $36,860 in nonmonetary perks. Mr. Dealy resigned in 1982. In a settlement, he received $500,000 immediately, with another half million to be paid out over five years. The benefits in his contract were honored through expiration date.

In certain cases the severance pay may be a spinoff.

Edward B. Moore resigned as a vice-president and director of EDO Corporation, an electronics firm, after thirteen years, receiving about $45,000 in cash and a consulting agreement worth $38,600. At the same time EDO sold to Mr. Moore and his wife the subsidiary—EDO-Aire—which Mr. Moore managed. The price was $803,000, described as approximately fair market value.

"NOTHING IN WRITING?" LOOK AGAIN

As numerous lawsuits have shown, an oral agreement is a contract. It just may be harder to prove than a written agreement.

However, even in the absence of a written contract or an oral agreement, you may still have a "contract" with the employer which covers certain areas, particularly that of severance pay.

One place to look for this kind of "contract" is in the printed orientation package handed to all new employees. This package often includes a booklet, produced by the personnel department, covering benefits, policies and procedures. Some people, notably executives, dismiss this stuff as being irrelevant and dull.

Don't. For example, one manager, fired after six years, was told he would receive severance pay amounting to one month's salary. The personnel booklet contained the sentence "It is the company's general practice to provide two weeks pay for every year of employment in case of termination..." That this practice had always been taken to apply to "non-exempt" personnel made no difference. The manager collected.

10

GOLDEN PARACHUTES

The wave of corporate mergers sweeping over American business for the past decade or so has been decisive in making employment contracts look like very desirable arrangements to senior executives. Top managers look out the window and see the takeover wolf approaching. Understanding fully that, whatever their brilliance, they are likely to be kicked out by the new owners, these executives have taken with unbounded enthusiasm to the kind of agreement that assures a lucrative severance deal in the event of termination following takeover. These contracts have come to be known as Golden Parachutes. For the moment, they tend to be distributed among the few managers at the very top of the corporation, but it is likely that the use of employment contracts among managers at diverse levels will grow significantly within the next ten years.

GPs are insurance policies given by senior managers to each other. They assure the members of this exclusive club that, in case of firing, the severance pay will be so magnificent that there will hardly be any pain at all. But there is a catch. GPs are not run-of-the-mill severance arrangements. They come into play only when the corporation undergoes a "change in control," typically through the medium of transfer of ownership of a large block of stock.

Here are two typical GPs:

September 10, 1979

Mr. L. C. Heist
187 Shore Road
Old Greenwich, CT 06870

DEAR WHITEY:

This letter will evidence the agreement of Champion International Corporation to make the payments and provide the benefits hereafter described in the event of termination of your employment following a change in control of the Company as defined below.

The Compensation and Stock Option Committee of our board of directors recognizes that, as in the case of many publicly-held corporations, there is the possibility of a change in control of the Company. This possibility and the uncertainty it creates in management may result in the loss or distraction of key officers to the detriment of the Company and its shareholders.

Despite the value that the Board attaches to your services and the fact that you are considered an integral part of management, the Board believes that the Company must remain free to effect changes in management and terminate employment to that end. However, in consideration of your continuing in the employ of the Company, the Company is prepared to agree and this letter will evidence such agreement on the part of the Company that, in the event of termination by the Company of your employment without cause following a change in control of the Company, as hereafter defined, you (or, in the event of your death, your legal representative) will be paid in a lump sum, no later than 30 days after such termination of employment, an amount equal to your full base salary for a period of 24 months, in addition to your full base salary for the month in which termination of employment shall take place. For this purpose, full base salary shall be computed at the highest monthly rate paid to you at any time during your employment with the Company.

During a period of 24 months commencing with the month

next following that in which termination of employment shall occur, you, together with your dependents, beneficiaries and estate, shall continue to be entitled to all benefits and service credit for benefits under all employee benefit plans of the Company for which key executives are eligible, including, without limitation, the Retirement Plan for Salaried Employees of Champion International Corporation, including related supplemental and excess benefit plans, group hospitalization, health care and dental care plan, life or other insurance or death benefit plan, and other present or future group employee benefit plans or programs of the Company for which key executives are eligible, in accordance with the provisions of any such plan or program, as if you had continued to be employed by the Company during such period. To the extent that such benefits or service credit for benefits shall not be payable or provided under such plans by reason of your no longer being an employee of the Company, the Company shall itself pay or provide for payment of such benefits and service credit for benefits. For the purpose of the foregoing two sentences, stock option and stock appreciation plans and agreements and savings or thrift plans shall not be considered employee benefit plans but you, your dependents, beneficiaries and estate will of course have all benefits and rights of a former employee under such plans and agreements.

The foregoing payments and benefits shall be made if your employment shall be terminated by the Company for any reason other than for "cause" and your employment shall be deemed to have been terminated for "cause only if termination of employment by the company shall have taken place as a direct result of an act or acts of dishonesty constituting a felony under the laws of the State of New York and resulting or intended to result directly or indirectly in gain or personal enrichment at the expense of the Company to which you are not legally entitled.

For purposes of this agreement your employment shall of course not be considered terminated by the Company if you voluntarily terminate your employment except in one of the following events:

1. Because you are not elected or reelected to or are removed from an office or position at least equal to that which you hold immediately prior to the change in control; or

2. Because of a material change in the nature or scope of the authorities, powers, functions, duties or responsibilities attached to your position without your express written consent as a result of which change your position with the Company shall be or become of less dignity, responsibility, importance or scope, or a reduction in base salary, which is not remedied within 30 days after receipt by the Company of written notice from you; or

3. Because of the liquidation, dissolution, consolidation or merger of the Company or the transfer of all or substantially all of its assets unless a successor or successors (by merger, consolidation or otherwise) to which all or substantially all of its assets have been transferred shall have agreed to continue your employment upon terms and conditions satisfactory to you.

Your employment shall be considered terminated by the Company for other than "cause" if you voluntarily terminate your employment in any of the events set forth in the above three paragraphs upon not less than 30 days' written notice to the Company.

For the purpose of the Company's commitment evidenced by this letter, a change in control of the Company shall mean a change in control of a nature that would be required to be reported in response to Item 5(f) of Schedule 14A of Regulation 14A promulgated under the Securities Exchange Act of 1934 as in effect on the date of this Agreement; provided that, without limitation, such a change in control shall be deemed to have occurred if and when any "person" (as that term is used in Sections 13(d) and 14(d) (2) of the Securities Exchange Act of 1934) becomes a beneficial owner directly or indirectly of securities of the Company representing 20% or more of the combined voting power of the Company's then outstanding securities.

It is suggested that you retain this letter with your stock option papers and other documents of value. For the Company's files please acknowledge receipt on the enclosed copy of this letter and return it in an envelope marked "Confidential" to Hazel Hansen.

Sincerely,

ACS:wgr

Receipt of the foregoing letter is hereby acknowledged this 17 day of September 1979;

_____

L. C. Heist

W. W. Clements
Chairman
Chief Executive Officer

This letter is to record our arrangement under which you may elect to receive termination pay in the event of a major change in the control, as set forth below, of Dr Pepper Company (the "Company"). In writing this letter to you, the management is endeavoring to assure and encourage in advance your continued attention and dedication to your assigned duties in the face of potentially disturbing circumstances. The Company is bound, in consideration of your continued services, as follows:

1. The Company, within ten business days of its knowledge of the happening of either one of the following events, will pay into an escrow account which will bear interest, at a major bank in Dallas, Texas (the "Bank"), an amount equal to your then current base salary for twelve months:

    a) Common shares of the Company have been acquired other than directly from the Company in exchange for cash or property by one person (as defined in Section 13 of the Securities Exchange Act of 1934) who thereby becomes the owner of more than 15% of the Company's outstanding common shares, if such acquisition did not receive prior approval by the Company's board of directors.

b) Any shareholder or other person or corporation had made a tender offer for, or a request or invitation for tenders of, common shares of the Company.

2. If, after either of such events, your employment with the Company terminates for any reason other than your death, permanent disability, retirement at age 65 or voluntary resignation, the Bank, on your written demand, will pay to you the amount, if any, so deposited (excluding accrued interest), at the time, in the manner and upon the conditions set forth below. Your resignation within 90 days following any action or inaction by the Company which results in a reduction of your base salary will, for the purposes of the preceding sentence, be deemed to be a termination for a reason other than voluntary resignation.

a) Your right to demand the payment will arise only when 33⅓% or more of the Company's outstanding common shares are owned by one person as defined in Section 13 of the Securities Exchange Act of 1934 and only if such person's acquisition of his shares resulted from an acquisition of the type referred to in subparagraph 1(a) without the prior approval referred to therein or from a tender offer, or request or invitation for tenders, of the type referred to in subparagraph 1(b) not recommended to the shareholders as contemplated by subparagraph 2(e).

b) The amount deposited for you will be paid, subject to withdrawal limitations so that the Company will not incur a loss of accrued interest from early withdrawal of invested funds, in equal monthly installments beginning on the first day of the month following your demand, and will continue for a total of twelve months.

c) The monthly amounts due you will be reduced by any salary or other remuneration you receive from anyone other than the Company or its wholly-owned subsidiaries for your service.

d) Your rights under this agreement will terminate upon the expiration of two years from the date of the deposit of funds with the Bank for your account unless you have become entitled to make and have made a demand within that time.

3. The Company may withdraw the amount so deposited when and only when two years have expired from the date of deposit and no demand has been made during that time. If, before the expiration of such period, there shall occur another event of the kind described in paragraph 1 above, the Company will not be required to make an additional deposit, but the two-year-period shall be measured from the date of the last such event.

4. The Company agrees to pay the usual charges of the Bank, for acting as escrow agent under this agreement and will be entitled to any interest or other income arising from the amount so deposited.

5. The escrow will be subject to the Bank's usual rules and procedures, and the Company will indemnify the Bank against any loss or liability for any action taken by it in good faith as escrow agent.

6. As used in this letter, the "Company" refers not only to Dr Pepper Company but also to its successors by merger or otherwise.

7. The Company retains the right to cancel and terminate this agreement for all purposes at any time prior to the occurrence of either one of the events described above in subparagraphs 1(a) and (b).

8. The arrangement with you created by this letter is confidential and is not to be disclosed by you to other persons unless required by law and the Company may cancel and terminate this agreement for all purposes should it reasonably believe that you have disclosed the

existence of this agreement in violation of this paragraph at any time prior to the occurrence of either one of the events described in subparagraphs 1(a) and (b) above.

Sincerely,

USING THE EXISTENCE OF GPs FOR A BARGAINING CHIP

While courts have generally found that management is within its rights in distributing Golden Parachutes, there is nevertheless considerable defensiveness about the practice among corporate top brass.

For the executive working at a level beneath that at which the GP is bestowed, the knowledge that the company makes this kind of arrangement may be of use in the negotiation. If the negotiating adversary says, "It's not our practice to give contracts to executives," the negotiator responds, "But I was under the impression that you do have contracts. In fact, your proxy statement says so." Since this is likely to be something of a sore point, top management may not be too adroit in defending it. The simplest response is the truth: "Those are Golden Parachutes, given only to our top people, and their purpose is just to provide substantial severance pay in case they are dismissed after a takeover of the company."

There are a number of possible rejoinders. The exaggeration ploy: "My God, I didn't realize that this company is in imminent danger of a takeover. Those of us who don't have the protection of Golden Parachutes better start worrying, etc., etc." The most likely comeback is reassurance that the firm is not directly under the takeover gun at this time. Unless the battle for control is actually under way, the party line is apt to be that the possibility should be soft-pedaled. If the employer contends that this is the case, the negotiator can express relief and then say something like "But since you give some managers contracts to cover something that probably won't take place, why should it be out of the question for me to ask for the same thing?"

The company's proxy statement is must reading if it mentions a GP, because it may very well spell out the terms. For example, Celanese Corporation's 1982 proxy statement specified that four senior managers would receive, in the event of termination after a change in control, benefits described as follows:

> The sum of his annual base salary at that time and his most recent annual bonus, multiplied by the lesser of four or the difference between his age at that time and 65; the equivalent of his benefits under the Executive Pension Plan as it existed prior to... the change of control...

What constitutes a change of control is not specified in this statement.

This is an interesting formula. The evident import is that the favored executive can get no less than the sum of base salary and latest annual bonus, and can receive as much as four times that amount. The negotiator can make use of the disclosure by arguing that it not only establishes a precedent for contracts, at least to the extent of covering severance arrangements, but also provides a formula for his own arrangement.

Besides fulfilling SEC requirements, why do companies tell about GPs? To an extent they may be reacting defensively to the image problem that the plan creates. Shareholders are often highly perturbed by the news that their top managers have presented to each other such a plush-lined safeguard against the financial pain of dismissal—pain that less fortunate persons must endure. Shareholders are even more outraged when they first learn of the parachute payouts after the change in control, when the treasury is being swiftly depleted by departing officers.

The conventional explanation for the GP is that it permits senior executives to make decisions calmly and judiciously when the possibility of a takeover appears. According to this reasoning, the top manager who fears that he will be thrown out into the cold, penniless, by the new controlling faction will fight tooth and nail to forestall the takeover. In many instances this would not be to the best interests of the shareholders, whose stock would go up in value if the change in control took place.

But there is another reason for GPs which companies often acknowledge in their proxy statements. The plan is presented as an "anti-takeover" measure, in language like this: "This proposal is likely to make the Company less vulnerable to an outside attempt to gain a controlling share..." The idea, of course, is that the would-be seizer of power will be deterred by the size of the bill that will have to be paid if the senior officials are dismissed.

Adoption of Golden Parachute plans may not always mean that the company is aware of a particular takeover threat. Sometimes the plan may be put into effect for more general insurance purposes, because there have been a great many takeovers in the industry and it's best not to wait until the last moment. And then there are those who claim that the adoption of a GP—or, more properly, the publishing of information that such a plan has been adopted—may be a device to send up the value of the stock, since the market is assumed always to react to a takeover possibility by bidding up the shares. The impact of this approach is probably not as great as some think. For one thing, observation shows that the market has grown so inured to takeovers—rumored and actual—that more is required than the news that Golden Parachutes have been passed out to send speculators scampering after the stock. Also, insider laws are supposed to preclude the taking of short-term gains on stock by executives.

Whatever the reason for the announcement of the creation of the GP plan—and whatever its effect—the fact that a firm has taken this step should offer interesting possibilities for maneuver to the person who is negotiating for a contract on his own.

WHERE THEY ANNOUNCE THE GOLDEN PARACHUTES

In negotiating for a contract it helps to know that the company gives

GPs to its top executives. That information is usually found in the proxy statement. Here's a typical passage, taken from the 1983 proxy statement of Perkin-Elmer, a high-technology company (1983 net sales of more than $1 billion) based in Norwalk, Connecticut.

Under the heading "Remuneration of Officers and Directors," the proxy statement tells what the top executives receive in salary, bonuses, exercise of stock options, etc. Then comes this paragraph:

> In addition, the Corporation has entered into certain deferred compensation contracts which, subject to earn-out provisions and certain other conditions, provide, after termination of employment with the Corporation (or in the event of an *involuntary termination of employment following a change in control of the Corporation*) for payments to be made for a maximum of ten years of $40,000 per annum to Mr. McDonell (President and COO), $12,000 per annum to Mr. Kelley (Executive Vice President), $12,000 per annum to Mr. Chorske (Senior Vice President, Optical Group), $12,000 per annum to Mr. Stashower (Senior Vice President), and $305,000 per annum to all present officers and directors as a group. The annual payment may be reduced if the recipient elects one of several optional forms of payment based on actuarial determinations.
>
> The Corporation has a deferred compensation contract with Mr. Sorensen (Chairman and CEO) which, subject to the condition that he remain in the employ of the Corporation until his normal retirement age or disability (or an involuntary termination of his employment following a change in control of the Corporation), and subject to certain other conditions, provides for annual payments after retirement, disability or such termination during his life of $100,000, and thereafter in the amount of $50,000 per year to Harriet K. Sorensen, his wife, for her life if she survives him. These payments of $50,000 per year will also be made to Mrs. Sorensen if Mr. Sorensen should die while in the employ of the Corporation.

There are a couple of noteworthy features in this text. One is the provision for the payment of $305,000 annually to "all present officers and directors as a group." The proxy statement does not specify how the payment will be divided among the members of the group.

A second interesting point is the provision of payments to the wife of the CEO if she survives him. While one cannot make any legal judgments, it is tempting to wonder what happens if, in such arrangements, the executive and his spouse divorced, particularly if the executive should marry again.

Proxy statements make rewarding reading for those who are curious about what corporations pay their senior managers.

CONSULTATION AGREEMENTS AS GOLDEN PARACHUTES

Some Golden Parachutes involve consulting agreements. The following GP, concluded between Axia Inc. and a number of senior officials, requires that the executive give ninety days' notice of termination. The payout provides the executive with a thirty-six-month consulting arrangement in case of termination after a change in control. Note that the executive can take another job, in which case the consulting fee is reduced by the amount of compensation from the full-time job. The consulting fee, which consists of monthly payments amounting to one twelfth of the highest annual compensation including bonuses, is to be paid whether or not any consulting services are performed, or whether the company wants any such services.

COMPENSATION CONTINUATION AGREEMENT

AGREEMENT made as of this 5th day of January, 1983 between AXIA Incorporated, a Delaware corporation (the "*Company*"), and _____(the "*Employee*").

In consideration of the premises and other mutual considerations, the receipt and sufficiency of which are hereby acknowledged, it is mutually agreed as follows;

1. Without the consent of the Company the Employee will not terminate his employment by the Company without 90 days prior notice to the Company.

2. In the event that:

(a) the Company is merged or consolidated with any other entity with the result that any voting securities of the Company which are outstanding immediately prior to the merger or consolidation are cancelled or are exchanged for or converted into cash (or cash equivalents), securities of another entity or non-voting securities of the Company; or substantially all of the Company's assets are sold; or thirty percent or more of the voting power of the Company's outstanding securities is acquired by a person or entity or an affiliated group of persons or entities; and

(b) within one year after the effective date of such merger, consolidation, sale or acquisition the Employee's employment by the Company is terminated (i) by the Company, or reduced to a position of significantly lesser responsibility by the action of the Company, for any reason other than the Employee's dishonesty or gross failure to perform the customary duties of his position, or (ii) voluntarily by the Employee;

then for a period of 36 months (the *"Consultation Period"*) after such termination the Employee shall serve as a consultant to the Company under the terms set forth in paragraph 3 below.

3. During the Consultation Period, the Employee will supply advice from time to time on reasonable advance notice with respect to the affairs of the Company, but the Employee may at his sole discretion serve as a full-time regular employee of any other business during the Consultation Period, and his consulting services shall not require his presence at times and places not compatible with such other full-time employment. For such consulting services the Employee shall be paid an amount per month equal to $1/12$th of the highest annual compensation (including bonuses and incentive compensation, but

excluding stock options and stock appreciation rights) received by the Employee from the Company in any twelve consecutive months preceding the termination date; provided that the amount payable hereunder for consulting services shall be reduced by an amount equal to the compensation received by the Employee from such other full-time employment, if any, during the Consultation Period. Unless and until the Employee shall have accepted full-time employment with another party during the Consultation Period, the Employee shall also be provided by the Company with such insurance benefits (including life and medical insurance) as the Company generally provides for any group or class of employee of which the Employee would have been a member had his employment continued.

The payments provided in this paragraph 3 shall be made without regard to whether the Employee is able to perform services for the Company during the Consultation Period or whether other full-time employment is available to the Employee or whether the Company desires consulting services from the Employee after the termination date. In the event of the death or disability of the Employee, the payments required by this paragraph 3 shall be made to his surviving spouse, and if he is deceased without leaving a surviving spouse, said payments shall be made to the estate of the Employee.

4. The Employee agrees that without the consent of the Company he will not at any time after the termination date (except as required by law) disclose to any person confidential information concerning the Company or any of the Company's trade secrets.

5. This Agreement shall be binding upon, and its benefits shall accrue to, the heirs, successors and assigns of the parties hereto.

6. This Agreement shall remain in effect until two years after notice of termination thereof is given to either party hereto by the other. Termination hereof shall not reduce or invalidate any rights or obligations accrued by termination of employment prior to the said expiration date of this Agreement.

IN WITNESS WHEREOF, this Agreement has been duly executed by the Employee and by the Company by its President thereunto duly authorized as of the day and year first above written.

AXIA Incorporated

By:_____

President

By: _____

Employee

"WE DON'T WANT YOU TO BE UPSET..."

One of the paramount justifications of the Golden Parachute is that the executive must not be made nervous by a takeover struggle. To soothe managerial nerves, the future is richly cushioned.

In the following agreement between Del E. Webb Corporation and one of its officers, the calming function of the parachute is spelled out. This agreement is signed by Robert K. Swanson, chairman and CEO. It might be noted that the following month Mr. Swanson's own employment agreement (a copy of which is included) was amended to provide a salary of $300,000 per year, immediate vesting of stock held more than twelve months, and changes in termination and death benefits.

July 29, 1982

Donald V. Upson
3800 N. Central Avenue
Phoenix, AZ 85012

DEAR DON:

The Board of Directors of Del E. Webb Corporation (the "Corporation") and the Compensation Committee (the "Committee") of the Board have determined that it is in the best interests of the Corporation and its shareholders for the Corporation to agree, as provided herein, to pay you termination compensation in the event you should leave the employ of the Corporation under the circumstances described below.

The Board and Committee recognize that the continuing possibility of an unsolicited tender offer or other takeover bid for the Corporation is unsettling to you and other senior executives of the Corporation. Therefore, these arrangements are being made to help assure a continuing dedication by you to your duties to the Corporation notwithstanding the occurrence of a tender offer or takeover bid. In particular, the Board and the Committee believe it important, should the Corporation receive proposals from third parties with respect to its future, to enable you, without being influenced by the uncertainties of your own situation, to assess and advise the Board whether such proposals would be in the best interests of the Corporation and its shareholders and to take such other action regarding such proposals as the Board might determine to be appropriate. The Board and the Committee also wish to demonstrate to executives of the Corporation and its subsidiaries that the Corporation is concerned with the welfare of its executives and intends to see that loyal executives are treated fairly.

In view of the foregoing and in further consideration of your continued employment with the Corporation, the Corporation agrees with you as follows:

1. *Limited Right to Receive Severance Benefits.* In the event that within 24 months after a change of control of the Corporation your employment with the Corporation is terminated you shall be entitled to the severance benefits provided in Section 3 hereof unless:

(a) you are given 12 months' advance notice of such termination (without any reduction in salary, bonus or other benefits during the notice period) or at the time of such termination you have a written employment contract with the Corporation extending at least 12 months from the date Notice of Termination is given you; or

(b) such termination is (i) because of your death or Retirement, (ii) by the Corporation for Cause or Disability or (iii) by you other than for Good Reason.

2. *Certain Definitions.* For purposes of this agreement:

(a) *Change in Control.* A "change in control" of the Corporation shall be deemed to have taken place if, as the result of a tender offer, exchange offer, merger, consolidation, sale of assets or contested election or any combination of the foregoing transactions (a "Transaction"), the persons who were directors of the Corporation immediately before the Transaction shall cease to constitute a majority of the Board of Directors of the Corporation or of any parent of or successor to the Corporation.

(b) *Retirement.* Termination by the Company or you of your employment based on "Retirement" shall mean termination in accordance with the Corporation's retirement policy in effect from time to time, including early retirement, generally applicable to its salaried employees or in accordance with any written retirement arrangement established with your consent with respect to you.

(c) *Disability.* If, as a result of your incapacity due to physical or mental illness, you shall have been absent from your duties with the Corporation on a full time basis for six months or more and within thirty (30) days after written Notice of Termination is given you shall not have returned to the full time performance of your duties, the Corporation may terminate this agreement for "Disability."

(d) *Cause.* The Corporation shall have "Cause" to terminate your employment upon (i) the breach by you of any employment contract between you and the Corporation, or (ii) the adjudication that you are bankrupt, or (iii) the indictment or conviction of you of a felony or crime involving moral turpitude (meaning a crime that necessarily includes the commission of an act of gross depravity, dishonesty or bad morals, or which results in the refusal to grant to or the cancellation or withdrawal of a casino or gaming license held by the Corporation or Subsidiary of the Corporation, by a casino or gaming authority).

(e) *Good Reason.* Termination of your employment by you for "Good Reason" shall mean:

(i) without your express written consent, the assignment

to you of any duties inconsistent with your positions, duties, responsibilities and status with the Corporation immediately prior to a change in control, or a demotion, or a change in your titles or offices as in effect immediately prior to a change in control, or any removal of you from or any failure to reelect you to any of such positions, except in connection with the termination of your employment for Cause, Disability or Retirement or as a result of your death or by you other than for Good Reason;

(ii) a reduction by the Corporation in your base salary as in effect on the date hereof or as the same may be increased from time to time;

(iii) the failure by the Corporation to continue in effect any thrift, incentive or compensation plan, or any pension, life insurance, health and accident or disability plan in which you are participating at the time of a change in control of the Corporation (or plans providing you with substantially similar benefits), the taking of any action by the Corporation which would adversely affect your participation in or materially reduce your benefits under any of such plans or deprive you of any material fringe benefit enjoyed by you at the time of the change in control (except for acceleration of stock options or restricted stock contemplated by this agreement), or the failure by the Corporation to provide you with the number of paid vacation days to which you are then entitled on the basis of years of service with the Corporation in accordance with the Corporation's normal vacation policy in effect on the date hereof; or

(iv) any purported termination of your employment which is not effected pursuant to a Notice of Termination satisfying the requirements of Section 2(f) hereof, and for purposes of this agreement, no such purported termination shall be effective.

(f) *Notice of Termination.* Any termination by the Corporation or you shall be communicated by written notice to the other party ("Notice of Termination"). With respect to any termination by the Corporation for Cause, Retirement or Disability, or any termination by you for Good Reason, the Notice of Termination shall set forth in reasonable detail the facts and circumstances claimed to provide a basis for such termination.

(g) *Subsidiary.* "Subsidiary" shall mean any corporation, partnership, joint venture or other entity in which the Corporation has a 20% or greater equity interest.

3. *Effect of Termination.* If you are entitled to receive severance benefits pursuant to Section 1 hereof, such severance benefits shall be as follows:

(a) You will be entitled to a cash payment in lump sum (or at your discretion, payable in 12 monthly installments without interest) equal to the highest annual base salary in effect at any time during the 12 months prior to the date the Notice of Termination is given plus an amount equal to the value of all bonuses paid to you during the 12 month period prior to the giving of such Notice of Termination; and

(b) Any stock options to purchase common stock of the Corporation held by you on the date the Notice of Termination is given which are not at that date currently exercisable shall on that date automatically become exercisable; and

(c) All shares of common stock of the Corporation held by you under the Corporation's 1979 Restricted Stock Plan which are still subject to restrictions on the date the Notice of Termination is given shall as of that date automatically become free of all restrictions; provided, however, that any such shares which have not been held by you for at least 12 months from the "date of grant" (as defined in such Plan) of such shares shall not be affected by this clause (c) of Section 3 hereof.

4. *Effect on Other Benefits.* Except with respect to stock to the extent specified in Section 3 hereof, this agreement shall not affect your participation in, terminating distributions and vested rights under, any pension, profit sharing or other employee benefit plan of the Corporation or any of its subsidiaries which will be governed by the terms of those re-

spective plans; provided that, in the event you elect to receive your termination payments under this agreement over 12 monthly installments, all group insurance benefits (other than long term disability and Senior Officer Medical Benefits) to which you are entitled on the date Notice of Termination is given will be continued for the installment payment period unless such continued coverage is barred under the group insurance policies of the Corporation, in which case the Corporation will use its best efforts to provide substantially similar benefits for such period.

5. *Entire Agreement.* In the event of the termination of your employment under circumstances entitling you to the termination payments hereunder, the arrangements provided for by this agreement, together with any written employment contract between you and the Corporation and any applicable benefit plan of the Corporation or any of its subsidiaries in effect at the time (as modified by this agreement), would constitute the entire obligation of the Corporation to you and performance thereof would constitute full settlement of any claim that you might otherwise assert against the Corporation on account of such termination.

6. *Successors and Assigns.* This agreement shall be binding upon the inure to the benefit of you, your estate and the Corporation and any successor of the Corporation, but neither this agreement nor any rights arising hereunder may be assigned or pledged by you.

7. *Miscellaneous.* No provisions of this agreement may be modified, waived or discharged unless such waiver, modification or discharge is agreed to in writing signed by you and such officer as may be specifically designated by the Board of Directors of the Corporation. No waiver by either party hereto at any time of the breach by the other party hereto of, or compliance with, any condition or provision of this agreement to be performed by such other party shall be deemed a waiver of similar or dissimilar provisions or conditions at the same or at any prior or subsequent time. No agreements or representations, oral or otherwise, express or implied, with respect to the subject matter hereof have been made by either party which are not set forth expressly

in this agreement. The validity, interpretation, construction and performance of this agreement shall be governed by the laws of the State of Arizona.

8. *Termination of This Agreement.* Prior to a change of control of the Corporation this agreement may be unilaterally terminated by the Corporation upon 12 months' prior written notice to you.

If you are in agreement with the foregoing, please so indicate by signing and returning to the Corporation the enclosed copy of this letter, whereupon this letter shall constitute a binding agreement between you and the Corporation in accordance with its terms.

Very truly yours,
DEL E. WEBB
CORPORATION

By_____
Robert K. Swanson,
Chairman of the Board
& Chief Executive
Officer

Agreed:

_____

_____
(Date)

SECOND AMENDMENT
TO
EMPLOYMENT AGREEMENT

This Second Amendment is entered into this *18th* day of *August*, 1982 by and between Del E. Webb Corporation, an

Arizona corporation (the "Company"), and Robert K. Swanson ("Employee").

The Company and the Employee hereby amend the Employment Agreement as first amended in a letter to R. H. Johnson, dated March 2, 1981, as follows:

AMENDMENT CLAUSE ONE: The following paragraphs appearing in numbered paragraph 10 at pages 7 and 8 of the Employment Agreement are deleted in their entirety:

"In the event the employment of Employee is terminated by the Company for reason other than death, permanent disability or for cause, the Company shall pay to Employee a termination allowance determined as follows:

(a) As to qualified stock options granted to Employee in accordance with paragraph 5(c)(i) hereof, the Company shall pay to Employee the amount by which the fair market value per share of the Common Stock of the Company on the date of termination of Employee's employment exceeds the option price of such shares multiplied by the number of shares which are unexercisable by the terms of said option on the date of termination of Employee's employment.

(b) As to the shares of restricted stock granted to Employee in accordance with paragraph (5)(ii) hereof, the Company will pay to Employee the amount by which the fair market value per share of the Common Stock of the Company on the date of termination of Employee's employment exceeds the price per share paid by the Employee to the Company for the grant of the restricted stock, multiplied by the number of shares as to which restrictions shall not have lapsed on the date of termination of such employment.

"The amounts payable under subclauses (a) and (b) of this paragraph 10 shall be paid in three (3) equal annual installments without interest commencing one (1) year following the date of termination of employment of Employee (for reasons other than death, permanent disability or for cause)."

AMENDMENT CLAUSE TWO: The following provisions are added as numbered paragraph 19 of the Employment Agreement:

"19. *Effect of Termination Without Cause*. Termination

of the employment of Employee by the Company for reason other than (i) death, (ii) permanent disability, (iii) cause or (iv) upon the expiration of the Employment Agreement as provided in numbered paragraph 4 hereof, shall have the following effect:

(a) Any such purported termination must be on 39 days' advance written notice to the Employee, whose employment shall continue during such notice period;

(b) Any stock options to purchase Common Stock of the Company held by Employee on the date notice of such purported termination is given ("Notice Date") which are not at the Notice Date currently exercisable shall on the Notice Date automatically become exercisable; and

(c) All shares of Common Stock of the Company held by Employee under the Company's 1979 Restricted Stock Plan which are still subject to restrictions on the Notice Date shall as of that date automatically become free of all restrictions; provided, however, that any such shares which have not been held for at least 12 months from the "date of grant" (as defined in the Plan) of such shares shall not be affected by this clause (c) of numbered paragraph 19.

The provisions of this numbered paragraph 19 are not to be construed as modifying in any way the termination provision of numbered paragraph 4 (as herein amended) of the Employment Agreement, nor as granting the Company the right to terminate the employment of the Employee other than for the permissible reasons specified in clauses (i) through (iv) of this paragraph; and the effects of such a purported termination specified in clauses (a) through (c) hereof shall be in addition to and not in limitation of any other rights the Employee has hereunder as a result of such purported termination."

AMENDMENT CLAUSE THREE: Subclause (iii) of paragraph 12 of the Employment Agreement is amended to read: "(iii) the benefits of paragraph 19 hereof."

AMENDMENT CLAUSE FOUR: The last paragraph of paragraph 10 on page 8 of the Employment Agreement is amended to read:

"In the event of termination of this Agreement upon advance written notice as provided in paragraph 4 (as herein amended), the Employee shall continue to be employed and he shall be entitled to the continuation of his then base salary as well as the employee benefits referred to in paragraph 5(b), including health and long term disability benefits and the other benefits as provided in the March 2, 1981 first amendment to this Employment Agreement, until the date of termination resulting from such notice."

AMENDMENT CLAUSE FIVE: The following paragraph 4 of the Employment Agreement is deleted in its entirety:

"4. *Term.* The term of this Agreement shall be thirty-six (36) months commencing on January 21, 1981, and ending on (and including) January 20, 1984 and shall be extended from year to year thereafter, subject to termination by either party at the end of the third year or any subsequent year by giving twelve (12) months advance written notice. In the event this Agreement shall terminate by reason of the death of the Employee the Employee's widow will be paid applicable death benefits to which she may be entitled under any then existing benefit plans of the Company, plus six (6) months salary at the Employee's then salary rate."

and the following is substituted therefor:

"4. *Term.* Notwithstanding anything contained in paragraph 2 hereof, the term of this Agreement shall be for the period beginning August 1, 1982 and ending on the date of the annual meeting of stockholders in 1985. In the event this Agreement shall be terminated by reason of the death of Employee, the Employee's widow will be paid applicable death benefits to which she may be entitled under any then existing benefit plans of the Company, plus six (6) months salary at the Employee's then salary rate."

AMENDMENT CLAUSE SIX: The following subclause (a) of paragraph 5 of the Employment Agreement is hereby amended, effective August 1, 1982:

"(a) The Employee's minimum base salary shall be Two Hundred Fifty Thousand Dollars ($250,000.00) per annum, payable as nearly as possible, in equal semi-monthly installments (except to the extent that Employee may have elected to defer payment pursuant to the provisions of the Company's Executive Deferred Compensation Plan or such other deferred compensation plan of the Company as may be in effect from time to time) subject to adjustment (but not below the minimum base salary provided above) in accordance with the regular procedures established by the Company for salary adjustments."

and by substituting therefor the following:

"(a) The Employee's minimum base salary shall be Three Hundred Thousand Dollars ($300,000.00) per annum, payable as nearly as possible, in equal semi-monthly installments (except to the extent that Employee may have elected to defer payment pursuant to the provisions of the Company's Executive Deferred Compensation Plan or such other deferred compensation plan of the Company as may be in effect from time to time) subject to adjustment (but not below the minimum base salary provided above) in accordance with the regular procedures established by the Company for salary adjustments."

IN WITNESS WHEREOF, this Amendment has been executed by the parties hereto in counterparts, each of which is deemed an original as of the date first written above.

DEL E. WEBB
CORPORATION

By:_____

    Alan P. O'Connor
    Vice President,
    Human Resources

ATTEST:

    _____

    Robert K. Swanson
    "Employee"

11

PROVISIONS RESTRICTING YOUR FREEDOM OF ACTION

The key segment in some contracts is the "noncompetition" paragraph, in which the executive agrees to stay out of certain money-making areas for a specified length of time after leaving the company:

> Executive agrees that for a period of two (2) years following termination of this Agreement for any reason, he/she will not, directly or indirectly, alone or as a partner, officer, director or shareholder of any other firm or entity, engage in any commercial activity in the United States in competition with any part of the Company's business...

WHY THE COMPANY WANTS THE NONCOMPETITION PROVISION

One of the most obvious examples of what the company is protecting itself against is the case of the executive who quits and either joins a competitor or goes into business for himself, taking one or more big customers with him. Such occurrences are well known in industries like advertising, where much of the contact with an important client is channeled through a particular account manager. The agency can't spread the contact around very much, since the client traditionally demands to be dealt with by one particular executive. The agency is therefore highly vulnerable. There have been spectacular lawsuits centering around the "stealing" of clients by account managers who move on.

A similar situation exists in publishing, where a successful author becomes more attached to an editor than to the publishing house, and is inclined to go where the editor goes.

A second major reason for the company's desire to restrict the future activities of managers is *knowledge*. We are not talking here about specific trade secrets—patents, formulas, inventions, etc. There are particular contract provisions which cover such discrete matters. Here we are concerned with the broader area of knowledge that a manager acquires about his company's structure, objectives, plans, philosophy, ways of doing business, and points of vulnerability. For example, in the soft-drink industry one of the hottest questions of 1982–83 was, Will our major competitor come out with a caffeine-free cola? In this highly volatile industry, driven by a market which exhibits illogical and sometimes capricious behavior in choosing one soft drink over another, any new departure by a competitor is a matter of vast concern. Even a minuscule change may provide enough of a crack for a wedge which is then hammered deeper by hundreds of millions of dollars in advertising billing, and may lead to an alteration of several points in market shares, which is an earthquake in the high-rolling consumer-goods business.

The soft-drink giants watched nervously while a smaller company introduced a no-caffeine product. This competitor was of no particular concern, no matter how good the drink tasted or how healthful it might be. The manufacturer was not big enough to spend the promotion money to create a big demand, nor was the competitor's distribution apparatus widespread enough to constitute a threat. But that left two questions for the cola titans: (1) Could the small company be absorbed by a larger company, not necessarily in the soft-drink business, which *would* possess the advertising clout to promote the new product? (2) Would the major competitor come out with such a drink, and if so, when?

Obviously, the purpose of this discussion is not to analyze the battle strategy and tactics of the global soda-pop antagonists (who ultimately felt compelled to bring out low-caf drinks), but to exemplify the kind of knowledge that is not so precise as the secret formula for a cola drink, but is nevertheless of decisive importance. Such information is highly prized in the consumer-goods industries. Facts about the performance of a new detergent in a test market, for example, would be welcomed by the brand managers of a competitor.

Another reason—less tangible but still significant—for the company to keep its managers from fleeing to the arms of a competitor: In the fall of 1983 an interesting example of the usefulness of a manager newly hired from a competing firm could be found in the computer commercials run by Burroughs. They feature earnest fact-to-audience discourse by a gentleman who explains that he was an IBM executive for many years, and it's not who's biggest but who's best, and so forth.

So there are a variety of reasons for companies to want to deter movement of managers to competing firms. In fact, if "pirating" of managers within industries were to be eliminated by mutual use of noncompetition agreements, many CEOs and human-resource directors would be a lot happier.

WHAT THE NONCOMPETITION PROVISION MEANS TO THE EMPLOYEE

Most provisions of the typical employment contract offer benefits to both parties, though the balance may swing to one side or the other. The noncompetition provision is strictly in favor of the employer, with no offsetting benefits to the manager. It keeps the manager from getting a job in the industry that he knows best and in which his contacts and reputation have been established.

Some executives believe that such a provision is unenforceable, or virtually so. While the wording of a particular paragraph may make it a little shaky as a legally binding proposition, the purely legal aspect is not the major point unless one really enjoys litigation.

If you have signed such an agreement you may have considerable trouble getting a job with a competitor. You may not disclose the existence of the contract if you are not asked directly, but its existence is likely to become known nonetheless; after all, the employer has gotten you to sign it for his self-protection, and he can often protect himself effectively by making that fact known. And then, whatever the ultimate enforceability, if you are the target of a suit you are up against an adversary with far more resources than you; furthermore, companies often do not rush to employ people who are being sued by their previous employers.

So it is realistic to regard the noncompetition provision as an effective measure which strictly favors the employer.

YOUR BARGAINING POSTURE

Your initial reaction to the paragraph should be, "Of course that must be removed." Why should you be in any way hampered in your pursuit of legitimate employment? By what right does the employer dictate your activities subsequent to the termination of your employment?

You may find little resistance to removal of the provision. Some organizations print such restrictive provisions in their standard contract forms. If the employee does not question them, they remain in place. The firm may have little or no intention of enforcing them. They are, however, available in the signed agreement if needed.

If your employer willingly strikes out the noncompetition clause, you may not be as important to him as you thought. If the employer holds out for inclusion of the provision, you have been given some interesting bargaining leverage.

Ask why the restriction is necessary. The answer is apt to revolve around the intimate secrets to which you will be privy. If that's the argument, it is a good tactic to say, "Well, then, why not say so? Let's have a paragraph that specifies the kind of secret that I am not entitled to give to somebody else. Once we have that provision on paper I can take a look at it," etc., etc. (Never say that if such-and-such a provision is written up you will *agree* to it. Just say you'll look at it.)

At the same time you suggest that the paragraph be rewritten to protect specific secrets, you insist that there be no limitations whatever on your activities following termination. What you want is for the employer to acknowledge that you are so important to the company (whatever the reasons) that it would be harmful to the firm if you went to work for a competitor.

That's a useful acknowledgment. It increases your bargaining power. You can use the added leverage to negotiate for higher compensation. You can also use it to get yourself considerably better severance provisions. Your argument: "This contract locks me in. It keeps me from considering a better offer from the people who are most likely to make me such an offer. Now, of course I have no intention of even taking seriously such an offer if it comes. I feel that my future is with this organization. But surely it's asking too much to expect me to cut myself off from all possibility of another job in this industry. I would be placing myself at your mercy." When they insist that the company requires such protection against the elopement of managers at your level to a competitor, then you insist on your own right of self-protection: "The severance arrangement will have to cover me completely for the time specified in the noncompetition section. That's only fair. My chances of getting a good job will be severely hampered by this clause in the event that I am compelled to leave...."

Your bargaining posture in obtaining a more favorable severance deal (covered in the relevant section) will include insistence on the arrangement's coming into play if you are terminated for any reason at all.

PULLING THE TEETH OF THE NONCOMPETITION SECTION

Having gotten all the mileage you can out of the company's desire to keep you from the arms of a competitor, you now want to limit the provisions of the restrictive paragraph.

One way is to introduce qualifications that render the prohibition invalid in certain instances. In Golden Parachutes, the ban on competitive activity is removed in case of a change of ownership. The parachuter not only receives munificent severance terms; he also enjoys freedom to compete with his former company.

Another qualification that you may want to introduce is one relating to the nature of the termination. Insist that termination by the company (i.e. firing) wipes out the clause. If they fire you they should not be entitled to dictate your activities. Furthermore, it isn't logical. The manager who is fired cannot be considered all that important, so how can he be so important to a competitor? (Do not accept the argument that the fired executive can deliver valuable secrets to the enemy, even though it is true. If the specific purpose of the agreement is to protect secrets, it should say so clearly. This paragraph focuses on "commercial activity... in competition...")

Another way of limiting the scope of the provision is to require that the agreement be more specific about the activity that constitutes competition. In the sample paragraph we quoted, on page 215, the employee agrees to avoid *any* competition "directly or indirectly, alone or as a partner, officer, director or shareholder..." This language could keep you from working as a consultant. It could even be construed as forbidding you to hold stock in a competitive firm.

Whittle down the scope. If the object is to keep you from going to work as, say, a marketing executive for a competitive firm, ask that the agreement say so, and limit its prohibition to this activity. You are unlikely to get it drawn so explicitly that it specifies the job title or the type of work (thus permitting a marketing manager to go to a competitor as an operations manager), but you may get the provision to confine itself to the taking of a full-time job. This could be important. Your experience and knowledge might make you valuable as a consultant, and you want to make sure that you have not signed away your right to consult in your field.

Still another way in which you can muffle the effectiveness of this paragraph is by insisting that it spell out just what company activities are to be shielded from competition. After all, in this day of conglomerates, a company may comprise units making shoes, turbines, frozen dinners, paper, pills, and condominiums, while selling services that range from security to surgery. A blanket non-competition provision signed with a gigantic global conglomerate could practically keep you out of work all over the world. So have the agreement spell out that the competition would exist only in a particular field, which you may want to define as narrowly as possible. One reasonable way to phrase such language is that the manager must refrain from competition "with any part of the Company's business that was under the Executive's direct supervision during the last year of employment..."

If the contract has a paragraph relating to confidential information, the noncompetition paragraph will (if it contains specifics at all) have a provision banning competitive activity "with respect to which Executive has Confidential Information as defined in paragraph 7..." There is no particular reason for you to want to eliminate the company's right to protect its legitimate secrets (and it might be unwise to imply that you would want to eliminate this right). Your position here, rather, is to acknowledge that this is a legitimate concern, but to eliminate if possible all other activity from the prohibition.

The noncompetition clause is paradoxical in that, while it is one-sided in favor of the company, it provides the employee with the chance to sweeten other parts of the agreement. It is certainly a manifestation of the company's feeling that you are an important executive.

PITFALLS IN THE JUNGLE OF JARGON

The following confidentiality clause may look like a parody of legal language, but it comes from an actual contract. The first few words carry a useful qualification. The rest of it is a maze of legalese that contains a potential trap.

Except to the extent reasonably required in conducting and carrying out of the business affairs of the Company, the Ex-

ecutive agrees that he will not at any time, in any fashion, form or manner, either directly or indirectly, divulge, disclose or communicate to any person, firm, or corporation in any manner whatsoever any information of any kind, nature or description concerning any matters affecting or relating to the business of the Company, including, without limiting the generality of the foregoing, the names of any of its customers, the prices it obtains or has obtained or at which it sells or has sold its products, or any other information of, about, or concerning the business of the Company, its manner of operation, its plans, processes, or other data of any kind, nature or description without regard to whether any or all of the foregoing matters would be deemed confidential, material, or important, the parties hereby stipulating that as between them, the same are important, material and confidential and gravely affect the effective and successful conduct of the business of the Company and its goodwill, and that any breach of the terms of this paragraph is a material breach hereof.

There are a couple of comments to be made here. Legal language has of course become a joke. Some lawyers do not seem to feel that a thing has been said unless it has been said at least three times. Some observers speculate that lawyers are so unsure of the meaning of simple English words that they cram all the possibly applicable words they know into a document, hoping that one will find its mark. This paragraph is a bizarre example of the extremities of prolixity to which some lawyers may be carried.

However, half hidden in the jungle of words there is a trap. The reader, plodding through the underbrush, might wonder what could possibly be confidential about the prices the company *used to* charge. The contract takes care of that a little later by saying, in effect, that no matter how public, trivial, or irrelevant a piece of information may be, the signer of this agreement stipulates that it is confidential, important, and relevant.

It is unwise to sign a contract that you might conceivably violate by making a casual reference to some unimportant matter. It is even more unwise to agree that anything you might say about the company is important and confidential even if everyone knows it already and no one gives a damn. The point is not whether the clause could be enforceable in court. The point is that you sign into being a potentially dangerous device that the company, or an ill-disposed superior, could use to harass you.

One way to handle the employer's request for such a clause would be to say, "Of course, I don't understand all the legalisms in here. Looks like a lot more words than I would use. But I see in general what it's saying and I have to ask, What's the point? If the company thinks I'm dumb enough to spill information that would be useful to a competitor, I shouldn't be hired. And I cannot believe you would think I'd disclose secrets deliberately. That doesn't mean I'm unwilling to sign a confidentiality clause. I understand the need to have it in any agreement like this, and I have no problem with that, because there is no way I would violate it, even inadvertently. But let's make it a straightforward, commonsense clause."

INTIMIDATION BY *IN TERRORUM*

Michael Roth of the influential New York law firm of Gould & Shea has negotiated many executive contracts. Roth says flatly that the vast majority of such agreements benefit the employee rather than the employer. The executive gets bonuses, perks, protection, and a severance agreement. The employer gets the hope that the employee will not want to work for someone else.

This is often a forlorn hope. And when an employee wants to make a move, it is likely to be consummated, whatever the contract states. This is particularly true in the case of noncompete clauses, in which the company tries to keep an individual from working for anyone else in the same industry for a stipulated number of years. Such provisions hit the headlines occasionally when prominent persons in show business or the media are tempted by lucrative offers. ABC tried to keep the sportscaster Warner Wolf from moving to WCBS, the competing New York station, by resorting to a noncompete clause, but the broadcaster negotiated the move with relatively little difficulty. When the New York *Daily News* was threatened with the defection of its longtime sports columnist Dick Young to the competing New York *Post*, Young's contract was cited. The columnist soon began appearing in the *Post*. (Mr. Young's frequent castigation of big-time athletes for playing fast and loose with contractual obligations was somewhat muted, but otherwise he was as acerbic as ever.)

While decisions vary from state to state, courts tend to be skeptical about noncompete contracts. Their opinions sometimes refer to "involuntary servitude" or "slavery."

However, this is not to say that noncompete provisions have no effect. Their major purpose may be deterrence through the threat of a lawsuit. The employee may be eager to flout the contract and make the move, but the new employer is likely to be unwilling to get involved in a lawsuit, whatever the outcome may be. Even if the new employer is not directly involved in the suit, the question of how fully the employee (who is being distracted by litigation) can devote himself to his job is a nagging one.

This effect of the noncompete provision leads lawyers to call it the *in terrorum* clause (free translation: it scares the hell out of you). The existence of the language in the contract makes the new employer nervous. Even if the chances are very high that the courts will uphold the employee's move, there is all that controversy and bad publicity to be considered.

So the "enforcement" of the provision comes indirectly. The prospective employer becomes aware of the clause. If the employer does not ask about it, as he should, he is probably told by the headhunter, who certainly does not want the client to have any unpleasant surprises. Failing that, the present employer will surely promulgate the fact that the agreement exists.

The employee who hopes to move says to his new employer, "My lawyer tells me that this clause is unenforceable." The employer nods and says, "Yes, that's what I understand, but we don't want any hard feelings or loose ends here. You go back to your company and get this straightened out."

There ensues a form of exit negotiation, in which the present employer may ask for concessions on benefits due the executive in exchange for a release on the noncompete language.

The *in terrorum* effect can sometimes be overlooked by a manager who, eager for the job or promotion and dazzled by the money and the perks, signs the noncompete clause along with the more congenial parts of the contract because of a feeling that it is not enforceable. The clause may not be legally enforceable, but it may be effective nevertheless.

It should be noted that comments on the dubious legal enforceability of such agreements do not apply to the noncompete provisions that are often included in the contract covering the sale of a business. For example, the owner of a store that has just been sold agrees not to open another store within a specific area. Inasmuch as the sale has included "goodwill," such a clause is logical and understandable. The same can be said about buyouts of nonretail enterprises, particularly service companies—consulting firms, public-relations houses, etc. On such agreements courts are much more likely to deem the noncompete clause legal and enforceable.

A HARD-NOSED APPROACH TO NONCOMPETITION

Here is a clause worded so as to put additional teeth into the non-compete provision:

> *Restrictive Covenant.* In consideration of the Company's agreements contained herein and the payments to be made by it to Employee pursuant hereto, Employee agrees, that during the period of his employment hereunder and for a period of one (1) year following the date of the termination of this agreement... Employee will not engage in a competing business within the geographical limits of any state... in which any of the businesses of the Company are being conducted on the date of any such termination. Employee acknowledges and agrees that, a breach by Employee of the provisions of this section will constitute such damage as will be irreparable and the exact amount of which will be impossible to ascertain and for that reason agrees that the Company will be entitled to an injunction to be issued to any Court of competent jurisdiction

> restraining and enjoining Employee from violating the pro-
> visions of this paragraph. The right of an injunction shall be
> in addition to and not in lieu of any other remedy available
> to the Company for such breach or threatened breach, in-
> cluding the recovery of damages from Employee.

A clause like this helps to explain why judges sometimes use the
word "slavery" with relation to noncompete provisions. But here the
"slave" helps to put on the shackles. However the matter might be
decided, it is not farfetched to imagine that the company, if it
wished, could find a judge willing to issue an injunction, since the
employee has expressly agreed that an injunction is in order. Perhaps
later the company would lose its case, but the injunction would
have had its effect. To many prospective employers the threat of
injunction surely is more than enough to discourage hiring the
executive in question.

It is exceedingly dangerous to sign contracts with such provisions.
The doubtful enforceability of noncompetition clauses notwithstanding, the agreement to an injunction considerably increases the
possibility that the firm really can stop the executive from working
at the new job, at least for a time. And the *in terrorum* effect is
undeniable.

NONCOMPETE LINKED WITH DEFERRED COMPENSATION

If the company is determined to try to limit what an executive does
after termination of employment, the executive ought to try to get
paid for accepting the limitation. Here is a clause that keys noncompetition to the receipt of "deferred compensation" which has
the effect of severance pay:

> *Noncompetition.* During the Active Employment Pe-
> riod... and for so long thereafter as he shall be living and

receive deferred compensation under paragraph 4(b) hereof, the Exccutive shall not... directly or indirectly render any services to or become employed by... any business which is at the time substantially competitive with the business of the Company...

Turning to paragraph 4(b) we find a provision to pay the employee (or beneficiary) $50,000 per year for two years and $25,000 per year for ten years thereafter.

The noncompete agreement may constitute a separate covenant, signed in this case on the occasion of the purchase of another company:

COVENANT NOT TO COMPETE

THIS AGREEMENT, made and entered into as of the *4th* day of *November*, 1982, by and between Roberson's Beverages, Inc. ("RBI"), its successors and assigns, W. R. Roberson, Jr. ("Covenantor"), and Dr Pepper Company ("Dr Pepper").

WITNESSETH:

WHEREAS, Dr Pepper recently purchased all of the outstanding shares of Roberson's Beverages, Inc.,; and

WHEREAS, Covenantor, a key managerial employcc of RBI, has skills which would allow him to compete with RBI or Dr Pepper; and

WHEREAS, Covenantor has represented to RBI and Dr Pepper that Covenantor will not compete with RBI or Dr Pepper in consideration of payments hereunder; and

WHEREAS, RBI desires that Covenantor enter into a non-competition agreement in the form hereof, and Covenantor is willing to enter into such an agreement;

NOW, THEREFORE, in consideration of the foregoing, of the mutual promises herein contained, and of other good and valuable consideration, the receipt and sufficiency of which are hereby acknowledged, the parties hereto agree as follows:

1. Covenantor covenants and agrees that, in order to protect Dr Pepper's and RBI's interests in the business, operations and assets of RBI, for a period of four (4) years from the date hereof

(the "Term of this Agreement"), Covenantor will not, without the prior written consent of Dr Pepper or RBI directly or indirectly:

(a) engage, whether by virtue of stock ownership, management responsibilities or otherwise, in the manufacture, marketing or sales or distribution of soft drinks or similar products which are competitive with the products currently manufactured, marketed, sold and distributed by RBI in the markets and geographic areas in which RBI now conducts its business (the "Area"), or

(b) become interested, whether as principal, owner, stockholder, partner, agent, officer, director, employee, salesman, joint venturer, consultant, advisor, independent contractor or otherwise, in any person, firm, partnership, association, venture, corporation or entity engaging, directly or indirectly, in any of the activities described in paragraph (a) above, or

(c) do any act which might injure the business or reputation of the business as now conducted by RBI or which might divert employees, customers or suppliers from such business.

2. Without limiting the generality of the provisions of Section 1 hereof, Covenantor agrees that he will not, during the Term of this Agreement, conduct in the Area a soft drink business under the name of "Roberson's Beverages" or "Dr Pepper" or any other trade names or trademarks used by RBI in the Area. None of the foregoing shall prevent Covenantor and members of his immediate family from collectively being holders of up to 5% in the aggregate of any class of securities of any corporation engaged in the prohibited activities described above, provided that such securities are listed on a national securities exchange or registered under Sections 12(g) or 15(d) of the Securities Exchange Act of 1934.

3. The limitation of Section 1 hereof shall apply whether or not RBI or Dr Pepper, or any of their successors or assigns, continue its business in its present name or form on or after the date hereof.

4. Covenantor agrees that his compliance with the covenants and agreements contained in Sections 1 and 2 hereof is reasonable and necessary for the protection of RBI's and Dr Pepper's interests in the aforementioned acquisition of RBI.

5. Covenantor recognizes and agrees that any violation of any of the covenants and agreements contained in Sections 1 and 2 hereof will cause irreparable and continuing damage or injury to Dr Pepper and RBI and RBI's business, assets and operations, the exact amount of which would be difficult to ascertain, and for which there will be not adequate remedy at law, and that, for such reasons, among others, RBI or Dr Pepper or both shall be entitled, in addition to termination of payments hereunder, to an injunction from any court of competent jurisdiction restraining any further violation as well as recovery from Covenantor of any and all costs and expenses sustained or incurred by RBI or Dr Pepper in obtaining such an injunction, including without limitation, reasonable attorneys' fees. Such right to an injunction (and to the recovery of such costs and expenses) shall be cumulative and in addition to any other rights and remedies in which RBI and/or Dr Pepper may be entitled.

6. Covenantor recognizes and agrees that, on and after the date hereof, he will not have the right to use for his own account any of the trademarks, trade names, licenses, labels, trade secrets or customers' lists owned by or licensed to RBI.

7. In consideration of the agreements contained herein, RBI shall pay to Covenantor cash payments over a period of ten (10) years commencing January 1, 1983. Such payments shall be in the amount of fifty-five thousand dollars ($55,000) per annum for the first five (5) years of the ten year period and one hundred and five thousand dollars ($105,000) per annum for the remaining five (5) years. The annual payments are payable in equal installments on the last day of March, June, September and December of each year commencing March 31, 1983 and ending December 31, 1992. For the first five year period the quarterly installments shall be thirteen thousand, seven hundred and fifty dollars ($13,750), and for the second five year period the quarterly installments shall be twenty-six thousand, two hundred and fifty dollars ($26,250) (both or either of which are referred to herein as "Installment Payments"). If RBI shall fail to make such payments without good cause, Dr Pepper agrees to make such payments to Covenantor.

8. If Covenantor should die before he shall have received all of the Installment Payments, then, subject to the provisions of Section 9 hereof, the remaining Installment Payments shall be paid when due to his estate or to such other person or persons as the executor or administrator of his estate shall designate (the estate and/or such designee hereinafter referred to as a "Successor in Interest"). This Agreement and amounts payable hereunder may not be sold, assigned or otherwise transferred except as provided herein.

9. If at any time or from time to time during the Term of this Agreement, Covenantor or any Successor in Interest shall be in breach of any of the provisions of this Agreement and shall continue so to be in breach for more than thirty (30) days after having received written notice thereof from RBI, then, in addition to any other remedies to which RBI may be entitled, RBI's obligations to make further Installment Payments shall be terminated.

10. If any provision or provisions hereof, or any portion of any provision hereof, shall be deemed invalid or unenforceable pursuant to a final determination of any court of competent jurisdiction or as a result of future legislative action, such determination or action shall be construed so as not to affect the validity or enforceability of the remainder of this Agreement and shall not affect the validity of any other portion of this Agreement.

11. No modification or waiver of any provisions of this Agreement and no consent by RBI or Covenantor to any modification or waiver shall be effective, unless such modification or waiver shall be in writing and signed by a duly authorized officer of RBI and by Covenantor.

12. This Agreement shall be construed in accordance with and governed by the laws of the State of North Carolina.

13. This Agreement may be executed by the parties in one or more counterparts, each of which shall be an original and all of which shall together constitute the Agreement.

14. This Agreement constitutes the sole and entire agreement of the parties hereto with respect to the matters covered hereby, and supersedes all prior negotiations and written, oral or implied representations, warranties, commitments, offers,

contracts and understandings between the parties with respect to such matters.

15. All notices, consents or other communications provided for herein shall be in writing and shall be deemed to have been given when personally delivered or sent registered or certified mail, return receipt requested, postage prepaid, addressed as follows:

if to RBI:

J. Scott Chase
P.O. Box 225086
Dallas, Texas 75265

if to Covenantor: or to such other person and place as RBI or Covenantor respectively, shall furnish by notice to the other party hereto.

IN WITNESS WHEREOF the parties hereto have caused this Agreement to be duly executed as of the day and year first above written.

DR PEPPER COMPANY   ROBERSON'S
                                  BEVERAGES, INC.

By_____   By_____
Title_____   Title_____

                                  COVENANTOR

                                  _____
                                  W. R. Roberson, Jr.

ARE YOU COMPETING IF YOU BUY STOCK?

Noncompete clauses tend to be very inclusive:

The Employee shall not, directly or indirectly, enter the employ of, or render any service to, any person, firm or corpo-

> ration engaged in any business competitive with the business
> of the Company or any of its subsidiaries or affiliates; he shall
> not engage in any such business on his own account; and he
> shall not become interested in any such business, directly or
> indirectly, as an individual, partner, shareholder, director,
> officer, principal, agent, employee, trustee, consultant, or any
> other relationship or capacity...

The executive who went immediately from the office to a Trappist
monastery might be reasonably sure of obeying to the letter all these
provisions. Any other course may, one way or another, lead to a
violation.

If there must be a noncompete clause it should be limited to
active competition that hurts the previous employer because the
executive puts specific knowledge of the company's activities to use
on behalf of a direct competitor. This might be done as an employee
of the competitor or as a consultant. It cannot be done inadvertently.
The former employee should not be held responsible for every
passing word or contact.

Nor should the former employee's rights to buy stock be unduly
restricted. After all, experience in the industry may have given the
executive a shrewd appreciation of the value of a competitor's shares.
Buying those shares is not equivalent to putting special knowledge
at the competitor's disposal.

So the noncompete provision might contain an exception like
the following:

> Nothing herein shall prevent or prohibit Employee from (i)
> owning not more than 2% of the outstanding stock or publicly
> held debt securities of any corporation whose stock is listed on
> any national securities exchange or reported on the NASDAQ
> system, or not more than 2% of the limited partner interests
> in any privately held limited partnership or (ii) acquiring in
> each year of the Term securities or other interests having an
> aggregate cost not in excess of $150,000...

Another problem with a sweeping noncompete clause is that the number of companies on the proscribed list can grow indefinitely as firms enter or acquire subsidiaries in the industry in question. The executive who signed such an agreement with a shoe company and later got a good offer from IBM might be chagrined to learn that IBM has just acquired a shoe business, thus putting him in violation of the covenant.

To forestall this possibility, language like the following is useful: "Nothing herein shall prohibit the Executive from rendering services to or becoming employed by or participating in any business that was not at the date of such termination substantially competitive with the business of the Company."

For many executives whose agreements are terminated, consulting is the logical course. They enjoy the freedom of action and have a chance to put their experience to work in a variety of situations. For some, consulting may be the only course. They're unable to land jobs and so must seek consulting assignments.

The existence of a noncompete clause can be very damaging in such cases. Therefore the executive who has no thought of doing consulting work at any time must be leery of signing a contract that expressly forbids doing it with companies in the industry the executive knows best.

Try to limit the noncompete clause to the actual taking of a job with a competitor, ideally a competitor whose name is specified. The bargaining approach might go something like this: "I see the point in your wanting to keep me from working for any of our main competitors. I'm good enough to make a significant difference to them. But then why don't we say what we mean? Let's have the contract say, 'The Executive is forbidden to enter the employ of the following companies...,' and name them. Wouldn't that take care of it?"

No doubt there would be opposition to this. One legitimate objection is that company names change. The executive might reasonably agree that the clause read: "... forbidden to enter the employ of any firm substantially engaged in competition with the Company at the date of termination of the Agreement."

Keep your options open, particularly the option to do consulting work. And exploit the company's insistence on such a clause. After all, it is an acknowledgment of your value.

HARD-TO-ENFORCE PROVISIONS

While the noncompete clause is one of the more prominently unenforceable provisions, it is by no means the only one. In fact, from one point of view the employer may have great difficulty in enforcing any of the provisions of a contract, except those which clearly enjoin embezzlement, etc.

In suing an employee for breach of contract, the company must usually prove damages. That's where the problem comes in. What are the damages? The employer may claim that an immense proportion of its success or failure depends on this one person, therefore the defection of the executive has materially damaged the firm's prospects. This admission would make stimulating copy for the business journals but would emphatically not enhance the value of the company's shares. Furthermore, the company that sues an executive for heavy damages stemming from the loss of his services is in the somewhat uncomfortable position of building the executive's market value while diminishing its own.

Because of this, the employer will try to write as much language into the agreement as possible in order to make violations by the manager easily visible. Moreover, the employer will prefer the kind of language that assesses damages for some action or omission by the executive, rather than simple removal of his services. For example, the firm decides to take a manager to court because he wishes to join a competitor. If the language of the contract is broad enough, the executive might be sued on the grounds of having violated company policy, and thus created damage, rather than on the basis of removal of services.

Employment contracts may in many respects be hard for the employer to enforce, but this does not mean the employee should blithely sign a tough and unwelcome agreement. It may be enforceable, and even if it is not, the company may be willing to go all out with a case that will hurt the employee a great deal, regardless of the outcome. The company is better able to pay lawyers than is the individual.

THE PROTECTION OF SECRETS

The struggle by organizations to prevent employees from disclosing secrets never ends. Governments do it; in 1983, the Reagan administration's suggestion that lie detectors be enlisted in the battle raised some dust, but the effort is age-old.

The desire to protect secrets has given impetus to the use of employment contracts in industries where the possession of inside information is considered a life-or-death matter from Silicon Valley to New York's dress design studios. But knowledge of a competitor's marketing plans, testing procedures, distribution networks, etc., is of great use in a variety of occupations. Therefore, the confidentiality clause is becoming a frequent feature of job agreements. As contracts for executives become more common, employers will tend to include such clauses. If the contract is heavily weighted in the direction of the employee, as many are felt to be, the employer can at least try to use the pact to protect some secrets.

The crux of the problem in protection of secrets is just how long the employer can keep the lid on. To what extent can the employee be prevented from making damaging disclosures after that employee has moved to another job? The possibility of that happening leads to the frequent coupling of confidentiality provisions with noncompete limitations, on the theory that the best way to keep an executive from divulging important information to a competitor is by keeping the employee from working for the competitor. As we discussed in the section covering noncompete provisions, these limitations often will not stand up in court. However, the threat of trouble over the provision may deter another employer.

Here's a clause that tries to do about as much as any employer would want it to do in terms of scope and duration:

Confidentiality. Employee convenants and agrees to hold in strictest confidence, and not disclose to any person, firm or corporation, without the express consent of the Company, any and all of the Company's confidential data, including but not limited to information and documents concerning the Company's business, customers and suppliers, market methods, files, trade secrets, or other "know-how" or techniques or information not of a published nature which shall come into his possession, knowledge or custody concerning the business of the Company, except as such disclosure may be required in connection with Employee's employment hereunder. This covenant and agreement of Employee shall survive this Agreement, and continue to be binding upon Employee after the expiration or termination of this Agreement, whether by passage of time or otherwise as long as such information and data shall remain confidential.

This clause (included in a contract between a financial executive and a corporation that owns food companies, hotels, and gambling casinos) would seem to limit what the employee can say about the employer for the employee's entire subsequent life, no matter what the circumstances. The enforceability of this contractual provision is, of course, a chancy proposition. It may be that one principal reason for the inclusion of such language in a contract is to impress upon the employee the fact that the employer is serious about protecting secrets. This is an effective technique in another area, that of bonding; the mere fact that the company bonds workers has a considerable effect in keeping down internal theft.

Here's another provision, in a contract signed by a financial corporation and a senior executive:

Confidential Information. During and after the term of this Agreement, Mr. _____ shall not disclose to any persons (other than another employee of the Company or any of its subsidiaries) any confidential information relating to the business of the Company or any of its subsidiaries, obtained by him

> while in the employ of the Company, without the consent of the Board, except as he deems necessary or appropriate in the discharge of his obligations to the Company, its subsidiaries and their respective shareholders.

Here the employee is given the discretion to speak of confidential matters if he deems it necessary or appropriate to do so. It is quite conceivable that the company might be horrified at what it considers to be a damaging breach of security by the executive who has told an executive of a competing firm about some of the company's plans. The employee in question could probably, under the language of this clause, advance the argument that in his judgment the disclosure was in the company's interests, since the other manager disclosed information of even greater value. The objective merits of this claim would not be the point. If it is a reasonable claim, or even an imaginable one, it would seem to be defensible.

The fact that the enforceability of a confidentiality clause may be dubious should not impel the manager to sign such a clause without questioning it. Some executives accept such provisions because they do not think of themselves as being in possession of hot intelligence. However, the employer is the judge of what must be kept confidential. If there were to be a dispute over some other provision of the contract, say severance payments, it might be possible for the employer to add to the employee's troubles by claiming breach of contract for a perfectly innocent activity like bringing home documents to work on them. Carried to a tough extreme, the provision could be used to harass the employee who is not well equipped to handle a lawsuit, whatever its merits. (The contract from which the second of the above excerpts was taken specifies that it shall be construed in accordance with the laws of the state in which the company's headquarters are located.)

So the first objective might be to eliminate the confidentiality clause altogether.

Elimination of the clause may not be possible. Moreover, it may not be near the top of the executive's priority list. If the company wants to impose a confidentiality rule it need not be accepted automatically, but it can be accepted as a trade-off, implicit or explicit, for more favorable handling of another section of the contract.

But the confidentiality clause should be circumscribed in its scope, and it ought to be terminated when the rest of the agreement is terminated. Whatever the enforceability may be, it is best not to go through one's career trailing contractual umbilical cords from the past.

Consider this clause (used by an oil company):

> In view of the fact that the Employee's work for the Company will bring him into close contact with many confidential affairs of the Company not readily available to the public, and plans for future development, the Employee agrees:
> 1. To keep secret and retain in the strictest confidence all confidential matters of the Company, including, without limiting the generality of the foregoing, trade "know how," secrets, investor lists, policies, operational methods, technical processes, geological methods, land holdings and prospects, research projects, and other business affairs of the Company... either during or after his employment...
> 2. To deliver promptly to the Company on termination of his employment... all memoranda, notes, records, maps, reports, manuals, drawings, blueprints and other documents (and all copies thereof) relating to the Company's business and all property associated therewith, which he may then possess or have under his control.

The first objective is to change the "during or after" limitation and make the contract read: "...during the Executive's employment" or "until termination of this agreement."

Then the manager would negotiate to limit the broad scope of both paragraphs. In the first paragraph the word "all" could be deleted. This would leave the focus on "confidential." Then the list of examples should be culled, since it includes items that vary considerably. Investor lists, technical processes, geological methods, land holdings, and so forth are things that a company is properly concerned with keeping confidential. Terms like "know how" and "business affairs" are vague catch-all phrases that should not be included in a document which is otherwise quite precise. Ideally the first paragraph would read: "To retain in confidence confidential matters of the Company, including investor lists, operational methods, technical processes, geological methods, land holding and research projects."

The second paragraph, concerning the return of materials, is a reasonable provision insofar as it applies to materials that are the property of the company. This paragraph becomes broad and vague when it refers to "all memoranda, notes," etc. Another problem is the phrase "have under his control." What does this mean? An assistant or associate might have possession of the material. Is the executive considered to nevertheless have it "under control" and thus be obligated to produce it?

The development of photocopying has made the proliferation of copies of documents virtually uncontrollable. When the company includes a paragraph asking that all copies of all relevant materials be returned it is trying to close the spigot a little bit. The larger purpose of the paragraph, however, is that it might provide a lever for use against the employee just in case. For example, it is not inconceivable that a manager who has been fired might find that the employer is holding up full payment of the severance because the manager has not—in the company's view—returned *all* materials under his control.

The second paragraph might better read: "To deliver to the Company on termination of this agreement materials which are the express property of the company, including manuals, maps, etc." This wording excludes "memoranda and notes," and it should. The manager's notes should remain his property. Any clause that raises the possibility that all his scribblings and doodlings may be subject to recall by the company makes the executive needlessly vulnerable.

Here is another version of the confidentiality provision:

Employee further agrees that he will not at any time, either directly or indirectly, divulge, disclose or communicate to any

> person, firm or corporation in any manner whatsoever any
> information of any kind, nature or description concerning any
> matters affecting or relating to the business of Employer.

If this provision were to be carried out fully the employee would
be forbidden to give the address of the office when he called to order
a pizza. Since the language is absurdly broad in scope, its purpose
must be to give the employer the option to accuse the employee of
violating the pact at practically any time.

Never sign an agreement to do anything that is beyond your
control. The above paragraph requires the signer to make promises
that no human being can be sure of keeping. The words "indirectly,"
"divulge," and "in any manner whatsoever" are paramount in cre-
ating that situation. The paragraph might more reasonably read:
"Employee agrees that he will not communicate to any person, firm
or corporation information the communication of which will be
harmful to the Company."

It is reasonable for the employer to require that employees not
give advantageous information to competitors. It is of course in the
employee's interest to keep the lid on secrets whose disclosure would
hurt the company. But that requirement should be confined to
deliberate disclosure, not inadvertency. A manager cannot be expected to spend a lot of time worrying about whether anything he
says or does, however innocent, may reveal a secret.

And the requirement for confidentiality should live only as long
as the agreement. What the manager says or does once all of his
contacts with the employer have been ended is his own business.
The employer's best means of keeping the executive from talking
about the business to a competitor is to keep the executive employed
and happy.

12

SIGNING BONUSES,
BUYOUTS,
SELLOUTS, AND
SPECIAL PROVISIONS

The up-front bonus has become a relatively commonplace tool in recruiting, useful for employer and manager.

Allan D. R. Stern, president of Haskell & Stern Associates, Inc., a New York–based search firm, observes that bonuses enable companies to offer an attractive money package without disturbing the existing pay structure. The company is eager to hire a vice-president of research, whose presence on board is necessary to the development of desperately needed new products. The range for people at that level, including VPs of marketing, manufacturing and finance, is $100,000–$150,000. To pay the new VP $250,000 would be to skew all the managerial ranges. To assume that the recruit can be paid more without the word getting around is naïve.

So the company gives the researcher a big lump-sum bonus up front. Since the practice of giving relocation bonuses to cover moving and cost-of-living differentials has become widespread, the fact of the bonus is not remarkable. Its size may be remarkable, but (the company hopes) the payment is less noticeable than if it were given as annual compensation.

Sometimes the front money needed to recruit senior executives is too big to fit under the heading "bonus." So the payment is made in the form of a loan, at low interest or perhaps no interest. Since the loan must be repaid, it serves as an effective set of Golden Handcuffs.

However, the loan need not always require repayment. For example, a firm which had decided that only one executive could meet its needs was having considerable difficulty in wooing him from his current affiliation. The answer was a $2 million loan. No repayment would be required. The loan would be forgiven according to a five-year schedule.

This executive negotiated a contract, which covered the usual conditions of employment, compensation, tenure, termination, and severance arrangements. The loan was not mentioned in the contract, which provided for generous base pay and bonuses, as well as options.

Companies that give executives large up-front bonuses usually do so because they want to buy a commitment of at least five years or a noncompete agreement. When the bonus takes the form of a loan, the manager is somewhat more closely bound to the company. However, it is simply not realistic to think that an executive can or should be kept against his will. If another company wants him enough, another up-front bonus will be arranged to enable him to buy out of his previous obligation.

The noncompete clause can be somewhat more effectively enforced, either by threat or by actual lawsuit. As noted, such clauses vary in their legal strength from state to state. However, *if the employer is able to tie a consideration*—the up-front bonus, for instance—to the inclusion of the clause, enforcement is easier. If it says in writing that the manager was paid to agree not to compete for a certain number of years after leaving the company, then life can be made pretty tough for him if he breaks the agreement.

The up-front bonus is an area that offers the manager considerable negotiating scope. When he perceives a situation in which the stumbling block is precedent and the stability of the present compensation structure, he may obtain a surprisingly high payoff by pushing hard on the bonus front. The employer, relieved of his worry that the existing salary ranges will be wiped out, may succumb in part to the "It's only money" syndrome which can be of such great benefit to the hiree.

It's best to offer plausible reasons for requesting a large bonus, rather than to simply say you want it instead of other forms of compensation. You can refer to the loss you may have to take on your home; the expense of enrolling the kids in good schools; the need to take care of various obligations. While the employer may realize that your demand is substantially greater than would be called for by these requirements, he may be willing to go along with the fiction.

The up-front bonus, once paid only to the most senior levels, is now used in recruiting managers down to and below the $100,000 levels. Bonuses range upward from $25,000. When the bonuses are in the five- or low-six figure level the company is unlikely to try to tie anything to them. They are simply used as bargaining chips in the recruitment process.

The cash in hand you get up front is in many ways the best kind of payment. You do your own investing, unencumbered by option plans or payout formulas.

It's frequently a good tactic to defer consideration of the up-front bonus, rather than settling it early in the negotiation. If you fall short in getting what you want under other headings, you return to the bonus and negotiate it up.

Note the up-front bonus provision in this contract between the Coastal Corporation and Executive Vice-President T. Gerald Harper.

1. Employer shall pay Employee a salary of Two Hundred Fifty Thousand ($250,000.00) Dollars per year during each year of this Agreement, one twenty-fourth of said sum being payable on the 15th and last day of each and every month. Such salary shall be adjusted upward from time to time by Employer if, in sole judgment of Employer, the Employee's performance merits such action.
2. A one-time cash payment of One Hundred Thousand ($100,000.00) Dollars shall be made August 11, 1980.

NEGOTIATING AN UP-FRONT BONUS

There are three basic reasons for the up-front bonus: (1) to reimburse the employee for out-of-pocket expenses connected with the move; (2) to recompense the manager for benefits lost because of the move (e.g., bonuses, long-term incentives, pension); (3) to entice the manager away from a good job by offering a "premium."

In negotiating for a "premium" bonus the manager should consider possible "future awards" as well as the more specific benefits in his present job. The extent to which "future awards" should be reflected in the up-front bonus is a matter for bargaining, but it should be reflected to some extent.

The up-front bonus may be a straight cash payment, a deferred cash payment, a stock-related award, or a combination of these methods of payment.

The manager must insist that the up-front bonus, whatever its form, be *fully vested*, i.e. that he will get the whole thing even if he walks away from the job. The thrust of the employer's negotiating will be to insist on forfeiture of these benefits or on prorated payment.

The cost of buying a house in a new location may be negotiated into the contract. If it costs more to live in the new location, this too may become part of the agreement.

Here is an example of a cost-of-living provision:

> ...the company will review the Annual Salary taking into consideration the Company's performance during the year ending June 30, 1983, the Executive's contribution thereto, changes in the cost of living index during such year for urban wage earners published by the U.S. Bureau of Labor Statistics for the Trenton, New Jersey, Standard Metropolitan Statistical Area (or a reasonably comparable successor index), and such other factors as the Company deems relevant (but not including the receipt of additional compensation pursuant to subparagraph (b) of this paragraph 2), and will adjust the Executive's Annual Salary retroactive to July 1, 1983 by an amount at

least equal to the aforesaid increase in such cost of living index. The Company will undertake a similar review in July, 1984, 1985 and 1986 with respect to a possible further increase in the Annual Salary effective July 1 in each of such years, but nothing herein contained will obligate the Company to any further increase in the Annual Salary, any such increase being entirely at the discretion of the Company.

Here are a couple of provisions relating to the purchase of a home:

When Squibb Corporation moved its headquarters from New York City to Princeton, New Jersey, the company provided senior executives with a relocation program which has Golden Handcuff features. Seven senior managers were entitled to receive loans (to a maximum of annual salary) for the purpose of buying or building a home near Princeton. Squibb holds a lien on the home and charges 9 percent per year. However, each year 20 percent of the loan is forgiven, unless the executive is fired for cause or quits. This program is in addition to the company's general relocation program, which offers interest-free equity loans for up to two years and mortgage financing for up to fifteen years at a maximum of 9 percent interest.

To the extent that the senior executives have to pay additional taxes because of the forgiveness of the loan, Squibb provides reimbursement up to 50 percent.

Humana Inc., the giant health-care company, gave Executive Vice-President Harold C. Rimes an interest-free $275,000 loan in 1978 when Mr. Rimes moved to California. In June 1981, Mr. Rimes was shifted to Louisville. He sold his California home to Humana for $645,000. The company retired the interest-free $275,000 loan made in 1978; assumed the $39,200 balance on a first deed of trust to a third party; and gave Mr. Rimes a new interest-free note for $330,000. Then the company paid Mr. Rimes $19,300 toward the purchase of a home in Louisville, reducing the note to $311,500. In September 1981, Humana loaned Mr. Rimes $116,000 at the prime rate, with principal and interest payable upon Humana's sale of the California home, or June 1982 at the latest. In May 1982, the company sold the California home, netting $604,954. Humana retired all the loans. Mr. Rimes reimbursed the company's $40,046 loss on the house.

Some contracts provide health- and life-insurance coverage after the employee leaves the company. This can be a very valuable perk. Here is the relevant section of an agreement between Phibro-Salomon Inc. and Hal H. Beretz:

> In the event that your employment terminates for any reason other than death prior to the time when you reach the age of 55, you shall from the date of termination until you reach the age of 55 be provided with the following insurance coverages under the company group insurance plan, if they are in force, as follows:
>   1. Medical and dental insurance for yourself and your eligible dependents.
>   2. Life insurance and personal accident insurance in the amount of the greater of $900,000 or twice the sum of your last salary plus your previous year's usual bonuses, subject to medical qualification if required by the insurer.

The quid pro quo for this extended perk is, in the case of Mr. Beretz, a confidentiality pledge plus an agreement not to recruit Phibro-Salomon employees:

> In consideration of the foregoing, you have agreed that you will maintain the confidentiality of all information concerning Phibro-Salomon Inc. and its subsidiaries and affiliates that you have received during your employment and that you will not disclose such information to any other person nor will you solicit any other employee for employment by a third party or

yourself. This paragraph will survive termination of your employment.

PAYMENT OF LEGAL FEES

If there is any possibility that an executive may be involved in litigation connected with the job, it may be well to put a provision into the contract to assure that the company will pay legal fees. This may be preferable to dependence on senior management or the board when the need arises.

It does come up. In 1982 the board of First National Supermarkets, Inc., authorized payment of legal fees for "certain officers and employees." The payment was in the form of "advances" without interest which must be paid back at the board's discretion. A principal beneficiary of this action was Richard J. Bogomolny, chairman and CEO. Mr. Bogomolny had pleaded nolo contendere to charges of price-fixing, thereby incurring a suspended six-year sentence and a fine of $200,000, of which $125,000 was suspended. The company entered the same plea, incurring a fine of $2 million, with $1.2 million suspended. At this time the company was also involved in several antitrust suits.

A contractual provision covering legal fees for criminal or civil actions arising out of the executive's duties (as distinguished from wrongdoing the executive might commit as an individual) might save embarrassment and make things run more smoothly at a troubled time.

BUYOUTS

When the owner of a company sells the firm to another company, part of the deal is often an employment agreement which calls for consulting services. The following is an example of such a pact.

CONSULTING AGREEMENT

This CONSULTING AGREEMENT (the "Agreement"), made this *4th* day of *November*, 1982, by and between Roberson's Beverages, Inc., its successors and assigns ("RBI"), W. R. ROBERSON, JR. ("Roberson"), and Dr Pepper Company ("Dr Pepper").

W I T N E S S E T H:

WHEREAS, Dr Pepper recently purchased all of the outstanding shares of Roberson's Beverages, Inc.;

WHEREAS, RBI and Dr Pepper desire to retain Roberson as an independent contractor in a consulting capacity; and

WHEREAS, Roberson desires to be so retained, and all parties desire to set forth in writing the terms and conditions of their agreements and understandings regarding this employment as a consultant.

NOW, THEREFORE, in consideration of the foregoing, of the mutual promises herein contained, and of other good and valuable consideration, the receipt and sufficiency of which are hereby acknowledged and confessed, the parties hereto agree as follows:

1. *Term.* RBI and Dr Pepper agree to retain Roberson in the consulting capacity set forth above, and Roberson agrees to accept such retention and to serve RBI and Dr Pepper in such consulting capacity. Such retention of Roberson shall commence on January 1, 1983 and shall terminate on December 31, 1984.

2. *Duties of Roberson.* In accepting the retention by RBI hereunder, Roberson agrees to consult and advise with, from time to time, the Board of Directors and officers of RBI, at their request, at reasonable times (whether in person, by telephone, or otherwise) with respect to the management, operations and business affairs of RBI, and to otherwise assist and advise RBI regarding such business matters that may arise at any time and from time to time during the term of this Agreement, including, but not limited to, the relations of RBI with its distributors, customers, potential customers and the general

public and any person or special group. RBI and Dr Pepper recognize that Roberson has substantial commitments and, while such commitments shall not diminish Roberson's obligation to render services hereunder, such commitments may affect his availability from time to time. During the term hereof, Roberson shall serve as a senior executive officer of RBI in the position of chairman of its Board of Directors.

3. *Compensation.*

a. As his compensation for services rendered to RBI under this Agreement, in whatever capacity or capacities rendered, RBI shall pay to Roberson the sum of Fifty Thousand Dollars ($50,000.00) annually (the "Fee"). The Fee shall be payable in equal quarterly installments of Twelve Thousand Five Hundred Dollars ($12,500.00) beginning on March 31, 1983, and continuing regularly thereafter on the last days of March, June, September and December until December 31, 1984.

b. The compensation provided for in this Paragraph 3 shall be the sole compensation receivable by Roberson for services to RBI pursuant hereto as a consultant, provided, however, that Roberson shall be entitled to reimbursement of expenses incurred in rendering services hereunder, if such services were requested by RBI or Dr Pepper and if the expenses are supported by documentation. Roberson and his spouse shall attend the annual Dr Pepper Bottlers Meeting, the annual National Soft Drink Association Meeting and the annual North Carolina Soft Drink Association Meeting whenever practicable during the term of this Agreement and shall be reimbursed for reasonable expenses incurred therefor.

c. If RBI shall fail to make such payments without good cause, Dr Pepper shall make such payments to Roberson.

4. *Extent of Services.*

a. During the term of this Agreement, Roberson shall not be required to render services outside of the licensed territory held by RBI without his consent.

b. Roberson shall perform all services required to be rendered by him hereunder to the best of his ability and with reasonable care and diligence.

c. Roberson covenants and agrees that, at all times during

the term of this Agreement, he will maintain the fiduciary duties of loyalty and care in rendering services to RBI.

5. *Burden and Benefit.* If Roberson should die prior to December 31, 1984, RBI shall continue to make the payments required hereunder to Roberson's heirs and/or personal or legal representatives. This Agreement may not be assigned by Roberson to any other party or entity.

6. *Governing Law.* It is understood and agreed that the construction and interpretation of this Agreement shall at all times and in all respects be governed by the laws of the State of North Carolina.

7. *Termination.* RBI may terminate this Agreement only upon a material, continuing, and wilful violation of this Agreement by Roberson and only after having given Roberson twenty (20) days prior written notice of such violation and provided that Roberson has not corrected such violation within such time.

8. *Severability.* The provisions of this Agreement shall be deemed severable, and the invalidity or unenforceability of any one or more of the provisions hereof shall not affect the validity and enforceability of the other provisions hereof.

9. *Notices.* Any notice required to be given hereunder shall be sufficient if in writing and sent by certified or registered mail, return receipt requested, to the other party.

10. *Entire Agreement.* This Agreement contains the entire agreement and understanding by and between RBI and Roberson with respect to the services herein referred to, and no representations, promises, agreements or understandings, written or oral, not herein contained shall be of any force or effect. No change or modification hereof shall be valid or binding unless the same is in writing and signed by the party intended to be bound. No waiver of any provision of this Agreement shall be valid unless the same is in writing and signed by the party against whom such waiver is sought to be enforced; moreover, no valid waiver of any provision of this Agreement at any time shall be deemed a waiver of any other provision of this Agreement at such time or will be deemed a valid waiver of any provision at any other time.

11. *Captions*. The captions appearing in this Agreement are inserted only as a matter of convenience and as a reference and in no way define, limit or describe the scope or intent of this Agreement or any of the provisions hereof.

ROBERSON'S
BEVERAGES, INC.

_____

W. R. Roberson, Jr.

By_____

Title:_____

DR PEPPER COMPANY

By_____

Title:_____

WHAT HAPPENS IF THE COMPANY IS SOLD?

Should the company change hands or be absorbed in a merger, the successor is, in the ordinary course of events, obliged to fulfill the provisions of the contract. Some contracts nevertheless carry provisos like the following:

Successors. The Company shall require any successor (whether direct or indirect and whether by purchase, merger, consolidation or otherwise) to all or substantially all of the business or assets of the Company, by an Agreement in form and substance satisfactory to the Executive, to expressly assume and agree to perform this Agreement in the same manner and to the same extent that the Company would be required to perform if no such succession had taken place.

WHEN THE PRESIDENT IS A CORPORATION

While it is unusual, executives are occasionally paid in whole or in part as corporate entities in their own right. For example, in fiscal years 1981 and '82 President Wayne G. Basler of AFG Industries Inc. was paid $250,000 annually in salary and bonus. Part of this ($150,000 in 1981 and $75,000 in 1982) was in the form of payments to the Basler Corporation, the president's wholly owned company, under a service agreement.

Following 1982 the contract between AFG and the Basler Corporation was terminated and Mr. Basler became an employee in full of AFG, being reimbursed more conventionally.

CONSULTING FOR BOARD MEMBERS

In a not-too-burdensome arrangement with Milton Rosenthal, an outside director, Phibro Corporation agrees to pay $300,000 per year for services described as follows:

> It will be your responsibility when requested to do so to advise the management on matters of policy affecting corporate decisions and to serve as representative of the Company in various important public functions. Your services in these matters will be consistent with your devoting the major part of your working schedule to other activities.
>
> You will be included in the management slate for election to the Board of Directors and as a member of the Executive Committee. You have agreed that your name be submitted for such elections and that, if elected, you will serve in these capacities.

FINANCIAL DISCLOSURE

Occasionally a contract will require financial disclosure by the executive. Here is such a provision in a contract between Mathematica, Inc., a company about to be acquired by Martin Marietta, and Mathematica executive Richard H. Cobb:

(c) During the Employment Period, the Executive will promptly disclose to officers of the company, in accordance with the Company's policies, full information concerning any interest, direct or indirect, of the Executive (as owner, stockholder, partner, lender or other investor, director, officer, employee, consultant or otherwise) in any business which, as reasonably known to the Executive, purchases or otherwise obtains services or products from, or sells or otherwise provides services or products to the Company or any of its subsidiaries or any of their respective suppliers or customers, provided that the Executive need not disclose any such interest by way of ownership of not more than 1% of the outstanding securities of any class of any corporation that are listed on a national securities exchange or traded in the over-the-counter market.

NEW AGREEMENTS FOR TEMPORARY JOBS

A manager who is called upon to fill a slot temporarily may be able to negotiate a new agreement extending beyond the point at which the assignment ends. While Clevepak Corporation searched for a president-CEO, Hubert McPherson, age sixty-eight, chairman of the board's executive committee, filled the job for nine months. He was paid $145,080 in salary and a bonus of $35,670. Then he returned to his old job, which, under the new agreement, paid a retainer of $75,000 plus deferred compensation of $40,000 for six years, along with benefits and other perks.

CONSULTING CONTRACTS FOR RETIREES

As retirement approaches, executives often resist the idea of being simply turned out to pasture. Nor are they eager to start new enterprises. They have a lot of experience and savvy to contribute to the company. Furthermore, they would like an arrangement that enables them to stay involved without working full time, and to make money while doing it.

This is why consulting contracts for retiring executives are becoming more popular. A few recent examples:

Raytheon Corporation's Beech Aircraft subsidiary gave retiring Vice-Chairman of the Board Frank E. Hedrick a $100,000-per-year consulting agreement for life, with an additional one-year fee of $200,000 from Raytheon.

Coca-Cola signed a former officer to a consulting pact calling for $375,000 over three years ending in 1984.

Prentice-Hall Vice-Chairman Howard M. Warrington retired and signed a contract for sixty days of consulting services in one year, at a fee of $60,000.

Ross Barzelay resigned as vice-chairman of General Foods in 1982 with an arrangement for consulting services through October 1, 1984, at an annual fee of $150,000.

Florida National Bank retained retiring Board Chairman Richard E. Ehlis as a legislative and industrial consultant for at least two years, paying his travel expenses and yearly compensation not expected to exceed $12,000.

Adams Drug entered a consulting-services agreement with retired Board Chairman Samuel Salmanson providing for consulting work up to 112 days per year, for $75,000 per year plus expenses. This contract provides also that Mr. Salmanson agrees not to compete with Adams Drug. (Retirement consultation agreements often carry a noncompete provision.)

The retirement contract is usually a simple document like the following agreement between Enstar Corporation and General A. A. Sproul:

September 2, 1982

General A. A. Sproul
P. O. Box 2006
Staunton, Virginia 24401

DEAR ARCH:

At its August 26, 1982 meeting the Board of Directors of ENSTAR Corporation approved the arrangement you and I have discussed earlier in August, with, as I have already mentioned to you, a slight modification; namely that the arrangement would exist for a year and be subject to reconsideration by the Board at that time. This letter will outline that understanding. If it meets with your understanding please sign a copy of this letter and return it to me, keeping the original for your files.

1. Following your retirement on September 30, 1982, the Company would pay you a consultant fee of $500 per day for each day that you are away from Staunton performing services for ENSTAR Corporation or any of its subsidiaries as requested by an officer of ENSTAR Corporation.
2. The Company would also reimburse your travel and other expenses incurred in such effort.
3. The above fee would not apply to any time you may spend in Staunton on affairs of the Company.
4. This arrangement will be for the period October 1, 1982 through September 30, 1983.

Should you have any questions concerning the above please let me know.

Sincerely,

OCH/t
Enclosure

I agree to and accept the terms described in this letter.

_____

Archibald A. Sproul

Date_____

Occasionally the consulting arrangement is part of a general employment agreement, as in this elaborate contract (dated April 1, 1977) between Esquire Inc., and A. L. Blinder:

(b) *Advisory Employment Period*. The Company will continue to employ Blinder in its business, and Blinder will continue to work for the Company therein, in an advisory and consultative capacity as hereinafter provided, for a period beginning immediately after the termination (for any reason other than Blinder's death) of the Active Employment Period and, unless such period of advisory and consultative employment shall be extended by agreement entered into between Blinder and the Company after approval thereof by the Board of Directors of the Company, terminating on the earliest of the dates specified below:

(i) The date five years after the termination of the Active Employment Period.

(ii) The date of Blinder's death.

(iii) If, in the opinion of the Board of Directors of the Company, Blinder shall become unable by reason of physical or mental disability to perform his duties under this paragraph 2(b) and such disability shall continue for a period of 12 consecutive months beginning after termination of the Active Employment Period, and the Company shall elect (which right of election is hereby reserved to the Company) to terminate the Advisory Employment Period for such cause, the date 30 days after the day on which the Company shall have given written notice of such election to Blinder.

(iv) If, for any reason or without stating a reason, Blinder shall elect (which right of election is hereby reserved to Blinder) to terminate the Advisory Employment Period, the date 30 days after Blinder shall have given written notice of such election to the company.

The period of such employment is herein called the "Advisory Employment Period."

Subject to the provisions of the following sentence, during the Advisory Employment Period Blinder (i) shall from time to time, as and when requested by the Chairman of the Board or the President of the Company, consult with and advise such officer to the best of his ability with respect to such matters within his knowledge involving the business, administration or policies of the Company or its subsidiaries or affiliated corporations as to which such officer may inquire of him and

(ii) shall, from time to time, as and when requested by the Board of Directors of the Company and duly elected (A) serve as a director of the Company and (B) serve as a representative of the Company on the governing body of any committee of any industry association which deals with matters within the experience of Blinder and of which the Company is a member. It is understood and agreed, with respect to the advisory and consultative services that Blinder shall be obligated to render pursuant to the provisions of the foregoing sentence, that (x) Blinder shall not be required to devote more than 35 hours in any one calendar month, and shall not be required to devote any time in at least three months in any one calendar year, to the performance of such services, to travel outside the United States in the performance of such services or to maintain a residence in any particular geographical location, (y) the officers desiring to consult Blinder or seeking his advice will, in so far as is reasonably practicable, consider the convenience of Blinder in respect of the timing of their requests and the places at which they request such services to be performed, and the failure or inability of Blinder, by reason of temporary illness or other cause beyond his control, because of absence for reasonable vacation periods or because of reasonable demands upon his time of other occupations permitted hereunder, to respond to such requests during any such temporary period shall not be deemed to constitute a default on his part in the performance of his obligation to render such services, and (z) Blinder's obligation to render such services shall not preclude him from engaging in any employment or occupation (not prohibited) by the terms of paragraph 5 hereof), either as an employee or on his own behalf, which does not interfere with his ability to render satisfactorily the advisory and consultative services contemplated by the foregoing provisions of this paragraph, and shall not preclude Blinder from receiving salary or other compensation for engaging in any such employment or occupation. At all times during the Advisory Employment Period, the Company will provide Blinder, at the Company's expense, with an office suitable to Blinder's position at its principal office in New York, New York, together with the services of a secretary. If Blinder shall require any other staff or technical assistance during the Advisory Employment Period in order to enable him to perform the services which he is obligated to render pursuant to the provisions of this paragraph 2(b), the company will provide such assistance at the Company's expense.

When you assume the status of a consultant under contract you have more latitude in certain respects than you did when you were an employee. For example, you may find it advantageous to incorporate and to have the consulting fees paid to a spouse or other relative.

As an independent contractor you are no longer eligible for perks like stock options and profit sharing. You may want to negotiate certain perks into the consulting contract. The use of an office, company clerical help, and transportation are reasonable perks. Another useful benefit, if it can be negotiated, would be continued coverage under the company's health plan.

If such an arrangement might interest you, do *not* wait until you're close to retirement to negotiate it. Last-minute consulting arrangements with senior executives are often trade-offs in exchange for concessions on the part of the employee. Bargain for your retirement/consulting contract while you're still a hot property.

13

GOLDEN STAIRWAYS, NOT GOLDEN HANDCUFFS

In the fall of 1983 a multinational fast-food and beverage company announced the introduction of a leadership course for senior managers. One of the salient features of the course was its emphasis on the retention of young, promising management talent.

For another company this would not be big news. For this firm, however, it was a revolution. Previously, the message to executives was sink or swim. The manager was given an assignment and was reviewed on the basis of one-year bottom-line performance. "If he doesn't cut it, he's gone," said a top executive. "We're not going to baby them. We just go out and get someone else." The shark-pool atmosphere fostered by this approach led to a near-paranoid level of suspicion and competition among the managers jostling for running room in the fast lane. But it undeniably elicited a high level of performance in the volatile consumer-goods area for those who survived.

Why is the company now going to the trouble and expense of training managers? And why is there sudden concern about keeping promising people on the payroll? One member of the top brass put it this way: "A few years ago we had the benefit of the baby boom. There were a lot of good people fighting for entry-level management jobs. We could afford to hire them and fire them. But now the crest has passed. Good people are a lot scarcer. For the sake of our future we need to develop a cadre of first-class managers we can count on to be around for a while."

It may be superfluous to add that this company, once totally uninterested in locking up-and-coming talent into Golden Handcuffs, is now talking about employment contracts.

This story exemplifies the increasing urgency with which companies large and small are looking for ways to assure that talented executives will remain with the organization. Human beings are now seen as a resource. Corporations now establish human-resource departments (steeply upgraded from the old-fashioned "personnel department," which was pretty much concerned with records and benefits) that are charged with planning for future disposition of people just as other departments plan five to ten years ahead for the availability of materials, the penetration of new markets, the building of plants, etc.

If your corporate planning tells you that you will require a mountain of potash five years hence, you can buy the potash, put a fence around it, and just let it sit there. But human beings are more mobile. The immensely gifted executive on whom you were counting to head up the new consumer-goods division as soon as he or she got a little more seasoning may get a better offer just as you are fully committed to the venture. Thus there has been increasing interest in building fences around people.

The concept of Golden Handcuffs—binding an individual to the organization by dangling future dollars—came into being around the mid-1960s (although, of course, the idea of eliciting loyalty or favor today by promising good things tomorrow is as old as human society).

There are a variety of Golden Handcuffs. In general, such plans include one or more of three basic ingredients. One element is the deferred cash bonus, in which "extra" money earned now is paid out over, say, five years. A second element from which the Handcuffs are forged is the deferred stock equivalent, in which the incentive is equity in the enterprise. Finally, there are variations on the basic retirement plan, in which certain people are enabled to look forward to far richer retirement benefits than those offered by the conventional plan.

Among young and growing companies the sharing of founder's stock is usually the only way to contrive Golden Handcuffs. *INC.* magazine (August 1983) quotes thirty-one-year-old Edward Esber, a former marketing vice-president for VisiCorp of San Jose, California: "I'm now able not to have to work the rest of my life, if I decide to do that." Esber had been granted stock in the software company when it was founded in 1978, and he was given a series of stock options through the following three years as the company made it big.

For the new company the continuing services of just one key person through the first five years can be a matter of life or death. Typically, the founder is a specialist who has a good idea and who attracts enough venture capital to go into business. It is well known that one of the main reasons for the early deaths of many firms based on a promising notion is that the founder tried to be a one-man band and could not bring it off. For example, he may be a marketing genius, but his lack of financial savvy causes him to undercapitalize so that he is unable to ride out the first cash-flow squall. More typically, the entrepreneur is a technical person with a better way to make something, but woefully deficient in marketing ability. Experienced providers of venture capital anticipate these problems and try to persuade entrepreneurs that they must bring in and keep talented people who can handle the essential jobs that the founder cannot do. The only inducement to the young, talented person is equity. So the pitch to the desired individual is, "Gamble with us. Put in five years and you might be rich beyond your wildest dreams."

The manager who is approached with such a proposition had better have the gambler's temperament. The short-term rewards are likely to be the exhilaration of participation in a high-risk venture and the chance to wield far more power than would be possible at an early stage of a career in a big company. If he or she would be devastated by the failure of the new company—which is, after all, likely—then the chance should not be taken.

Larger, established companies can offer a wider range of incentives in exchange for the commitment to stay. The big firm can put together a package that might include—for the younger manager—bonuses worth 50 percent of base salary spread over five years, with an increase each year, plus options on an amount of stock presently worth $200,000, with no more than 20 percent allowed to be converted in any one year. While younger managers are almost invariably uninterested in retirement benefits, older executives find that this perk may loom much larger. While there are limitations on what the person can expect from the regular pension program, and while there may be time-of-service requirements for vesting, there is no reason why the firm cannot set up a supplementary program for an employee. The vesting requirements can be circumvented by setting up an IRA into which the company pays and which, of course, does not require any vesting period.

Another form of Golden Handcuffs—which is particularly favored by banks, but is used by many organizations—is the company loan. The arrangement may restrict the use of the loan to the buying of company stock, as is frequently the case with stock plans. But it may give the employee a low-interest loan that is to be paid back over five years. Young executives who are short of cash may be enabled to buy expensive houses with company loans.

The company's motives are obvious. The Golden Handcuffs bind the promising employee to the firm. At least that is the theory. However, as George H. Orgelman of Kensington Management Consultants, Stamford, Connecticut, points out, "Any set of Golden Handcuffs can be broken. There is no way that a firm can absolutely guarantee itself the future services of a high flyer, no matter how much of his compensation may be deferred." This is why people such as consultant Richard R. Conarroe view employment contracts for executives as a one-way street, with the traffic invariably flowing in the direction of the employee. Conarroe is among those who believe that the company should avoid making contracts with managers unless they are designed to protect the company in some specific way, for example against the appropriation of secrets or customers. This view is understandable—after all, no one in business wants to be bound to commitments if they can be avoided—but the need to attract and keep talented employees often takes precedence. Dubious employers are often prodded into willingness to offer Golden Handcuff contracts by search consultants. The headhunter locates someone who would be perfect for the job, but who insists on guarantees. The headhunter implies that the guarantees will be forthcoming. Then the headhunter tells the client that the prize recruit can be gained only by means of a contract. It is in this way that many companies have abandoned precedent and, for the first time, concluded written employment agreements with managers. Managers who are the target of recruiting efforts can use headhunters to help them get favorable contracts, since the headhunter's primary interest is in filling the job with the right person, without reference to what the company has to pay.

Reasonably sophisticated employers know that while they may have to enter into contracts to increase the chances of keeping desirable employees around, they cannot be certain that the contracts will hold up. It is very difficult to hold someone against his will, no matter how freely he entered into the contract a few years ago. The attitudes of star athletes toward contracts typify on a grand scale what happens more modestly in other forms of business. The hard-hitting outfielder signs a five-year contract for $1 million per year. If he has two good years he insists that he be given a new and better contract. If he has two bad years he does not give back the money or tell the team that he would like another agreement for a lower salary. Although the team may take a tough stance initially, it is usually the player who wins.

Human-resource experts are aware of the dangers in trying to tie up people beyond the point at which they want to be free. Gilbert T. Walker, former director of human-resource planning for Benton & Bowles, observes, "The guy who sticks with you only because you have him locked in financially is worse than nothing. He is a liability. Subconsciously, or even consciously, he resents the company so much that he wants it to go down the drain."

This is what makes the low-interest loan one of the most dangerous forms of Golden Handcuffs from the company point of view.

If the employee wants to leave, it is a lot tougher to work out a loan agreement than it is to work out a harmonious conclusion of the contract in terms of bonuses or stock. And if the person is forced to pass up an advantageous offer principally because he still owes $200,000 to his employer, imagine the frame of mind in which he does his work.

For the employer, there are equally real, though perhaps less drastic, drawbacks in trying to keep an unwilling employee whose contract involves deferred bonuses or stock options. Since what the company wants to retain is the manager's talent, not his or her physical presence, and since the exercise of talent may be severely affected by festering resentment, the sullen employee of today may be quite different from the eager individual who happily signed the contract three years back. From the company's point of view it would probably be just as well to let the contract be broken.

What may be the strongest stimulus in making the company fight to enforce a contract, in spite of the fact that the employee may be so alienated as to be not worth clinging to, is precedent. Once, the company reasons, a precedent is set that manifests the idea that people may make contracts and then break them with impunity, the firm is at a terrible disadvantage. Often employees who want to get out of agreements cannot understand this. They feel that the firm is simply being obstinate and nasty in insisting on fidelity to an agreement. That's unfair to the company, and, more to the point, it is a mistake in perception that is a drawback when one is trying to negotiate one's way out of a contract.

Precedent is of considerable importance to the employer—at least if the employer is a company of some size—in negotiating any contract. While the fiction may be maintained that the lid of secrecy will be kept on the extraordinary provisions of the agreement, the realistic employer must assume that others in the company will come to know about special deals that have been given in terms of bonuses, stock or retirement. The employer must then steel himself to be asked for similar provisions by other executives who consider themselves equally deserving. Moreover, people who have worked for years without written contracts, never dreaming that such things were in the cards, may be impelled to demand them when they learn that a colleague has been so favored.

Once the employer gets over his reservations about precedent, he may be surprisingly openhanded in offering deferred compensation. He is apt to be far less willing to give the employee, however talented, a greatly increased share of power. The import of some employment contracts—whatever their intentions—is to buy off the gifted manager with enough money to not only keep the manager around but tone down the manager's demands for a piece of the action.

Here's how the money-versus-power conflict operates. With today's accelerated trend toward the establishment of autonomous units and profit centers, there are a great many more opportunities for younger executives to win independent commands early in their careers. However, the supply of such opportunities is not infinite, no matter how big the company may be. Top management may have earmarked twenty-eight-year-old Audrey Brown for big things ten years down the road. To make sure that Ms. Brown stays on board, the company is willing to pay her very well and to try to lock her in with handsome stock options and bonuses. The company assumes that she will ultimately be running a profit center. However, top management has no spots open, and would like to retain its own options about when and where to give her the chance. Ms. Brown, however, is more impatient. She feels that she is ready for bigger things right now, or that she soon will be. She would like to be assured that she will be in charge of her own autonomous operation within five years.

Under pressure, top management gives her even more glittering Golden Handcuffs. She accepts. But the money is not what she really wants. She certainly enjoys getting it, and she is reassured to know that the company thinks so much of her, but she is really interested in power.

Kenneth A. Meyers, former president of Golightly & Co. International, a global consulting firm, has observed that companies often lose their best people because they try to bribe them to be patient instead of telling them when they may expect to accede to power. Golden Handcuff agreements that are concluded without reference to the question of power can be traps for both parties.

Why isn't management more willing to conclude an agreement that would tell the executive where he might be in five years? To some degree it is paternalism. The top brass are willing to share the dollars with younger managers, especially if it's necessary in order to keep talented people around, but there is a natural tendency to want to keep the reins in experienced hands.

Another reason given by senior executives for not being precise about career paths is, "We don't want to let him know how important he is to us. If he knows that, he has us over a barrel." This is an unrealistic fear—if the younger manager is as good as all that he already knows he's important—but that doesn't make it any less influential.

The big reason for top management's heartfelt unwillingness to outline career paths in writing is the *instinctual avoidance of sharing of power*. The capable young manager may find that the employer is willing to go a long way in committing future dollars, particularly if they are "contingency" dollars, bonuses based on performance or stock options that have value only if the stock goes up. But employers shy away from saying that subordinates will be given a specific amount of say in the decision-making process by a specific time.

An increasing number of observers feel that this tendency must be modified if companies are to keep their best people. The manager who can be locked in with Golden Handcuffs is not likely to be as good in the long run as the manager who insists on being assured of a position of responsibility in which he or she can take risks to win rewards. Allan Stern, president of the search firm of Haskell & Stern, says, "Suppose the economy were to get into such a state that wage controls were imposed? Where would the Golden Handcuffs be then?" Stern adds that, whatever the likelihood of controls, companies are well advised to think about their mechanisms for retaining talent as if there were not unlimited money. If money is limited, then the Golden Handcuffs have to be made of some other material. Stern suggests that this material is the *promise of power*. He tells senior managers to go through three steps: identify the high flyers; give them the lion's share of the money available; make the risk of future commitment.

The young executive who is approached about agreeing to Golden Handcuffs can be sure he has been identified as a high flyer. He should recognize that the company is trying to lock in his future services by committing money while avoiding the commitment of power. Stern observes of the young executive, "He is probably at least as interested in learning when he will achieve a position of power as he is in money. Tell him. Lay out the track for him. Your willingness to make a commitment may be just what it takes to keep him on board—even if the money is not what he'd like."

The company's priorities in negotiating a Golden Handcuff agreement are, first, to try to lock the employee in with "soft" dollars, payments that are contingent on performance; second, to lock the employee in with whatever dollars it takes, soft or hard; third, to reduce the employee's options by binding him to the firm while keeping the firm's options open by avoiding the commitment of power.

Before agreeing, the employee who is asked to consider putting on the Golden Handcuffs should think about where he wants to be in five years. This is the time to get the employer to talk about career paths and how best to prepare the employee for the designated assignment. The employer will of course maintain that no one can know what the situation will be in three months, let alone five years, so there is no way to guarantee a certain job. But that's not what the employee should want. The objective is commitment on the employer's part to a job that has certain degrees of authority and responsibility. These can be described—for example, "unit manager of a profit center grossing no less than $20 million annually." Once the commitment has been made, the career path can be discussed in terms of whether or not each successive step is designed to prepare the employee for that goal.

Such a demand will be firmly opposed by any employer on the ground that it infringes upon his freedom to assign personnel as he sees fit. The employer's objective in making a Golden Handcuff agreement is to lock in the employee while keeping management's options intact. The employee who does not particularly want an exceptional amount of power should, in bargaining, keep that fact to himself, using it as a bargaining chip in order to win more money.

Golden Handcuffs give the employer reasonable assurance of an important resource into the future. It's up to the employee to make the employer pay for that assurance.

CONTRACTING FOR BENEFITS NOT CONNECTED WITH PROMOTION

The term "Peter Principle" became a part of the language because it describes a phenomenon with which we are all familiar: the tendency for people to continue to be promoted until they reach their level of incompetence. American corporations, by and large, have focused on promotability as a most desirable commodity, frequently more desirable than competence. The manager is judged less by how well he does his present job than by how rapidly he seems to be approaching his next job.

One result of this emphasis has been that managers who do not go all out for promotion are considered deficient. One does not have to refuse a promotion to have the question mark placed next to one's name. An executive who demurs at a sideways transfer that involves a difficult relocation often permanently impairs his career. No matter how good he may be at what he does, he is dismissed as lacking in ambition, and he is highly vulnerable to being fired. At the same time, a far less efficient manager may survive and prosper because he displays a lust for corporate guerrilla warfare and the kinds of cosmetic qualities ("coming across well," etc.) that make a good impression.

Promotion is the standard reward for excellence, which is why thousands of happy and effective salesmen have been elevated to become unhappy and ineffective sales managers. The inevitability of promotion to a more resounding title has been accepted by generations of executives.

Today, however, many younger people in business are unwilling to buy without question the "up or out" philosophy. At the same time, managements badly in need of more talented performers see the merit in keeping people in jobs they like and do well, particularly if the people want to stay there.

Those among this new generation who want to make money and live a satisfying life—and are willing to work for businesses but not willing to "sell their souls" to their employers—are looking for ways to get maximum benefits from their own efforts. Often these people are individualistic and confident enough to want an entrepreneurial setup, in which they are rewarded on the basis of their own efforts.

People who want salary, bonuses, and perks without necessarily being promoted into distasteful jobs will enter into contracts that give them what they want. The essence of the entrepreneurial arrangement is to find a basis on which the pay plan can be based. The salesman, of course, is most easily paid on the basis of individual effort. His compensation may depend entirely on the volume he produces. Most people who are not in sales (or in piecework) cannot be paid on the basis of individual production. For those people the principle is to base a portion of compensation on the smallest possible unit whose performance is measurable and logical as a basis for payment. The middle manager may seek a pay scheme that is tied to the performance of the unit rather than the company as a whole. For this individual to try to gear the compensation plan to a smaller body, say a department, would be illogical, since the performance of the department cannot be viewed separately from the unit or division of which it is a part.

The measurable performance on which payment is partially based may be volume, cost savings, earnings, total production, etc. The person making the agreement should be certain that his or her work will be decisive in assuring better performance. If, no matter how well you do, the bottom line of your division can be swamped by the mediocrity of others, you should not voluntarily hitch your compensation to it.

Stock and stock options are useful forms of compensation for individual efforts in two ways. You can earn more of them depending on your effectiveness; and they appreciate in value depending on how well the company does.

People who are interested in living rewarding and satisfying lives rather than reaching the pinnacles of power will make contracts that place more emphasis on perks than do many conventional agreements. The use of company cars and boats, travel, recreation, and time off are vital in the all-around lifestyles of these people. These perks can be described in written agreements.

The employment contract, as it comes into more general use, will be found to serve as a flexible instrument which can be made to apply to the wide variety of needs—employer needs and employee needs—that will have to be served.

APPENDIX

The full texts of contracts in this section (many of which have been referred to in the body of the book) make interesting reading and give the reader an opportunity to become more familiar with the variety of provisions and arrangements possible.

ABC

This contract between ABC and Frederick S. Pierce carries an interesting deferral provision along with a stipulation that it is "personal and non-transferable":

AGREEMENT entered into this last day of March, 1983 as of the 10th day of January, 1983, between AMERICAN BROADCASTING COMPANIES, INC., a New York corporation (herein called the "Corporation"), and FREDERICK S. PIERCE (herein called "Mr. Pierce").

WITNESSETH:

1. The Agreement dated as of September 1, 1981 between the Corporation and Mr. Pierce is hereby amended in its entirety to read as follows:

"FIRST: The term of this Agreement shall be for a period commencing September 1, 1981 and ending August 31, 1985. The Corporation hereby employs Mr. Pierce during the term of this Agreement, subject to his election as such by the Board of Directors of the Corporation (herein called the 'Board'), as Executive Vice President of the Corporation until January 10, 1983 and as President and Chief Operating Officer of the Corporation for the balance of said term.

"Mr. Pierce's principal office shall be at the Corporation's headquarters.

"Mr. Pierce hereby accepts such employment and agrees to perform such services. Mr. Pierce shall perform such duties to the best of his ability and, during the period of his employment hereunder, shall not enter into or conduct any business other than that of the Corporation.

"SECOND: The Corporation shall pay to Mr. Pierce, and Mr. Pierce shall accept from the Corporation for the services described in Article FIRST above, a salary of $400,000 per annum through January 2, 1983 and $460,000 per annum for the balance of said term, or such higher amount as the Board shall from time to time determine, such salary to be paid in accordance with the usual manner of payment of executive salaries by the Corporation. It is anticipated that the Key Employees Incentive Plans Committee of the Board will review Mr. Pierce's salary level on a regular annual basis (as well as at any time when Mr. Pierce's duties are increased). Any increase in salary, however, shall be made only in the sole discretion of the Board. Nothing herein contained shall affect Mr. Pierce's eligibility to participate in the Key Employees Incentive Compensation Plan of the Corporation, the 1975 Restricted Stock Bonus Plan of the Corporation, or any pension, profit sharing, stock option or stock purchase plan or any group insurance, hospitalization or other incentive plan now in effect or hereafter adopted by the Corporation.

"THIRD: The Board will review the provisions of this Agreement at the end of the first three years of its term and also in the event that Messrs. Goldenson and Rule are no longer employees of the Corporation, if such event shall occur during the term hereof, it being understood, however, that any changes in such provisions shall be made only in the sole discretion of the Board.

"FOURTH: If at any time after January 10, 1983 and during the balance of said term the Corporation shall fail to re-elect Mr. Pierce as President and Chief Operating Officer of the Corporation, or shall remove Mr. Pierce from such office (other than for cause or other than because Mr. Pierce is unable by reason of physical incapacity [including mental disability or illness] to substantially perform his duties hereunder), Mr. Pierce shall have the right, upon written notice to the Corporation specifying in detail the alleged breach and given within thirty (30) days after such occurrence of any such event, provided that the Corporation has not cured such alleged breach within thirty (30) days after receipt of said notice, to select the alternative set forth in Paragraph (a) of this Article FOURTH; in the event that Mr. Pierce fails to give such notice the alternative specified in Paragraph (b) of this Article FOURTH shall apply:

"(a) Mr. Pierce's employment with the Corporation shall terminate on a date thirty (30) days after receipt of said notice by the Corporation and the obligations of the Corporation under this Agreement shall cease on such date, but for the period from such date to August 31, 1985, the Corporation shall make bi-weekly payments to Mr. Pierce at the most recent rate provided for in Article SECOND above. The amounts payable to Mr. Pierce pursuant to the preceding sentence shall be deemed liquidated damages hereunder and shall not be diminished by reason of any earnings by Mr. Pierce subsequent to such date of termination.

"(b) Mr. Pierce may continue in the employ of the Corporation as an employee and perform such duties as the Board or the Chairman of the Board may assign to him, such duties to be of a character and dignity appropriate to a senior executive of the Corporation, upon the terms and conditions specified in this Agreement, including the most recent compensation specified in Article SECOND above.

"FIFTH: The rights to receive payments hereunder are hereby expressly declared to be personal and to be non-assignable and non-transferable."

2. The Agreement dated as of September 1, 1981, as hereinabove amended, shall remain in full force and effect.

IN WITNESS WHEREOF, American Broadcasting Companies, Inc. has caused these presents to be signed by its duly authorized officers and Frederick S. Pierce has hereunto set his hand, this 1st day of March, 1983 as of the 10th day of January, 1983.

AMERICAN
BROADCASTING
COMPANIES, INC.

Attest:

_____   By_____
Secretary

_____
FREDERICK S. PIERCE

MATHEMATICA, INC.

This contract is one of several concluded by Mathematica, Inc., with key executives in anticipation of the acquisition of Mathematica by Martin Marietta:

EMPLOYMENT AGREEMENT

AGREEMENT, dated May 31, 1983, between Mathematica, Inc., a New Jersey corporation (the "Company"), and Richard H. Cobb (the "Executive"), residing at 121 Braeburn Drive, Princeton, New Jersey 08540.

The Executive presently is in the employ of the Company and, in the course of such employment, performs services for the Company and one or more of its subsidiaries. The Company has entered into an Agreement in Principle with Martin Marietta Corporation ("MMC"), dated May 12, 1983, which contemplates the merger of the Company with a subsidiary of MMC (the "Merger"). The parties now wish to provide the Executive's continued employment subsequent to the Merger upon the terms and conditions herein set forth, it being understood (without in any way limiting the provisions of paragraphs 14 and 17) that the Company's obligations hereunder will be assumed upon the merger by the surviving corporation in the Merger, and the Executive's obligations hereunder will be to such surviving corporation.

NOW, THEREFORE, in consideration of the foregoing, and for other good and valuable consideration, it is agreed:

1. (a) The Company hereby continues the Executive in its employ for the period (the "Employment Period") which shall commence as of the date of consummation of the Merger and, unless sooner terminated by the Executive's death, or as hereinafter provided in this Agreement, or unless extended pursuant to subparagraph (b) of this paragraph, shall end on the fourth anniversary of said date.

The Executive hereby accepts such employment and agrees to devote his full working time and best efforts to the services of the Company in such senior executive capacity, consistent with his experience and abilities, as the Board of Directors and President of the Company may from time to time reasonably designate. Unless the Executive otherwise consents, the principal place of the Executive's employment shall be within a 50-mile radius of Princeton, New Jersey, or Bethesda, Maryland.

(b) The Employment Period herein may be extended beyond the date specified above by mutual agreement of the parties.

2. (a) During the Employment Period, the Company shall pay to the Executive for all services rendered by him in any capacity (a) a salary at the rate of $114,300 per annum (the "Annual Salary"), payable in equal semimonthly installments, plus (b) such additional compensation in the form of salary or bonus as the Board of Directors of the Company in its sole

discretion shall authorize or agree to pay, payable on such terms and conditions as it shall determine. As used herein, the term "Annual Salary" shall include any such increases in salary (but not bonus) which are in effect at the time. As soon as reasonably practicable following the Merger the Company will review the Annual Salary taking into consideration the Company's performance during the year ending June 30, 1983, the Executive's contribution thereto, changes in the cost of living index during such year for urban wage earners published by the U.S. Bureau of Labor Statistics for the Trenton, New Jersey, Standard Metropolitan Statistical Area (or a reasonably comparable successor index), and such other factors as the Company deems relevant (but not including the receipt of additional compensation pursuant to subparagraph (b) of this paragraph 2), and will adjust the Executive's Annual Salary retroactive to July 1, 1983 by an amount at least equal to the aforesaid increase in such cost of living index. The Company will undertake a similar review in July 1984, 1985 and 1986 with respect to a possible further increase in the Annual Salary effective July 1 in each of such years, but nothing herein contained will obligate the Company to any further increase in the Annual Salary, any such increase being entirely at the discretion of the Company.

(b) The Company shall pay to the Executive, as additional compensation, the sum of $1,569,963.00, said sum to be paid as follows: an initial payment of 20% to be paid upon consummation of the Merger and the balance of 80% to be paid in four equal installments on the first through the fourth anniversary dates of said consummation. The Executive shall not, however, be entitled to receive any installment if he shall not be an employee of the Company on the date such installment becomes due because he shall have theretofor voluntarily terminated his employment in violation of this Agreement or because the Company shall have theretofor terminated his employment pursuant to paragraph 4.(b).

3. The Executive is authorized to incur reasonable traveling and other expenses in connection with the business of the Company and its subsidiaries in accordance with Company policy. The Company will reimburse the Executive monthly

for all such expenses upon presentation by the Executive of an itemized account in substantiation of such expenditures.

4. (a) If the Executive is unable to perform his duties hereunder by reason of mental or physical illness or other incapacity continuing for a period of six consecutive months, the Company may, at any time after the expiration of such six-month period and prior to his recovery from such illness or incapacity, elect to terminate the Employment Period hereunder by giving written notice of such election to the Executive.

(b) If the Executive (i) is convicted of a criminal offense involving dishonesty or a felony giving rise to a sentence of imprisonment or (ii) wilfully disobeys instructions reasonably given to him in the course of his employment or (iii) wilfully commits any serious breach of any of his obligations under this Agreement, the Company may summarily and forthwith terminate the Employment Period, and in such event the Annual Salary shall be paid and if necessary apportioned to the date of such termination, and payment made for any then unreimbursed expenses incurred pursuant to paragraph 3. If subsequent to any such termination of the Employment Period for a reason specified in clause (i) the Executive's conviction is reversed on appeal, the Executive shall, if he so requests, be reinstated as an employee whereupon, commencing with such reinstatement, he will be entitled to payments in accordance with this Agreement, but with the time periods appropriately extended to take account of his absence, and no payments shall be made retroactively except as the Company in its sole discretion may determine.

5. If the Employment Period shall terminate by reason of the death or disability of the Executive, the Company shall pay (a) in the case of disability, to the Executive, or (b) in the case of death, to the beneficiaries designated by the Executive in his sole discretion in writing to the Company, or in the absence of such designation, to the Executive's estate: (i) for the balance of the month in which such termination occurred, the amount that would otherwise have been payable as Annual Salary pursuant to paragraph 2.(a), (ii) thereafter, for a period of two years, payments at the annual rate of 60% of the Executive's Annual Salary, payable in equal monthly install-

ments, and (iii) any unpaid installments of additional compensation called for under paragraph 2.(b) as they become due. In the event any beneficiary designated in writing by the Executive pursuant hereto shall become entitled to receive payments hereunder and shall die prior to the completion of such payments, then the remainder of such payments shall be made to such other beneficiary or beneficiaries as such deceased beneficiary shall have designated in writing to the Company or, in the absence of such designation, to the estate of such deceased beneficiary.

6. (a) The Executive agrees that (a) during any period payments are being made to him pursuant to paragraphs 2.(a) or 6.(b), or would be made to him pursuant to paragraph 6.(b) but for his violation of any of the provisions of this paragraph 6 (without regard to the Company's option in the proviso immediately following clause (iii) of paragraph 6.(b)), and (b) during any period payments are being made to him pursuant to clause (i) or (ii) of paragraph 5, he will not, without the prior written consent of the Company, directly or indirectly:

(i) engage or become interested (whether as an owner, stockholder, partner, lender or other investor, director, officer, employee, consultant or otherwise) in any business or enterprise that shall, at the time, be in whole or in part competitive with any part of the business conducted by the Company or any of its subsidiaries during the period of the Executive's employment with the Company or any of its subsidiaries (except that ownership of not more than 1% of the outstanding securities of any class of any corporation that are listed on a national securities exchange or traded in the over-the-counter market shall not be considered a breach of this clause (i));

(ii) participate in the solicitation of any business of any type conducted by the Company or any of its subsidiaries during the period of the Executive's employment with the Company or any of its subsidiaries from any person or entity which was a customer of the Company or any of its subsidiaries during the period of the Executive's employment with the Company or any of its subsidiaries, or a prospective customer of the Company or any of its subsidiaries from which the Company or any of its subsidiaries solicited business (or for which a proposal for submission was prepared) during the period of one year immediately preceding the point in time when the Executive ceases to be employed by the Company or any of its subsidiaries;

(iii) knowingly employ or retain, or knowingly arrange to have any other person or entity employ or retain, any person who was an employee of the Company or any of its subsidiaries at a base compensation rate of at least $25,000.00 per year at any time during the period of one year immediately preceding such employing or retention of such person.

(b) For a period of two years after termination of the Employment Period (one year if such termination was on or after the third anniversary date of the Merger) the Company shall, unless it is making payments to the Executive pursuant to clause (i) or (ii) of paragraph 5, make payments to the Executive at the following rate:

(i) For the first six months, payments at an annual rate equal to 20% of the Executive's Annual Salary at the time of termination of the Employment Period, payable in equal monthly installments;

(ii) For the second six months, payments at an annual rate equal to 40% of the Executive's Annual Salary at the time of termination of the Employment Period, payable in equal monthly installments; and

(iii) Thereafter, if applicable, payments at an annual rate equal to 30% of the Executive's Annual Salary at the time of termination of the Employment Period, payable in equal monthly installments;

provided, however, that, at the Company's option, the Company may terminate the payments to be made to the Executive pursuant to this paragraph 6.(b) at any time after one year so long as it gives the Executive 60 days prior written notice of its intention to so terminate. The Company's obligation to make any payments as aforesaid shall terminate in the event that the Executive shall in any way, directly or indirectly, violate any of the provisions of this paragraph 6; and the Company shall have no obligation to make such payments if the

Employment Period shall have been terminated pursuant to paragraph 4.(b).

(c) During the Employment Period, the Executive will promptly disclose to officers of the Company, in accordance with the Company's policies, full information concerning any interest, direct or indirect, of the Executive (as owner, stockholder, partner, lender or other investor, director, officer, employee, consultant or otherwise) in any business which, as reasonably known to the Executive, purchases or otherwise obtains services or products from, or sells or otherwise provides services or products to the Company or any of its subsidiaries or any of their respective suppliers or customers, provided that the Executive need not disclose any such interest by way of ownership of not more than 1% of the outstanding securities of any class of any corporation that are listed on a national securities exchange or traded in the over-the-counter market.

(d) During the Employment Period and for such further period as Executive is obligated pursuant to paragraph 6.(a), the Executive will promptly furnish in writing to the Company any information reasonably requested by the Company in writing (including any third party confirmations which can be obtained with reasonable efforts) with respect to any current activity or interest of the Executive in any business.

(e) The Executive agrees that during his employment with the Company or any of its subsidiaries and at all times thereafter, he will not disclose to others, directly or indirectly, other than in the ordinary course of business of the Company and its subsidiaries, any confidential or secret information relating to the business, research activities or other interest of the Company or any of its subsidiaries (including, without limitation, any confidential programs, techniques or work products, any trade secrets, any reports, recommendations or conclusions or any information as to present or future business plans or finances, or with respect to any products, services, suppliers, customers or prospective customers) or use any such information unless such information is used (i) solely on behalf of the Company or any of its subsidiaries, or (ii) after he is no longer employed by the Company or any of its subsidiaries and after such information becomes generally available to oth-crs in the business, other than those acquiring rights thereto under arrangements contemplating maintenance of confidentiality or through unauthorized disclosures thereof. At such time as he is no longer employed by the Company or any of its subsidiaries, the Executive shall promptly surrender to the Company any and all programs, work papers, reports, drawings, blueprints, manuals, documents, photographs and the like (including all negatives, originals and copies, whether in document form, on computer discs or otherwise, thereof) in his possession, custody or control which relate in any way to the business of the Company or any of its subsidiaries, whether prepared by him or by others.

(f) If any of the provisions of the foregoing subparagraphs of this paragraph 6 is held to be unenforceable because of the scope, duration or area of its applicability, the court making such determination shall have the power to modify such scope, duration or area or all of them, and such provisions shall then be applicable in such modified form.

7. Obligations of the Company for payments hereunder shall be deemed satisfied if such payments are made by any affiliate of the Company for whom the Executive performs services.

8. The Executive shall promptly disclose to the Company or its designees any and all knowledge possessed by him which he may legally impart relating to any and all work product or copyrightable material (hereinafter referred to as "said material") or to any and all inventions, developments or innovations (hereinafter referred to as "said inventions"), whether patented, patentable or unpatentable, developed or acquired by him, either solely or jointly with others, either prior to the effective date of this Agreement or during the term of his employment, and which in any way relate to the business of the Company or any of its subsidiaries. The Executive will not disclose to any person or entity (other than in the ordinary course of the business of the Company and its subsidiaries) any information concerning any of said material and said inventions.

9. The Executive hereby assigns and agrees to assign to the Company, its successors and assigns, his entire right, title and interest in and to any of said material and any of said inven-

tions, whether patented, patentable or unpatentable, which the Executive has on the effective date of this Agreement, or which he may conceive of, acquire or make while in the employ of the Company or any of its subsidiaries, which are in any way related to the business of the Company or any of its subsidiaries. Said material and said inventions shall be the property of the Company. The Executive shall, without further compensation, do all lawful things, including, without limitation, rendering assistance and executing necessary documents, as requested, which may be convenient or necessary or proper to enable the Company or any of its nominees and designees to perfect title in said material and in said inventions and to obtain and maintain effective patent and copyright protection in the United States and foreign countries thereon.

10. The Executive may not assign, pledge or encumber his interest in this Agreement without the written consent of the Company.

11. In the event of a breach or threatened breach of any of the provisions hereof (other than those providing directly for the performance by the Executive of his services hereunder), the Company shall, in addition to all other remedies, be entitled to a temporary or permanent injunction and/or a decree for specific performance, in accordance with the provisions hereof, without showing any actual damage or that monetary damages would not provide an adequate remedy.

12. Nothing contained herein shall affect such rights as the Executive might otherwise have during the Employment Period, or thereafter, to participate in and receive benefits from any pension plan, profit-sharing plan, or other employee benefit plan or plans of the Company or any of its subsidiaries or affiliates, as the same may now or hereafter exist and under the terms thereof as the same may be amended from time to time, nor shall any payment under any such plan be deemed to constitute a payment to the Executive under this Agreement.

13. Any and all notices or consents required or permitted to be given under any of the provisions of this Agreement shall be in writing and shall be deemed to have been duly given three days after mailing, if mailed by registered or certified mail, return receipt requested: if to the Executive, at his address

appearing above, and if to the Company, at its principal office at that time. The Executive may change his mailing address for the purpose of this Agreement by notice to the Company as herein provided.

14. In the event the Company shall at any time be merged or consolidated with or into any corporation or corporations or in the event that all or substantially all of the business and assets of the Company shall be sold or otherwise transferred to another corporation, the provisions of this Agreement, including the provisions of this paragraph, shall be binding upon and inure to the benefit of the successor of the Company resulting from such merger, consolidation, or sale of assets.

15. The Company agrees to indemnify the Executive for any and all liabilities to which he may be subject as a result of his service as an officer, director or other corporate agent of the Company, or of any other enterprise at the request of the Company, or otherwise as a result of his employment hereunder, as well as the expense (including, without limitation, reasonable counsel fees) of any proceeding brought or threatened against the Executive as a result of such service or employment, to the fullest extent permitted by law. Such counsel fees shall, to the fullest extent permitted by law, be paid by the Company in advance of the final disposition of the proceeding upon receipt of an undertaking of the Executive satisfactory to counsel for the Company to repay such fees unless it shall ultimately be determined that he is entitled to be indemnified with respect thereto.

16. In the event that any provision of this Agreement would be held to be invalid, prohibited or unenforceable in any jurisdiction for any reason unless narrowed by construction, this Agreement shall, as to such jurisdiction, be construed as if such invalid, prohibited or unenforceable provisions had been more narrowly drawn so as not to be invalid, prohibited or unenforceable. If, notwithstanding the foregoing, any provision of this Agreement would be held to be invalid, prohibited or unenforceable in any jurisdiction for any reason, such provision, as to such jurisdiction, shall be ineffective to the extent of such invalidity, prohibition or unenforceability, without invalidating the remaining provisions of this Agreement

or affecting the validity or enforceability of such provision in any other jurisdiction, except that, to the extent that the provisions of paragraph 6.(a) may be held invalid, prohibited or unenforceable, the Company's obligation to make payments under paragraph 6.(b) shall terminate.

17. Except as otherwise provided herein, this Agreement shall be binding upon and shall inure to the benefit of the parties hereto, and their respective heirs, successors, assigns and personal representatives.

18. This Agreement shall be governed in all respects by the internal laws of the State of New Jersey without giving effect to principles of conflict of laws.

19. Effective with the consummation of the Merger, this Agreement constitutes the entire understanding between the parties hereto relating to the services to be performed by the Executive hereunder and supersedes all prior Employment Agreements and other agreements and undertakings, oral and written, between the parties hereto with respect to the subject matter hereof, except that the following agreements signed concurrently with this Agreement shall remain in full force and effect: (i) the agreement among the Company, Mathematica Products Group, Inc. ("MPG") and the Executive captioned "Agreement" and relating to the termination of a Stock Option Agreement between the Executive and MPG, and (ii) the agreement between the Company and the Executive captioned "Agreement Amending Phantom Share Agreements" and relating to the Company's Long-Term Incentive Compensation Plan. Except as otherwise specifically provided herein, no change, modification or addition shall be valid unless in writing and signed by or on behalf of the parties hereto.

20. This Agreement shall take effect upon consummation of the Merger and shall not be effective prior thereto.

IN WITNESS WHEREOF, the parties have executed this Agreement as of the day and year first above written.

MATHEMATICA, INC.

By_____

_____
Executive

COASTAL

This contract requires written notice of termination:

EMPLOYMENT AGREEMENT

Employment Agreement dated as of the 18th day of January, 1982, between The Coastal Corporation, a Delaware corporation with its principal executive offices at Houston, Texas (the "Company"), and Frederick N. Otto, whose Houston, Texas, address will be 14 Greenway Plaza, Suite 16R (the "Executive").

The Company and the Executive hereby agree as follows:

1. *Employment; Period of Employment.*

The Company hereby agrees to employ, engage and hire the Executive and the Executive does hereby accept and agree to such hiring, engagement and employ, for a term of five (5) years commencing on the 18th day of January, 1982 (the Period of Employment), in accordance with the terms and provisions hereof.

2. *Position, Duties, Responsibilities.*

a. During the Period of Employment the Executive shall continue to serve as an officer of the Company or as an officer of one of the companies which will result from the proposed restructuring of the Company into three or more separate companies to be owned by the holders of Coastal common stock as announced by the Board of Directors following the October 15, 1981, meeting, with the office and title and with duties and responsibilities as follows: as Senior Executive Vice President, with Executive exercising supervisory responsibilities over the Company's domestic refining, marketing, supply, terminal and related activities.

b. Throughout the period of Employment the Executive shall devote his fulltime efforts during normal business hours to the business and affairs of the Company, except during reasonable vacation periods and periods of illness or incapacity, performing such duties as may be reasonably assigned to him, diligently and faithfully to the best of his abilities. The Executive shall at all times during his employment hereunder conduct himself in a manner consistent with his position with the Company and shall not knowingly perform any act contrary to the best interest of the Company.

c. Executive expressly agrees that during the term of this Agreement, he will not engage in, either directly or indirectly, any business in competition with Employer's business. Nothing contained herein shall be deemed to prevent or limit the right of Executive to invest any of his funds in the capital stock or other securities of any corporation whose stock or securities are publicly owned or are regularly traded on any public exchange, nor shall anything contained herein be deemed to prevent Executive from investing or limit Executive's right to invest his funds in real estate.

3. *Termination, Effect of Termination and Notice of Termination.*

a. *Termination.* This Agreement shall terminate on the occurrence of any one of the following events:

(i) the death of the Executive;

(ii) termination by the Company due to the permanent disability of Executive. For the purpose of this Agreement, Executive shall be deemed to have permanently become disabled if at any year during the term hereof, because of ill health, physical or mental disability, or for other causes beyond his control, he shall have been continuously unable or unwilling or have failed to perform his duties hereunder for 120 consecutive days, or if, during any year of the term hereof, he shall have been unable or unwilling or have failed to perform his duties for a total period of 180 days either consecutive or not. For the purpose hereof, the term "any year of the term hereof" is defined to mean any period of 12 consecutive months during the Period of Employment;

(iii) termination by the Company at its sole right and election at any time after the expiration of two years from the date of this Agreement;

(iv) termination by the Company for willful breach of duty by the Executive which is materially detrimental to the Company;

(v) termination by the Executive for Good Reason. As used

in this section, Good Reason shall be the willful breach by the Company of any of the obligations imposed on it under this Agreement.

b. *Effect of Termination.* In the event of termination of this Agreement prior to the completion of the Employment Period for any reason other than by the Company pursuant to Section 3.a.(iii) above or the Executive pursuant to Section 3.a.(v) above, the Executive shall be entitled to compensation earned by him prior to the date of termination as provided in this Agreement, computed pro rata up to and including such date, plus an additional sum equal to the Executive's base salary for a one month period. If this Agreement is terminated by the Company pursuant to Section 3.a.(iii) above or by the Executive pursuant to Section 3.a.(v) above, the company shall pay to the Executive in cash and as full liquidated damages, a sum equal to the lesser of (i) the Executive's base salary for a one year period or (ii) a sum equal to the Executive's base salary for the remaining term of the Period of Employment if the remaining term of the period of Employment is less than one year.

c. *Notice of Termination.* Any termination by the Company pursuant to Section 3.a.(ii), Section 3.a.(iii) or Section 3.a.(iv) above or by the Executive pursuant to Section 3.a.(v) above shall be communicated by written Notice of Termination to the other party hereto. For purposes of this Agreement, a "Notice of Termination" shall mean a notice which shall indicate the specific termination provisions in this Agreement relied upon and shall set forth in detail the facts and circumstances claimed to provide a basis for termination of the Executive's employment under the provisions so indicated.

4. *Compensation.*

As compensation (inclusive of Director's fees and Committee fees, if any) for services rendered to the Company during the Period of Employment, the Executive shall receive compensation provided for in this section.

a. *Salary.* Salary will be at the rate of Three Hundred Twenty-Five Thousand Dollars ($325,000.00) per annum, payable in cash not less frequently than monthly and not later than the 16th day following the expiration of the month in question, provided, however, such salary shall be reviewed periodically by the Executive Compensation Committee or such other group as is hereafter designated by the Board of Directors of the Company.

b. *Stock Option.* The Executive shall be granted an option pursuant to the Company's September 28, 1980, Stock Option Plan to purchase 15,000 shares of the Company's stock under the form of stock option agreement currently being used by the Company in connection with such plan.

c. *Company Automobile.* The Executive shall be provided with a Company automobile under arrangements at least equivalent to those currently in effect with respect to other Company Senior Executives.

d. *Country Club Membership.* The Company will reimburse the Executive for his initial membership fee and monthly dues (during the Period of Employment) for one country club membership to be approved by the Company. Upon conclusion of the Period of Employment, the Executive's right to such membership shall terminate with all rights thereunder reverting to the Company; if requested to do so, the Executive shall execute such assignments as necessary to accomplish this result.

5. *Nondisclosure of Information Concerning Business.*

Except to the extent reasonably required in conducting and carrying out of the business affairs of the Company, the Executive agrees that he will not at any time, in any fashion, form, or manner, either directly or indirectly, divulge, disclose, or communicate to any person, firm or corporation in any manner whatsoever any information of any kind, nature or description concerning any matters affecting or relating to the business of the Company, including, without limiting the generality of the foregoing, the names of any of its customers, the prices it obtains or has obtained or at which it sells or has sold its products, or any other information of, about, or concerning the business of the Company, its manner of operation, its plans, processes, or other data of any kind, nature, or description without regard to whether any or all of the foregoing matters would be deemed confidential, material, or important, the parties hereto stipulating that as between them, the same are important, material, and confidential and gravely affect the effective and successful conduct of the business of the Company and its goodwill, and that any breach of the terms of this paragraph is a material breach hereof.

6. *Successors.*

The Company shall require any successor (whether direct or indirect and whether by purchase, merger, consolidation or otherwise) to all or substantially all of the business or assets of the Company, by an Agreement in form and substance satisfactory to the Executive, to expressly assume and agree to perform this Agreement in the same manner and to the same extent that the Company would be required to perform if no such succession had taken place. As used in this Agreement, "Company" shall mean the Company as defined in the preamble to their Agreement and any successor to its business or assets which executes and delivers the Agreement provided for in this paragraph or which otherwise becomes bound by all of the terms and provisions of this Agreement by operation of law.

7. *Notice.*

For the purpose of this Agreement notices and all other communications provided for herein shall be in writing and shall be deemed to have been duly given when delivered or mailed by United States Registered or Certified Mail, Return Receipt Requested, postage prepaid, addressed as follows:

If to the Executive:
Frederick M. Otto
14 Greenway Plaza
Suite 16R
Houston, Texas 77046

If to the Company:
The Coastal Corporation
9 Greenway Plaza
Houston, Texas 77045
Attention: Corporate Secretary

or such other address as any party may have furnished to the others in writing in accordance herewith, except that notice of change of address shall be effective only upon receipt.

8. *Governing Law.*

The validity, interpretation, construction and performance of this Agreement shall be governed by the laws of the State of Texas.

9. *Miscellaneous.*

No provision of this Agreement may be modified, waived or discharged unless such waiver, modification or discharge is agreed to in writing signed by the Executive and the Company. No waiver by either party hereto of, or compliance with, any condition or performance of this Agreement to be performed by such other party shall be deemed a waiver of similar or dissimilar provisions or conditions at the same or any prior or subsequent time. No agreement or representations, oral or otherwise, express or implied, with respect to the subject matter hereof have been made by either party which are not set forth expressly in this Agreement or in a letter dated December 22, 1981, from Harry L. Blomquist, Jr. to Frederick M. Otto, a copy of such letter being attached hereto as Exhibit A and incorporated herein by reference; the Exhibit A letter is still relevant with respect to the statements contained in the following paragraphs: Paragraph one on page one, numbered paragraph 6. on page two, and the first unnumbered paragraph on page two. Otherwise, the Exhibit A letter is superseded and replaced by this Employment Agreement.

10. *Separability.*

The invalidity or unenforceability of any provisions of this Agreement shall not affect the validity or enforceability of any other provisions of this Agreement, which shall remain in full force and effect.

11. *Counterparts.*

This Agreement may be executed in one or more counterparts, each of which shall be deemed to be an original, but all of which together will constitute one and the same Agreement.

12. *Withholding of Taxes.*

The Company may withhold from any benefits payable

under this Agreement, all federal, state, city or other taxes as shall be required pursuant to any law or government regulations then in effect.

EXECUTED and entered this 6th day of July, 1982.

_____

"Executive"

_____

For

_____

"Company"

CONTROL DATA CORPORATION

Here's a characteristic Golden Parachute (in the form of a blank agreement), which also contains an extensive confidentiality section.

CONTROL DATA CORPORATION
EXECUTIVE EMPLOYMENT AGREEMENT

PARTIES

Control Data Corporation (a Delaware Corporation)
8100 34th Avenue South ("CDC")
Minneapolis, Minnesota 55440

_____

("Executive")

Date_____19_____

RECITALS

A. The parties desire to provide for the employment of Executive by CDC, which, for the purposes of this Agreement, includes CDC or any subsidiary or affiliated corporation or entity that is at least 51% owned directly or indirectly by Control Data Corporation.

B. Executive desires to be assured of a secure minimum compensation from CDC for Executive's services over a defined term (unless terminated for cause), and to be protected in the event of a change in the control of the company.

C. CDC desires reasonable protection of CDC's confidential business and technical information which has been developed over the years by CDC at substantial expense and assurance that the Executive will not compete with CDC for a reasonable period of time after termination of employment.

D. CDC and Executive, each intending to be legally bound, covenant and agree as follows:

1. Employment. Upon the terms and conditions set forth in this Agreement, CDC hereby employs Executive, and Executive accepts such employment. Except as expressly provided herein, termination of this Agreement by either party shall also terminate Executive's employment by CDC.

2. Duties. Executive shall devote his or her full-time and best efforts to CDC and to fulfilling the duties of his or her position which shall include such duties as may from time to time be assigned him or her by CDC, provided that such duties are reasonably consistent with Executive's education, experience and background.

3. Term. Subject to the provisions of paragraphs 6 and 11, Executive's employment shall continue until June 30, 1984, and shall be automatically extended for an additional year on June 30th of each year following the date of this Agreement unless either party gives written notice of termination to the other in which case no further automatic extensions shall occur. In any event, the Agreement shall automatically terminate without notice when the Executive reaches 70 years of age. If employment is continued after the age of 70 by mutual agreement, it shall be terminable at will by either party.

4. Compensation.

(a) Base Salary. For all services rendered under this Agreement during the term of Executive's employment, CDC shall pay Executive a minimum Base Salary ("Base Salary" shall mean regular cash compensation paid on a periodic basis exclusive of benefits, bonuses or incentive payments) at the annual rate currently being paid or, if Executive is not currently in CDC's employ, at the amount specified in the written offer of employment. If the Executive's salary is increased during the term of this Agreement, the increased amount shall be the Base Salary for the remainder of the term and any extensions.

(b) Bonus and Incentive. Bonus or incentive compensation shall be in the sole discretion of CDC, provided that if Executive is currently employed by CDC he/she shall continue to participate in those bonus or incentive plans in which he/she currently participates. CDC reserves the right to alter, amend or eliminate any bonus or incentive plans in accordance with their terms without compensation to Executive.

5. Business Expenses. CDC shall, in accordance with, and to the extent of, its policies in effect from time to time, bear all ordinary and necessary business expenses incurred by the Executive in performing his or her duties as an employee of CDC, provided that Executive accounts promptly for such expenses to CDC in the manner prescribed from time to time by CDC.

6. Early Termination. Subject to the respective continuing obligations of the parties, pursuant to paragraphs 7, 8, 9, 10, 11, 12 and 13, this Agreement may be terminated prior to expiration of its term as follows:

(a) CDC may terminate this Agreement immediately for cause, including without limitation, fraud, misrepresentation, theft or embezzlement of CDC assets, intentional violations of law or company policies or a breach of the provisions of this Agreement, including specifically the failure to perform his or her duties as required by paragraph 2.

(b) Either Executive or CDC may terminate this Agreement without cause on seventy-five (75) days' notice.

(c) This Agreement shall terminate in the event of death or disability of the Executive. Disability shall mean the inability of Executive to perform his or her duties under this Agreement because of illness or incapacity for a continuous period of five (5) months.

7. Remedies for Early Termination.

(a) In the event of termination pursuant to paragraph 6, Base Salary shall be paid as follows:

(i) In the event of termination pursuant to paragraph 6(a), Base Salary shall continue to be paid on a semi-monthly basis prorated through the date of termination specified in any notice of termination.

(ii) In the event of termination pursuant to paragraph 6(b), compensation shall continue to be paid as follows: (A) if the notice of termination is given by Executive at any time or by CDC to be effective on or after Executive's 65th birthday, Base Salary shall continue to be paid on a semi-monthly basis prorated through the date of termination specified in such notice; (B) if the notice of termination is given by CDC and effective prior to Executive's 65th birthday, Executive shall receive the same compensation and shall have the same rights as would apply in the event of a termination pursuant to the provisions of paragraph 11.

(iii) Base Salary shall terminate automatically upon termination of this Agreement by reason of Executive's death and shall be prorated through the date of death.

(iv) In the event of disability, Base Salary shall be terminated as of the end of the month in which the last day of the five-month period of Executive's inability to perform his or her duties occurs.

(b) In the event of termination by reason of Executive's death or disability (clauses (a)(iii) and (a)(iv) above), Executive shall receive a pro rata portion (prorated through the last day Base Salary is payable pursuant to clauses (a)(iii) and (a)(iv), respectively) of any bonus or incentive payment (for the year in which death or disability occurred), to which he/she would have been entitled had he/she remained continuously employed for the full fiscal year in which death or disability occurred and continued to perform his/her duties in the same manner as they were performed immediately prior to the death or disability.

8. Confidential Information.

(a) For purposes of this paragraph 8, the term "Confidential Information" means information which is not generally known and which is proprietary to CDC, including (i) trade secret information about CDC and its products; and (ii) information relating to the business of CDC as conducted at any

time within the previous five years or anticipated to be conducted by CDC, and to any of its past, current or anticipated
products, including, without limitation, information about
CDC's research, development, manufacturing, purchasing,
accounting, engineering, marketing, selling, leasing or serv-
icing. All information which Executive has a reasonable basis
to consider Confidential Information or which is treated by
CDC as being Confidential Information shall be presumed to
be Confidential Information, whether originated by Executive
or by others, and without regard to the manner in which
Executive obtains access to such information.

(b) Executive will not, either during the term of this
Agreement or any time following expiration or termination of
this Agreement, use or disclose any Confidential Information
to any person not employed by CDC without the prior written
authorization of CDC and will use reasonably prudent care to
safeguard and protect, and to prevent the unauthorized disclosure of, all such Confidential Information.

9. Inventions.

(a) For purposes of this paragraph 9, the term "Inventions"
means discoveries, improvements and ideas (whether or not
in writing or reduced to practice) and works of authorship,
whether or not patentable or copyrightable, (i) which relate
directly to the business of CDC, or to CDC's actual or demonstrably anticipated research or development, (ii) which
result from any work performed by Executive for CDC, (iii)
for which equipment, supplies, facilities or trade secret information of CDC is utilized, or (iv) which were developed during
the time Executive was obligated to perform the duties described in paragraph 2.

(b) Executive agrees that all Inventions made, authored
or conceived by Executive, either solely or jointly with others,
during Executive's employment with CDC or within one year
after the termination of this Agreement, shall be the sole and
exclusive property of CDC. Upon termination of this Agreement, Executive shall turn over to a designated representative
of CDC all property in Executive's possession and custody and
belonging to CDC. Executive shall not retain any copies or
reproductions of correspondence, memoranda, reports, note-

books, drawings, photographs or other documents relating in any way to the affairs of CDC which came into Executive's possession at any time during the term of this Agreement.

(c) Executive will promptly and without request by CDC fully disclose to CDC in writing any Inventions. Executive will assign (and by this Agreement, hereby assigns) to CDC all of Executive's rights to such Inventions, and to applications for patents or copyrights in all countries and to patents and copyrights granted in all countries. Upon the request of CDC, Executive will apply for such United States or foreign patents or copyrights as CDC may deem desirable, and Executive will do any and all acts necessary in connection with such applications for patents or copyrights, or assignments, in order to establish in CDC the entire right, title and interest in and to such patents or copyrights. If Executive renders assistance to CDC under this paragraph 8(c) after termination of this Agreement, CDC shall pay a reasonable fee as determined by CDC for Executive's time and expenses.

NOTICE: Pursuant to Minnesota Statutes §181.78 the Executive is hereby notified that this Agreement does not apply to any invention for which no equipment, supplies, facility, or trade secret information of CDC was used and which was developed initially on the Executive's own time, and (1) which does not relate (a) directly to the business of CDC or (b) to CDC's actual or demonstrably anticipated research or development, or (2) which does not result from any work performed by Executive for CDC.

10. Non-Competition. Executive agrees that for a period of two (2) years following termination of this Agreement for any reason (except in the case of termination of this Agreement pursuant to paragraph 11 because of a Business Combination) he/she will not directly or indirectly, alone or as a partner, officer, director or shareholder of any other form or entity, engage in any commercial activity in the United States in competition with any part of CDC's business (a) that was under the Executive's management or supervision during the last two (2) years of employment by CDC; or (b) with respect to which Executive has Confidential Information as defined in paragraph 8 of this Agreement.

11. Business Combination. For purposes of this paragraph 11, a "Business Combination" shall mean the merger or consolidation of CDC with, the sale of all or substantially all the assets of CDC to, or the ownership of twenty percent (20%) or more of the total voting capital stock of CDC then issued and outstanding by, any person or entity not affiliated with CDC as of the date of this Agreement. It is expressly recognized by the parties that a Business Combination would necessarily result in material alteration or diminishment of Executive's position and responsibilities. Therefore, if, during the term of this Agreement, there shall occur, with or without the consent of CDC, a Business Combination, Executive shall have the option to terminate this Agreement on ten (10) days' notice. It is expressly recognized that Executive's position with CDC and agreement to be bound by the terms of this Agreement represent a commitment in terms of Executive's personal and professional career which cannot be reduced to monetary terms and necessarily constitutes a forebearance of options now and in the future open to Executive in CDC's areas of endeavor. Accordingly, in the event that Executive elects to terminate the agreement because of a Business Combination under this paragraph 11:

(a) Executive shall be under no obligation whatever to seek other employment opportunities during any period between termination of this Agreement under this paragraph 11 and expiration of Executive's unexpired term of this Agreement as it existed at the time of termination, and Executive shall not be obligated to accept any other employment opportunity which may be offered to Executive during such period.

(b) During such unexpired term of employment, Executive shall continue to receive on a semi-monthly basis, 200% of Executive's Base Salary in effect upon the date immediately prior to CDC's breach hereunder.

(c) In lieu of the continued compensation provided in paragraph 11(b), Executive may elect in writing the payment to Executive by CDC of a lump sum settlement in any amount equal to one hundred fifty percent (150%) of the total aggregate Base Salary payments (at the rate in effect immediately prior to the Business Combination) that would have been payable under this Agreement for the remaining term of this Agreement.

(d) Executive's termination of this Agreement by reason of a Business Combination described in this paragraph 11 and the receipt by Executive of any amounts pursuant to subparagraphs 11(b) and (c) shall not preclude Executive's continued employment with CDC, or the surviving entity in any Business Combination, on such terms as shall be negotiated between CDC (or such surviving entity) and Executive following such termination.

12. No Adequate Remedy. The parties declare that it is impossible to measure in money the damages which will accrue to either party by reason of a failure to perform any of the obligations under this Agreement. Therefore, if either party shall institute any action or proceeding to enforce the provisions hereof, such person against whom such action or proceeding is brought hereby waives the claim or defense that such party has an adequate remedy at law, and such person shall not urge in any such action or proceeding the claim or defense that such party has an adequate remedy at law.

13. Miscellaneous.

(a) Successors and Assigns. This Agreement shall be binding upon and inure to the benefit of the successors and assigns of CDC, whether by way of merger, consolidation, operation of law, assignment, purchase or other acquisition of substantially all the assets or business of CDC and shall only be assignable under the foregoing circumstances and shall be deemed to be materially breached by CDC if any such successor or assign does not absolutely and unconditionally assume all of CDC's obligations hereunder. Any such successor or assign shall be included in the term "CDC" as used in this Agreement.

(b) Notices. All notices, requests and demands given to or made pursuant hereto shall, except as otherwise specified herein, be in writing and be delivered or mailed to any such party at its address which:

(i)   In the case of CDC shall be:
        Control Data Corporation
        8100 34th Avenue South
        Minneapolis, Minnesota 55440

Attention: General Counsel

(ii)   In the case of the Executive shall be:

At the address listed on the first page of this Agreement. Either party may, by notice hereunder, designate a changed address. Any notice, if mailed properly addressed, postage pre-paid, registered or certified mail, shall be deemed dispatched on the registered date or that stamped on the certified mail receipt, and shall be deemed received with the second business day thereafter or when it is actually received, whichever is sooner.

(c) Captions. The various headings or captions in this Agreement are for convenience only and shall not affect the meaning or interpretation of this Agreement.

(d) Governing Law. The validity, construction and per-formance of this Agreement shall be governed by the laws of the State of Minnesota and any and every legal proceeding arising out of or in connection with this Agreement shall be brought in the appropriate courts of the State of Minnesota, each of the parties hereby consenting to the exclusive juris-diction of said courts for this purpose.

(e) Construction. Wherever possible, each provision of this Agreement shall be interpreted in such manner as to be effective and valid under applicable law, but if any provision of this Agreement shall be prohibited by or invalid under applicable law, such provision shall be ineffective only to the extent of such prohibition or invalidity without invalidating the remainder of such provision or the remaining provisions of this Agreement.

(f) Waivers. No failure on the part of either party to exercise, and no delay in exercising, any right or remedy here-under shall operate as a waiver thereof; nor shall any single or partial exercise of any right or remedy hereunder preclude any other or further exercise thereof or the exercise of any other right or remedy granted hereby or by any related document or by law.

(g) Modification. This Agreement may not be and shall not be modified or amended except by written instrument signed by the parties hereto.

(h) Entire Agreement. This Agreement constitutes the entire agreement and understanding between the parties hereto in reference to all the matters herein agreed upon; provided, however, that this Agreement shall not deprive Executive of any other rights Executive may have now or in the future, pursuant to law or the provisions of CDC benefit plans.

IN WITNESS WHEREOF, The parties hereto have caused this Agreement to be duly executed and delivered as of the day and year first above written.

Executive

_____

CONTROL DATA
CORPORATION
By_____

Title_____

HERTZ

The following agreement exemplifies the contract concluded between a corporation and the head of a subsidiary. Frank A. Olson is chairman of the board and chief executive officer of Hertz, a subsidiary of RCA.

Mr. Frank A. Olson
827 Morningside Road
Ridgewood, New Jersey 07450

April 7, 1982

Dear Mr. Olson:

The Management Compensation, Incentive, and Stock Option Committee of the Board of Directors (the "Committee") of RCA Corporation ("RCA") has approved a contract of employment with the Hertz Corporation ("Hertz") for your services upon the terms set forth in this letter. In accordance with this action of the Committee, I am pleased on behalf of Hertz to submit to you the following offer.

1. Hertz agrees to employ you during the period commencing March 1, 1982, and ending February 28, 1985. During your employment you shall serve, at the pleasure of Hertz' Board of Directors, as the Chairman of the Board and Chief Executive Officer of Hertz. If, however, Hertz ceases to be a subsidiary of RCA and thereafter the Board of Directors of Hertz shall fail to elect you Chairman of the Board or Chief Executive Officer of Hertz or, without your prior written consent, shall remove you from either office or position or prevent you from functioning in such capacities, for any reason other than a failure or refusal on your part to perform your duties hereunder or a disability entitling Hertz to terminate your employment under paragraph 5 hereof, you shall have the right to terminate your employment and receive payments hereunder equal to those you would have received under paragraph 3 hereof had your employment continued until February 28, 1985. Your right to terminate shall be exercised by you by written notice to the Secretary of Hertz given within 30 days of the date on which you cease to be, or are prevented from acting as, Chairman of the Board or Chief Executive Officer of Hertz.

2. During the period of your employment under this agreement you agree to perform the duties of any position you may hold in an efficient and competent manner and to devote your skill and best efforts to the business and affairs of Hertz and its subsidiaries. It is understood that you are and, while Hertz is a subsidiary of RCA, expect to continue to be a senior officer of RCA and that you have and expect to continue to have substantial duties and responsibilities to perform for RCA that do not involve Hertz or its subsidiaries. It is agreed that you may continue to perform such duties and responsibilities without breach of this agreement so long as Hertz is a subsidiary of RCA.

3. Your salary during the period of your employment under this agreement shall be at the rate of $325,000 per annum, or such other amount, not less than that figure, as the Board of

Directors of Hertz shall from time to time determine in light of your performance and responsibilities, payable in equal semimonthly installments. Any such determination in respect of salary shall be final and conclusive upon you and Hertz. In addition, if Hertz shall cease to be a subsidiary of RCA, you shall be entitled to participate throughout the remaining term of the agreement in any bonus, incentive, or similar plan that may be provided for Hertz officers and to receive a bonus, award or similar entitlement thereunder commensurate with the position of Chief Executive Officer of Hertz.

4. If during the period of your employment under this agreement you shall become temporarily disabled, through illness or otherwise, from performing your duties hereunder you shall be entitled to a leave of absence from Hertz for the duration of any such disability, up to but not exceeding an aggregate of one year and not past February 28, 1985. Your employment hereunder shall continue during any such leave of absence. If any such disability shall at any time appear to the Board of Directors of Hertz to be permanent or your leave of absence for disability shall continue for more than one year in the aggregate, Hertz will thereupon have the right to terminate your employment.

5. Nothing contained herein shall prevent your participation, while Hertz is a subsidiary of RCA, in any present or future incentive or other plan that may be provided by RCA or Hertz for Hertz employees and for which you may qualify.

6. This agreement sets forth the entire agreement between us. The terms of this agreement may not be changed orally.

Sincerely,
THE HERTZ CORPORATION

By_____
    George H. Fuchs

Accepted:_____ Date:_____
    Frank A. Olson

The undersigned RCA Corporation and Frank A. Olson hereby agree that the agreement of June 18, 1980, for Mr.

Olson's services to RCA Corporation is hereby terminated effective upon the execution of the foregoing agreement between the Hertz Corporation and Mr. Olson.

RCA CORPORATION

By_____   _____
   George H. Fuchs   Frank A. Olson

INDEX

ACKNOWLEDGMENTS

The number of people who helped me write this book is so great that comprehensiveness is impossible and selectivity is unfair. Since I can do the unfair but not the impossible, I shall mention in particular Judy Fischer and the staff of Executive Compensation Reports; Charlotte A. Krasman, a patient and understanding compensation analyst; Ann Glickman of the Securities and Exchange Commission; Dave Meredith; Michael Roth; Gary Stromberg; Joni Evans and Allen Peacock for belief, support, and editorial astuteness; and above all to Paul Fargis, who had the idea in the first place and who did more than one would believe could be done to make it come out right.

To everyone who helped, I am grateful with all my heart.

John Tarrant writes about life and work: how our jobs impact on our lives; the meaning of success and the ways of achieving it; the customs, folkways, and intricacies of American business. He has written more than a dozen books, most of them on various aspects of business and the corporate life. His articles appear in a wide range of magazines, including *Dun's, Smithsonian, Savvy, Family Circle, Nation's Business, Cosmopolitan, New York,* and *Working Woman.* He has worked as a consultant for General Electric, Texaco, Combustion Engineering, Pepsi-Cola, Mutual Life, Chase Manhattan Bank, J. P. Stevens, and *The New York Times.* Tarrant lives in Westport, Connecticut, with his wife, Dorothy.